Astrology for the
Light Side of the Future

Astrology for the Light Side of the Future

Kim Rogers-Gallagher

ACS Publications
5521 Ruffin Road
San Diego, CA 92123

International Standard Book Number 0-935127-45-3

Cover design by Lightbourne Images

Printed in the United States of America

Published by ACS Publications
5521 Ruffin Rd.
San Diego, CA 92123-1314

First Printing, September 1998

Praise for Kim Rogers-Gallagher's first book:
Astrology for the Light Side of the Brain.

"It's fun, it's brief, and it covers almost all of astrology's basic territory. I can't think of a better place for lighthearted beginners to wet their feet."
–Steven Forrest, Author of *The Inner Sky, The Changing Sky, Skymates* and *The Book of Pluto*

"...this is a delightful, easy to read and fun to learn with book. ...Kim Rogers-Gallagher is a good astrologer who has found the right mixture of cajoling students along with a smile and yet teaching them real astrology."
–Marion March, author of The Best Selling Series, *The Only Way to Learn Astrology*

"...wonderfully humorous book."
–James A. Cox, Midwest Book Review

"...the most refreshing approach to learning astrology I've ever encountered. Gallagher shows exceptional mastery of the subject and has managed to present astrology in a rare fashion that is playful, humorous, and highly readable."
–Jackie Harvey, Eye of the Vortex Bookstore

"I recommend this book for those new to astrology as well as those with experience who may find inspiration in the freshness of Kim Rogers-Gallagher's approach. Enjoy!"
–Steve L., Viewpoints

"As wonderful as Davison, Hand, Leek, Adams and Oaken have been—yours was tops. I will recommend it to every student I encounter on the topic of astrology. It is a breath of fresh air. Thank you."
–Mark S., Bridgeport, CT

"It's humorous and funny, yes, but it's also uncannily accurate at pinpointing the essence of the signs, houses and planets."
–Jaline K., Viewpoints

Also by Kim Rogers-Gallagher

Astrology for the Light Side of the Brain

It may sometimes seem complex, but astrology can be lots of fun. Here is a very serious introduction to all of the basics of astrology, with even a few intermediate techniques. All are presented in a witty, irreverent and even flippant style that will leave you laughing while you are informed and enlightened.

The author has a colorful way of bringing astrology alive through imagery and imagination. You'll be impressed with the completeness and good, solid content of this text for beginners with a refreshing new view for the rest of us.

Millennium: Fears, Fantasies and Facts
Astrologers Predict 2000

Forewarned is forearmed! Protect yourself in the years ahead. Four astrologers (Zipporah Dobyns, Maritha Pottenger, Kim Rogers-Gallagher and Maria Simms) predict 2000 and beyond, including disaster scenarios, the meaning of 2000, the Aquarian Age and cycles in human history. Marion March provides a timely foreword which comments on Nostradamus' prophecies.

Dedication

This book is dedicated with the greatest of affection to my Muses, the critters who share my life and my home, inspire me as they sit their shifts on my lap (or my shoulder) while I write, and provide me with the most unconditional love an Aquarian Moon could ask for. Most especially to Katie, who gave me 20 years of purrs and snuggles, Miss Lilly Mae Blacke, the best dog in the world, and Zuni, who adopted me one day in a convenience-store parking lot in Gallup, New Mexico.

Thanks and Appreciation

Once again, I've got to tell you that the best part of creating a book is being able to publicly mention some of the special beings who've contributed their charts, their experiences, their love and their support during the Birth Process.

First off, For Garth/Sir Gareth: The one and only Sit Babe....

To Dana, Jill, Deadra, Allison, Mary, Erin, and Michelle, who made working at The True Grit a lot more like play. Most especially to Dana Hagenson, the most solid, wonderful Taurus I've ever had the pleasure of being best buds with. Thank You for everything, darlin'—for being Other Mother to Lillie Mae, and for being the most unbeatable confidante a girl could ever ask for. I love you to pieces.

To all my friends from The Big Barn. Most especially, with much, much love and all kinds of respect, to Dennis and Gerry Weaver, and their son, Rusty, (my all-purpose bud) who always wears the very best of shirts.

For Rick Levine, with undying loyalty, love and affection, for always providing me with a 'nest' whenever I return home to Seattle.

For my sweethearts, Edie and Lee-Lee, the mothers of two beautiful little ladies, Sophie and Amazing Gracie—for all the great dinners, great wine, and great conversation.

To Laura Gerking, for always providing hugs, and a bit of Capricorn reality when it's necessary.

To my Sagittarian Astro-Bro, David Pond, his wife, Laurie, and their lovely family.

To Phillip Sedgwick, my Coyote Brother. A truly great astrologer, and an even better friend.

To Roxana Muise, the loveliest Libra Lady in the world, for the patience it takes to edit *anything* with a Mercury in Sag, and the ability to surprise me by saying the damndest of things at the damndest of times.

To Demetra George, beloved ancient sister who saw fit to reincarnate as my present-day Temple Partner and conference wife.

To Diana Rieboldt, my travellin' dancin' partner, (AKA 'Darla Mae,' the other half of the Soon-To-Be-Famous cast of 'Them Girls'), for all the rollickin' good boot-scootin' and the perpetual laughter.

To Ronnie Grishman and Jack Petty.

To all the fine medieval folks I've come to love throughout my transits to the 13th century. First of all, for m'Lady Debra Dubois Debouf, a forever friend if ever there was one. To Her Ladyship Elana the Wandering, (AKA 'Bob—JustBob') for sharing her green sweater with me on the coldest of nights. To Her Ladyship Katerina Hawkswood, (who may someday be Sir Rini, if I have my way). To Her Excellency Baroness Elizabeth Cameron Campbell, (who'll raise her pinky finger even in the most sedate of Court situations), and Her Grace Duchess Anna Ophelia Holloway Tarragon, (my partner in the struggle to beat Jose once and for all, and the light of so many lives). With love to Baroness Jovanna of ICOD—(don't ask)—for her hospitality each and every August. To all the M.A.P.S., and all members of The Sacred Order of the Pit Viper. Vivat! Huzzah! And so forth… With hugs and love to Baron Richard and Baroness Sorscha of Green Briar Keep.

To all the wonderful citizens of Pennsic, my much-loved medieval family I see all too seldom.

For Martha Barron Barrett, the best writing teacher in the world, who, I'm sure, will smile smugly when she sees this, and say "Told you so…".

For Elesha, my youngest reader, pen-pal, and late-night phone bud.

Table of Contents

Introduction xiii

Chapter One
An Overview: Introduction to Astrology 1
    The Universe and Its Seasons: 'As Above, So Below' 1
    A Few Words On Prediction in General 3
    …And Why We So Love To Do It 4
    Change—And Your Transits 5
    The Importance of Knowing The Chart
    You're About To Predict From 6

Chapter Two
So, What's A Transit? 7
    The Standard Disclaimer 8
    First, Finding Transits—
    And Seeing What They're 'Doing' 8
    Inner Planet Transits and Outer Planet Transits—
    Very Different Critters 9
    Evolution is quite the process. 10
    A Bit About Orbs and Retrogrades, Too 12
    What's an 'orb'? Well, let's cover that next 12
    Now, about Retrogrades 13
    Hindsight And Learning Transits 15
    How Transits Work—and 'Don't' Work 16
    A Few More Tips 17
    Fate vs. Free Will—
    The Truth of the Matter 18
    Planning Your Trip 20
    The Difference Between 'Hard' and 'Easy' Aspects 22
    And Speaking Of Transits Through The Houses 23

Chapter Three
The Sun 25
    Your Sun Transit Kit: 25
    The Sun—Let's Talk About You—
    What Do You Think Of Me? 25
    The Sun Through The Houses 26
    Sun/Sun Transits 34

Chapter Four
Transits of The Moon 45
   Your Moon Kit: 45
   Moon Transits 46
   The Moon Through the Houses 46

Chapter Five
Mercury 67
   Your Mercury Kit: 67
   Mercury Transits: Life In The Fast Lane 68
   Mercury Through The Houses 68

Chapter Six
Venus 85
   Your Venus Kit: 85
   Venus Transits 86
   Venus Through The Houses 86

Chapter Seven
Mr. Feisty Goes To The Gym 103
   Your Mars Kit: 103
   Mars Transits: Don't Step On My Blue Suede Shoes 104
   Mars Through The Houses 106

Chapter Eight
Jupiter 127
   Your Jupiter Kit: 127
   Jupiter Transits: Up, Up and Away 128
   Jupiter Through the Houses 129

Chapter Nine
Saturn 159
   Your Saturn Kit: 159
   Saturn Transits: What Goes Around, Comes Around 160
   Saturn Through The Houses 161

Chapter Ten
Intermission 193
   The Outer Planets and 'I Will Never' Syndrome 193
   Picture this scene, if you will: 194

Chapter Eleven
Uranus: A Visit From The Loon 199
    Your Uranus Kit: 199
    Uranus Transits: Just Get Yourself Free 199
    Uranus and 'Buffers' 201
    Uranus Through The Houses 202

Chapter Twelve
Neptune 231
    Your Neptune Kit: 231
    Neptune Transits: Dream A Little Dream Of Me 232
    Neptune Through The Houses 233

Chapter Thirteen
Pluto 261
    Your Pluto Kit: 261
    Pluto Transits: Just Let Go 261
    Pluto Through The Houses 263

Chapter Fourteen
Good-Bye 297
    And In Conclusion 297

INTRODUCTION

Well, hello again. Welcome to my book. If you've already been to *Astrology for the Light Side of the Brain*, and you're back here for a return trip, I'd just like to say thanks. Apparently, we've developed something of a relationship, and I want you to know I appreciate both the time you've already invested in listening to me and the time you're about to invest. It's wonderful to know that there's someone Out There as I go on at length about my favorite subject. Now, as you've probably already noticed, this book has the word Light in the title, just like its predecessor. Just so we don't get our signals crossed, then, and before we go any further, I'd like to address that fact.

See, I'm a Sag, and as such, a card-carrying clown. That means I tend to see the Lighter Side of things. Everything. It's my job. I just want to make sure that you don't think I'm being disrespectful of astrology when I take a Lighter tone with it, because I'm not. I love astrology. Truly. It never ceases to amaze me. It explains everything—even things I didn't know I didn't know. It makes me aware, constantly, of my connection to every single living thing in the Cosmos, and reminds me to be understanding of Others who are out there simply doing their astrological jobs. Even if they're different from me...even if they're Virgos. (Oh, stop, now—I'm only kidding...)

At any rate, we're gathered here to talk about prediction this time. So I'd like to make a prediction of my very own: I predict that you're going to go immediately to the section on the transit you're currently suffering under—for a little comic relief. Further,

I predict that it's either Saturn or Pluto that's the symbol of your distress. How'd I know that? Hey, I'm an astrologer—we know these things. I'm also a human—and I know just how terrible a Saturn or Pluto transit can feel...Since learning astrology, however, I've also learned how good the aftermath of those transits can be, when you're far away enough from them to say, 'Well, it may have been tough while it was going on, but if it hadn't happened, I never would have.....'—you fill in the blank. So I see my job, this time out, as this: to be honest with you about what to expect from every transit—to get you up and around, even during those notoriously easy, lazy, Jupiter trines, and to try to get you to smile a little during even the toughest Pluto times.

Before you start flipping towards the chapters on specific transits, then, do me a favor and take a peek at these first few chapters, just for the heck of it. For a review—for a bit of my own personal philosophy of astrology and life—and so you'll understand where I'm coming from. If it's especially hectic transits you're having—say a long-term stay from Uranus, coupled with a visit from Mr. Mars—and you just can't wait, then stop back later. Just do me one favor as you read this book: keep in mind that no matter how good or bad a transit feels, nothing lasts forever. The idea is to plan ahead for the future, and to Get what the present is all about. Good luck. Write if you're so inclined. Here's the address:

PO Box 141
Ridgway, CO 81432-0141

CHAPTER ONE

AN OVERVIEW: INTRODUCTION TO ASTROLOGY

All right, then. Let's get started. First, we'll need to do a bit of a review. Nothing serious, just basic stuff, to make sure we understand each other—because my view of the planet tends to be, oh,... a bit 'different,' let's say. Now, even if you consider yourself already quite accomplished in the basics, and even if you have read AFTLSOTB, that doesn't mean that you've been excused and you can skip along to chapter three. That goes for you fire-signs, especially. (Remember, I'm fire, too, so I know how you get.) Regardless of how long you've been at this, hearing The Basics from the perspective of several different Mercurys is the very best way to learn astrology—and to keep learning it. Besides, I'm prepared to promise you that this entire book will be fun. Oh, and informative, too—not to worry. It's what a ninth-house Sag Sun, Aquarian Moon and Aquarius Ascendant most want to pass out. So settle down, get comfortable, and prepare, as per, to see astrology from what I hope will be a very different, mind-expanding perspective.

The Universe and Its Seasons: 'As Above, So Below'

First off, a word about the Universe in general. What an amazing place, huh? Tilt your head back some clear evening and consider just exactly what you're looking at—but unable to see. The sky above you—and what's beyond it—is absolutely chock full of all kinds of amazing heavenly bodies. There are stars, asteroids, planets and comets Out There, all whizzing along through space, all constantly in motion and constantly changing. Although there are lots of theories as to where those heavenly bodies originated and lots of folks who profess to understand The Cosmos and its inner workings, no one's really got a handle on it—no matter what they say. We may understand the effect of some of the energies the Universe is kind enough to keep consistent for us to keep our confusion level down—take light, sound, and magnetism, for example—but we'll probably never understand the why of it all. Perhaps that's because we're not meant to know more than we need to know—any more than an amoebae is meant to know, or needs to know, why it lives on our body.

What we do know after centuries of observation is that what happens Upstairs with the planets and the other heavenly bodies—their cycles, as well as the angular relationships they form to one another as they move through those cycles—is an amazingly accurate indicator of what happens down here on Planet Number Three. That's not to say that the planets "do" anything, or cause anything to happen, you understand—but their movements certainly do mirror the natural processes of life on this planet. Or, as They say, As above, so below...

Now, this correspondence between what happens Upstairs and what happens Down Here is not a brand new concept. It's all about working with the seasons, and gardeners have been hip to it for years. Well, astrologers are gardeners, too. Astrology simply allows us to make use of all of the planets' seasons—instead of just the Sun and the Moon. It's a system that's tried and true, that's been around for about as long as humans have, studied and used by such legendary figures as Ptolemy, Johannes Kepler, Carl Jung, and even, um,... Ronald Reagan. It's a blend of science, magic and mathematics, expressed through symbols, interpreted by those of us curious enough to study these Cosmic 'smoke-signals.'

It's not a religion, so you don't have to start or stop believing in anything, and you don't need to believe in it for it to 'work,' any more than you need to "believe" the Sun will set to make it so. There's no hocus-pocus involved, no channeling critters from another plane, and no Psychic Friends—although using it for a while certainly does help to fine-tune your perceptive abilities. Astrology validates our hunches about ourselves, supports what we already knew, and gives us the ability to get to know ourselves even better. It allows us to see why Others act the way they do, and gives us insight to help accept them as they are—(even if our Mars is square to theirs, and they're always picking on us).

Astrology is a language, a symbol set, a guide to understanding the world, your life, the Cosmos. Consider yourself fortunate that you found it, pat yourself on the back for being, like, speerichually evolved enough to recognize that there's really something to all this, and read on.

A FEW WORDS ON PREDICTION IN GENERAL...

Okay, so, if it's a fact that astrology is really just the study of the planets and the other heavenly bodies and their seasons, doesn't that put astrologers on the same plane as meteorologists? Well, yes. You bet it does. We're both in the business of drawing parallels between cycles Upstairs and cycles Down Here. It stands to reason, then, that just like meteorologists, astrologers are capable of not just understanding the cycles—the seasons, that is—but also of predicting them by using the tools they've learned. There's no way we wouldn't be able to predict—it only makes sense. The heavenly bodies are real—all of them, not just the Sun. They're so real, in fact, that their movements are consistent and recordable—enough so to be put into tables. So how could the seasons of one heavenly body—the Sun—be so amazingly accurate for predicting what's under it's astrological job description—life, growth, creation and procreation—if the rest of the planets are just 'dumb notes'? It's just not logical to believe that—the Universe is far too orderly.

No, the only real difference between the type of prediction We do and the type of prediction They do is that We use all the planets, and the asteroids, and a comet or two. That means that astrologers are able to work on a larger scale. We're not confined to predicting only physical things—like tides, weather, and climate. We understand the relationship between each planet and the innate human urges or needs it represents, so we can predict all kinds of things. Everything from job changes to relationship issues, to financial stuff, for individuals. We can even predict the outcome of elections by looking at the charts of the candidates along with the chart of the place that's holding the election. Pretty amazing stuff....

Now, nobody's saying that we're infallible in our predictions— but, then, neither are meteorologists. Both astrologers and weather-folks are interpreters, first of all, and humans, secondly. Both those facts mean that we're subject to error. That's why prediction is such a touchy matter—no matter what you're predicting.

...AND WHY WE SO LOVE TO DO IT

So if prediction—of any kind, weather-wise or otherwise—comes with a built-in Nothing-Is-Set-In-Stone clause, why do we do it? Well, perhaps it's because we feel that prediction gives us an edge—and if we do our interpretations properly, that's a very valid thing to feel. Predicting astrologically allows us to figure out the best way to surf the Cosmic waves that are en route by glancing at our own tidal tables—our ephemerides—and figuring out when the next tide is due in—or out. Predicting astrologically is all about planning for what's coming—just the same way we plan our days by making a list, our budgets by what we're expecting in our paychecks, or our schedules by keeping a date book. (In fact, like most astrologers, when I'm trying to choose a date for an event, I don't reach for my calendar until I've reached for my ephemeris. I mean, why bother being in The Biz if you're not going to use the tools?)

Okay. We've seen the absolute logic and sensibility in wanting to predict. Apparently, it's not just okay to do it, it's downright prudent to try to anticipate the future. It's just another form of planning — and we all know that planning is a good thing. That's the legitimate reason for attempting to predict what's up ahead. But, let's be honest. We're not into prediction because we're all so responsible. We're into it because we love it—because we're fascinated by it. But why is that? Why are we all so darned interested in knowing what's going to happen before it happens? Why can't we settle for just living in the moment? Would knowing The Future really change anything, alter anything, or make our decisions easier? After all, everything each of us has ever done has made us who we are, right now. If we're happy with ourselves, we've got to give equal credit to each and every person and event that's come our way throughout life. So why bother stressing out about The Future? Why not just relax and accept whatever comes at us as part of our evolutionary process?

Well, because unless you're an Ascended Master or a practicing Buddhist, it's not that simple. Sure, most of us realize that there's a purpose for everything that happens—but that doesn't mean we have to like all of it. Especially the stuff we didn't vote for. We reach for the tarot cards or the runes or the astrology chart when we're unsettled here in the present and uncertain or worried about the future. Basically, we look to prediction to help us deal with humankind's least favorite topic—Change.

CHANGE—AND YOUR TRANSITS

Yes, gang, it's fairly common knowledge that Our Kind are not notoriously good at Change—mainly because it doesn't always happen when and how we think it should. We want Out of our present circumstances—now, thank you very much—and nothing seems to be happening. Or we don't want Out of our present circumstances, and yet we feel them slipping away. See, more than anything, we humans hate to be reminded that we're not omnipotent. It's unnerving. Makes us set to wondering about death, taxes, and other Inevitables we know are on our list of Things To Do This Lifetime, that we nonetheless aren't exactly looking forward to. So when we feel as if life circumstances are truly beyond our control—when we feel as if Change is happening without our seal of approval—we're not happy about it. We look to prediction at those times because we feel powerless, because it seems that there are Powersomethings That Be out there who aren't listening to what we're ordering. More than anything, we look to prediction because we want to know when things are going to start going our way again—dammit.

Regardless of why we do it, however, if we actually can find a way to catch a glimpse of The Plan, (if there is one), and if that glimpse helps us to cooperate with it, we can help ourselves to maximize good experiences and minimize unpleasant experiences—which sounds to me like a great way to go through life. If we're going to do it anyway, then, I vote for doing prediction well, by using accurate, reliable methods, and by seeking out reputable professionals to help interpret for us until we've learned and we're capable on our own. Astrology, of course, is the system I'm fondest of, mainly because I've seen how accurate, how rich in meaning and how full of options it is.

Now, the most popular method of astrological prediction is Transits. The word 'transit' technically means 'to pass through or over.' Working with transits involves inserting the planets, wherever they happen to be, on a particular date, into the framework of a natal chart to see how what's happening Upstairs (as the planets 'pass through' our houses 'or over' our planets) is symbolically representative of what's happening—and what's about to happen—in the life of the chart's owner. Transits are great because they're relatively easy to find and just as easy to learn to interpret, but the best part of working with them is the fact that because they describe potential situations, they automatically provide built-in 'antidotes' or 'remedies' for potentially difficult situations. Just because your Moon is about to be contacted by Mars, for example, doesn't necessarily mean you have to have a fight (Mars) with your Mom (Moon). You can spend the day working (Mars) at home (Moon), or do something strenuous (Mars) with your Mom (Moon). You might also simply take the initiative (Mars) to express your true feelings (Moon). Through finding the most positive use of a planet or sign, transits provide options to make the best of every moment—and that's what it's all about, isn't it?

The Importance of Knowing The Chart You're About To Predict From

Another thing that will make or break your ability to predict successfully from any chart is how well you know it. In other words, if you're going to form an opinion on what might happen to someone or something, you've got to know an awful lot about it, starting with the nature of the beast, in general. Once you're familiar with an entity, then you'll be able to make more educated guesses about its reactions to upcoming circumstances based on past situations and what happened last time a particular planet was in the neighborhood.

If you've already read AFTLSOTB, you're ready to dig in. If you haven't, go get yourself one so we're all on the same page here. We'll wait till you get back before we start, but you've got to read fast. As an added inspiration for all you impatient fire-signs out there, remember that you can't pass go (and you can just forget about that $200, too), if we are not all on the same page. So review your basics if you're shaky, and then we'll move along.

CHAPTER TWO
SO, WHAT'S A TRANSIT?

As I mentioned last chapter, transits are inarguably the number one favorite way to do astrological prediction. They're easy to use, fun to monitor, and they give an awful lot of information quickly—it's like immediate astrological gratification. They're done by comparing what's happening today—or on any date you're curious about—to your own chart, usually by penciling the transiting planets in around the edges of your natal chart in the appropriate spots, then looking at the houses and planets they're affecting. A good rule of thumb when you're trying to decide what this transit will bring is to remember that transiting planets describe symbolic incoming influences and events that your natal planet will be asked to handle—a tide of sorts that's about to wash over your life.

The nature of the transiting planet describes the types of situations that will arise, and the nature of your planet tells which 'piece' of you you're working on at the moment. Basically, transits are another way of describing growth cycles. They represent periods of change, times when you're in the mood to stretch, to grow, and try something new. No matter how difficult they seem to be, by the way, no transit is meant to be gotten through, or endured. Each and every touch of a transiting planet to one of your own is there for a reason, because you're supposed to be learning something. After a transit has passed, your natal planet will usually be very different, too—especially if the transit is from an outer planet. Every transit you undergo adds knowledge and experience to your personality. It's why maturity and age naturally bring wisdom, and why it's true that life is the greatest teacher.

THE STANDARD DISCLAIMER

One more thing—before we get started. The first and most important thing to remember when you're attempting to predict is also the hardest—this goes double when you're predicting for yourself, but it works when you're doing unto others, too...The first step, and the one that may even save you all the rest of the time you were about to spend, is to look at the natal chart and see if you can find a description of the event you're wondering about. Because if it's not in there, it's not In There. If it's going to happen, it has to have an Honorary Mention in your chart. It has to be part of The Story of Your Life, that is. So, for example, before you check your transits to find a great time to invest that hunk of money you've been saving in coffee cans for 12 years, make sure you own the type of chart that indicates good fortune in the market. (Then call an expert financier/astrologer like Ray Merriman or Jeanne Long to plan it for you.) Both those strategies might save you a couple of bucks.

First, Finding Transits— And Seeing What They're 'Doing'

Okay, let's try it. Get out your chart—which should be folded and living permanently inside your ephemeris by now. Open your ephemeris to today. Look at the planets' placements and pencil in each one around the outside of your wheel, in the appropriate signs and degrees. When you're finished, take a look at where in your chart each of the planets is positioned. If Mercury is penciled in just before your Ascendant, for example, we would say that Mercury is transiting through your 12th house, and will soon be transiting your Ascendant and your first house. The same goes for all the other planets and the Moon. Wherever they turn up in your chart is the spot they're currently transiting—i.e. "going across"—in your chart. That's how you "find" transits, and how you figure out which 'room' in your house—or area of life— is being visited by which planetary guest. Next, take a look at any aspects the transiting planets might be making to your natal planets. (Don't forget your Midheaven and your Ascendant degree, too.) Start with Pluto, and work backwards to the Moon.

Inner Planet Transits and Outer Planet Transits—Very Different Critters

Okay. You've made your list up, and you've seen where in your chart each of the planets is, right now. But how long will each of those visits last? Well, that brings me to another good point to remember—about the difference between transits of the Outers—(Uranus, Neptune, and Pluto)—and transits of the Inners—(everybody else.) See, not all transits were created equal—and that applies especially to Inner vs. Outer planet transits. There are several reasons for this, but the most obvious one is that transits of the outer planets just plain old last longer than transits of the inner planets. As a result, they're also more representative of bigger changes in your life.

Think of it this way: Pluto can hang around one particular degree of the zodiac for as long as 4 months, while the Sun takes only one day to cover a degree, and the Moon whizzes through a degree every two hours. If that same degree Pluto happens to be occupying for a whole season also happens to be the degree of one of your natal planets, that planet will have a Plutonian 'feeling' to it for that entire time, and the types of experiences Pluto corresponds with—intensity, passion, power struggles, and complete overhauls of your present life circumstances—will also last for that entire length of time.

In general, outer planet transits are rather like stage backdrops in a play. You don't notice them after you've been watching the play for awhile, but they still color everything else that goes before them. Inner planet transits act like 'triggers' for the Outers.

Think of what you were doing three years ago. Or ten years ago. It's easy—now—to see that you were in the middle of some major, sweeping changes back then. You didn't realize it, of course, because you were busy living your life from day to day, but whatever you were going through at that time, for better or worse—is very much a part of who you are right now. That's what the Outer planet(s) who were setting the backdrop at the time had in mind as they pulled up to your natal planet, then backed away, then returned. Long-term, subtle—but permanent—change.

The Inners, because they whip along so quickly, relatively speaking, are more immediately responsible, (symbolically speaking), for the actual events that occur—so although it's the specific events that you'll remember, as symbolized by The Inners, it's the Outers who set up the 'tone' or 'theme.' It's quite a process. As the Outer approaches our natal planet or point, we turn towards the Big Issues it illuminates in our life, at first on an internal level. The closer the Outer gets to the actual degree of our natal planet, the more the transits of the Inners correspond with events that bring home the actual lesson the Outer Planet inspires. We incorporate the memory of those events into our being, and we grow from the experience. The really amazing thing to remember is that we're just about always in the middle of one Outer Planet transit or another—so all of us are always changing from one moment to the next.

EVOLUTION IS QUITE THE PROCESS.

Now, as I said, any of the three Outers can hang around a natal planet or point for up to three years. They usually touch a degree three times, but occasionally, depending on whether or not they 'hit' close to the spot of your planet or point when they retrograde, they can come within 'orb'—within Astrological Shouting Distance, that is—as many as five times. (We'll talk about orbs in the next section, by the way.) Since an awful lot can happen in three years (and three to five 'hits' of an Outer), and since, as we've seen, the Outers like to set 'themes,' these three are notorious for being on stage when Big Stuff—AKA major life changes—come along. We make decisions about relationships, life direction, family matters, and the way we present our Selves when the Outers are around. We often feel as if we are watching ourselves reacting to situations and responding to outside circumstances in entirely new ways when they're visiting, too.

Needless to say, then, a Pluto transit carries a lot more long-term wallop than a Moon transit. That's not to say Moon transits aren't as important as Pluto transits, you understand—they're each orchestrated perfectly, and timed just as they should be. Pluto represents the idea that old forms need to "die" to make way for the new. That's not a quick process. On the other hand, the Moon comes and goes, mirroring our moods and the constant fluctuation of feelings we experience as we move through a single day.

Planet	Approx. Cycle	Approx. Daily Motion	Approx. Retrograde Period	Duration
Sun	1 year	1 degree	None	about 25 days
Moon	27-29 days	12-15 degrees	None	6 weeks
Mercury	Approx. 1 year	1.5-2 degrees	3 per year	11 weeks
Venus	Approx. 1 year	1 degree 15 minutes	about 18 months	
Mars	1.88 years	42-48 minutes	every 24-26 months	3-4 months
Jupiter	12 years	8-14 minutes	about once a year	4-5 months
Saturn	29.5 years	6-8 minutes	about once a year	5-6 months
Uranus	84 years	2-4 minutes	about once a year	5-6 months
Neptune	165 years	1-2 minutes	about once a year	5-6 months
Pluto	248 years	1-2 minutes	about once a year	

That is a quick process. Pluto's transits, then, will be a part of your life for an awful lot longer than will the Moon's.

A Bit About Orbs and Retrogrades, Too...

If you really want to get a feel for how long each planet will take to touch off a point or planet in your chart, take a look at the diagram above. It shows a couple of things it's really handy to get a fix on when you're trying to plan for tomorrow—or next week, or next year. The first column shows approximately how long each planet takes to make an orbit—which is one loop around your chart. The second column lists how many degrees a planet covers, on average, in a day—which is really helpful when you're looking at the transits of some of the faster planets, like the Moon and Mercury. The third column shows how long each of the planets spends retrograde, or apparently backwards, from our point of view here on Earth. That's good to know because if your planet or point happens to be smack in the middle of a planet's retrograde path, your transit is going to last much longer than it would ordinarily because you'll get three 'hits'—and maybe five—from that planet before it really passes out of the 'orb of influence' of your planet.

WHAT'S AN 'ORB'?
WELL, LET'S COVER THAT NEXT.

Basically, orbs are 'point spreads'—they're extra degrees that tell you how far you can stretch a transit and still expect to 'feel' something. In other words, if you have the Sun at 14 Aquarius, and you use a five degree orb for transits, you'll be experiencing situations that reflect the nature of the transiting planet for however long it takes to cover 10 degrees of sky. Think of the transiting planet as a wood stove someone's wheeling towards you. The closer it comes to you—that is, the closer the transiting planet gets to the exact degree of your planet—the hotter you're going to feel. So from the time it reaches 9 degrees of a sign until it gets past 19 degrees of a sign, you'll be experiencing symbolic events that reflect the nature of the transiting planet. The 5 degrees it takes to reach the degree of your planet is called the Approaching Transit, and the 5 degrees it covers after the degree of your planet is called the 'Separating' Transit.

Although some folks disagree on this, other folks seem to think that events that occur during Approaching Transits are symbolic warm-ups arranged by the Universe to get your attention directed towards The Subject of your transit. Events that come up when your planet is being touched Exactly by the transiting planet are closer to the point of the transit, and Separating Transits often are the afterward stage of a transit, when you're assimilating or dealing with the aftermath of events. Think of the 5 degrees approaching as a time of preparation for an event, the exact transit as the event itself, and the 5 degrees separating as clean-up time.

NOW, ABOUT RETROGRADES

Although 'retrograde' literally means 'backwards,' none of the planets ever really throw their engines in reverse and move backwards. All of them but the Sun and Moon appear to be going backwards periodically, however—from the perspective of the Earth, for varying amounts of time. Very basically, what's happening is that we're moving either faster or slower than the planet that's ' retrograde,' and since we have to look over our shoulder to see it, we refer to it as retrograde—egocentric little critters that we are.

That's what retrograde means, (very loosely), in terms of celestial mechanics. The way it seems to play out in our affairs as it's happening is a bit more involved. Retrograde planets 'act' a bit differently than planets moving forward. (Steven Forrest says it's because they're a bit unsure of themselves—strangers in a foreign country who aren't quite sure of how to act yet.) In Mercury's case, the planet with the most famous retrograde of all, it means that the Head of the Communications Department isn't paying close attention to where he's going—he's watching where he came from. So the details Mercury usually handles so easily aren't tended to as carefully. Keep in mind that Mercury correlates with Hermes, (the original Trickster), and you'll understand how cleverly disguised some of these errors can be. If Mercury touches one of your planets during this time, you might experience all kind of things. Communications relative to the nature of your planet become confused, delayed, or misunderstood. If it's your own Mercury, your letters could be lost, sent to Auckland instead of Oakland, or end up under the car seat for three weeks. If it's Venus, you might sign a contract or agreement and find out later that you didn't have all the correct information, and what you signed was misleading in some way.

There are other Mercury retrograde symptoms you might notice if it's touching off key areas in your chart. You might be late for appointments due to circumstances beyond your control, like traffic, accidents, or roadblocks. You may try repeatedly to reach someone via telephone but be unable to catch them, or your communications devices themselves may break down or garble information in some way. The written word falls victim to Mercury's retrograde, too, via typos, false information, or partial information. Your timing may feel a bit off, so short trips often become more difficult to make, too, especially if the directions to where you're going are at home, or written down incorrectly—other possible symptoms.

So what's the point? Is there a constructive use to this time period? And aren't all planetary energies good for something? Well, yes, indeed, they are. Astrologer Erin Sullivan has noted that the ratio of time Mercury spends moving retrograde (backwards) and direct (forward) corresponds beautifully with the amount of time we humans spend awake and asleep—about a third of our lives. So this period seems to be a time to take stock of what's happened over the past three months, and assimilate our experiences—just as sleep is how we assimilate our daily experiences. Moving forward with new plans doesn't work as well as it ought to when Mercury's retrograde because we're not supposed to be moving forward yet—just reviewing the past in preparation for our next stage of activity. A good rule of thumb, in fact, with Mercury Retrograde, is to try to confine our activities to those that have "re" attached to the beginning of a word. Reschedule, repair, return, re-write, re-decorate, restore, replace, renovate, renew.

As for the other planets, their retrogrades seem to work the same way—again, especially if the retrograde is very close to a natal planet or point. With Venus retrograde, (every 18 months for 6 weeks), it's relationships and money matters that can be delayed or muddled. With Mars, (retrograde 11 weeks, direct for 22 months), actions initiated are often rooted in confusion, or end up to be at cross-purposes to our original intentions. Typically, under Mars retrograde, the aggressor or initiator of a battle is defeated.

Jupiter retrogrades for 4 months, and is direct for 9. Saturn retrogrades for about the same amount of time. Each of the outer planets, Uranus, Neptune, and Pluto, stays retrograde for about 5 or 6 months of every year. In general, remember that actions ruled by a particular planet may often need to be repeated, or done over, when that planet is retrograde—and make sure that whatever you're planning is something you don't mind doing twice. Also remember, that if you've been trying to contact someone, or finish up on a project, now is the time to do the editing.

Now just because retrogrades are a great time to redo anything that needs it, doesn't mean that you can't ever take a step forward. It's very rare to find all of the planets retrograde at one time, first of all, and as long as somebody's charging ahead, your projects will too. Just make sure that you tend very carefully to details when the planet ruling your upcoming activity is in reverse. And think of what happens when you back up along a path you've previously traveled. You are able to see it from another side, from a different perspective. In general, then, that's the best way to use retrogrades: to use the different perspectives the universe is providing to help you see all sides of an issue, especially things you may have missed the first time around.

Hindsight And Learning Transits

Now, whether you've just gotten into astrology, or you're just new to prediction, here's a really good way to learn all about transits, and about how each of the planets seems to affect your particular chart when it comes along. Get out your ephemeris and go back to all the major days in your life. Check out where all the planets were when you got married, had a child (a whole separate birth-chart that's really just a set of transits to your chart, if you can wrap your mind around that one), started a new job, or moved to South Africa. See what was happening. It's educational, and unbelievably accurate. It will make you laugh, cry, and remember things you haven't thought of in years. Best of all, it will take your attention away—a little—from the obsessive task of Scanning the Globe to see what will happen tonight, and tomorrow, and in an hour—something that's just about inevitable once you realize that you really can pick up the "flavor" of a day from the ephemeris.

This type of obsession is a natural stage in your astrological education, by the way—it's like realizing that you can walk when you're a few months old. You want to walk everywhere—nonstop. It's the same with any new toy. After a while, you'll calm down and resume going about your business without checking the Moon's position every hour. You'll settle for taking a peek into your Moon-sign calendar once or twice a day.

HOW TRANSITS WORK—AND 'DON'T' WORK

Now, the truly educational part of the Obsessive Stage is that we all come out of it knowing that Stuff doesn't automatically happen when it "should," nor does it hardly ever happen the way we think it will. Practice, in fact, shows over and again that the outcome of our transits is hardly ever as dramatic as we imagine. Once again, don't forget that if it's not In There, it's not In There. Period.

So how do transits work? Well, let's review. It's like this: first of all, as we've said before, the planets don't "do" anything—not even Pluto. (Although he'd like you to think he does.) They just show you where your interest will be drawn to at a particular time. When a transiting planet comes along and makes itself comfortable on one of your planets, then, like we've already talked about, you'll find yourself dealing with Symbolic Situations. Remember, the transiting planet represents Incoming Influences and Events that your natal planet is asked to handle. The nature of the transiting planet describes the types of Situations that will arise, and the nature of your planet shows which "piece" of you you're working on at the moment.

You can think of transiting planets as if they were Exercise Trainers. Their visits coincide with periods where you'll feel as if the strength and fitness of one of your personal Qualities is tested, when you'll get to see just exactly what you can handle. Your natal planet gets a good workout, and you learn what you're capable of and what you're not—yet. In other words, if your planet is strong—that is, if you're already operating that side of you at optimum capacity—the events symbolized by the transiting planet will provide opportunities for you to make your planet even stronger. If, on the other hand, your natal planet isn't working at optimum, the weakness in it will be brought to your attention. Either way, you'll find yourself in situations that will provide you with report cards, if you pay attention—evaluations of your natal planet's performance.

As time goes on and you adjust to your current set of circumstances, your planet will strengthen, as if it's on a workout program designed especially to build its muscles. Remember, the idea behind transits is to incorporate the qualities associated with the transiting planet into your natal planet—for however long the transit lasts. It's like you're being lent a tool to work with through a particular task. So if your Moon, for example, is about to be conjoined by Pluto, your emotions, as symbolized by the Moon in your chart, are about to undergo a very, very intense time—via Pluto. Your topic is Emotional Control and Intensity, Taking Charge of Your Own Feelings, and Understanding Emotional Manipulation. You may encounter power struggles with women, you may be forced to move from your home, or you may realize just how intensely you care for someone—at any rate, the point of the transit is to get you aware of the fact that your emotional nature is deepening. Basically, all transits are Growing Cycles—they represent spurts of change.

A FEW MORE TIPS...

1) First off, remember that since at least some of the planets in your chart are hooked together by aspect, your transits won't usually happen one at a time. So you can pretty much count on working through a couple of different projects from the Universe at once—which makes things Interesting, as the Chinese say. How so? Well, think back on just exactly what an Aspect 'does' to two or more planets. Again, it joins them together or hot-wires them—so that one never acts without the other. Transits to planets in your chart that are in aspect will show up in several Life Departments, then. Transits, in fact, are quite an interesting way to really see your aspect patterns. Depending on your natal chart set-up, transits to Yods, Grand Trines, T-Squares or other major aspect patterns can quite literally indicate periods when every part of you will be tested or pushed to change in some way.

2) When you're trying to judge whether or not a particular transit will go well for you or your client or Other, remember that everybody gets to have favorite planets. Some folks like Saturn (yes, honest to God, some people do), and some people don't like Jupiter (I know-I don't get it, either). In other words, what you're

already familiar with—because it's in your natal chart—is going to have a lot to do with how well you handle visits from particular planets. Folks with Capricorn stellia are going to be a lot happier about Saturn transits than folks with Sag stellia. Trust me on this.

3) Another thing to keep in mind is that the last transit of an Outer Planet that touched your planet by hard aspect is going to be the one your planet carries, or remembers, until the next transit of an Outer by hard aspect comes along. Honest. I've watched this for some time now, and it works. In other words, after your Venus has spent some time with Saturn squaring it, it's going to feel a bit more frugal than it may have in quite a while. It's going to stay that way, too, until the next Outer comes along—maybe a conjunction from Uranus, for example—and it symbolically 'hears' an entirely different message.

It's kind of like learning a hard lesson. It sticks.

4) There are certain major transits (involving Saturn and the Outer Planets) that everyone experiences around the same age—i.e., the Saturn Return, at about age 29, the Uranus opposition Uranus at age 42, etc. These are major milestones that come with the package as part of being a human down here on Planet Number Three.

5) Stuff is most likely to happen when a whole bunch of factors come together at one time. So if you're waiting for an event to happen, and you're trying to predict when that might be, look for a day, or a week, when just about every body Upstairs is matching just about everybody in your chart—and that's when your event will most likely occur...

Fate vs. Free Will—
The Truth of the Matter...

Now, given that we have ephemerides and we can see Pluto sidling up to our Mars, or Mars sidling up to our Pluto—or both—we have the ability to make choices. That's the whole idea behind astrology, and the whole point of this book—to take charge of our lives by "doing" our charts instead of letting Stuff Happen to us. Of course, even astrologers are subject to an awful lot of things that we can't change, situations that we can only affect by our response to them. So what do we do when we see that Pluto\Mars transit coming—and as a matter of fact, can we really "do" anything?

Well, it's like this: there are two distinct schools of thought on the subject of transits: One is led by those folks who believe that nothing is carved in stone, that we are all In Charge of our own destinies, and that anything can be positive—if you just "use" it right. Which sounds good, except that when something bad happens to you, you end up feeling awfully guilty and even more confused, wondering what you did to bring this on yourself. Like maybe, somehow, if you'd only done something differently, maybe that flood wouldn't have carried away your home. Not a happy state of mind—and not a very rational one, either, in my humble opinion.

Then there's the second school of thought—run by The Fatalists, a real fun crew who believe the contrary is true, that you have absolutely no control over your transits—zero. In their minds, everything has been pre-paid in the eyes of the Universe, and that's that. From this perspective, we're all speeding down a mountainside with no breaks, totally out of control, completely at the mercy of those Powersomethings that Be. In which case you've got to wonder why you'd bother to learn astrology at all, if you're really just condemned to be a spectator to what the planets "Do" to you for the rest of your life.

Personally, I tend to waffle a bit on this point. I believe you usually get six of one and a half-dozen of the other with transits, mainly because although you certainly can make decisions that affect the outcome of any situation in a Major League kind of way, you certainly can't stop other people from doing what they're doing— and sometimes those other people's paths do cross your own. So if someone drives through your living room wall one night while you're sitting there innocently munching on popcorn and watching a Star Trek rerun, I don't want you to think for a moment that it's your fault. It's not. Other People have Mars transits and agendas of their very own, which sometimes include us— regardless of whether or not we missed a work-out that morning. So. The best way to handle all your transits is to take charge of the situation as much as you can, to be as conscious of what's going on as possible, and to stay aware of what you might expect from others.

Think of your natal planets as symbolic containers where you store all the different energies that come together to form You.

Your Mars, for example, is where you store all your Assertion Impulse. Each planet is like a glass full of water, sitting right in the middle of a hallway. When you see what looks like a tough transit coming through the door, right at your planet, then, rather than leaving the glass right there in the way, you can run over to your planet, pick it up, and start pouring your energy out, a little at a time. That way, by the time the transiting planet does get to your planet, although there still may be a bit of a spill, it's definitely not going to be as bad as it could have been.

Let's pretend the planet in question is your Mars, and that a long-term Uranus transit that's been on for months is about to be set off, Big Time, by the added oomph of transiting Mars. You look in the ephemeris and see that they're on the way, and you start thinking about all that stuff in the Olde Bookes about being beheaded, dying of The Plague, and so forth. Well, the first thing to keep in mind is that there aren't nearly as many opportunities to be beheaded as there used to be, and the Black Plague isn't running nearly as rampant, either. Still, rather than just sitting there waiting for the executioner to arrive, get busy. Get out all your new books and start circling your favorite Uranus\Mars activities—experiences that are the astrological equivalent of a Thunderstorm. Sudden, exciting things. Anything you've never done before qualifies—especially if you never thought you'd dare to try it.

See, when your Mars is being transited, your physical energy level is high—'way high. You've got to find a way to use that energy—an Antidote, you might say, specially designed to tap it off. Remember, your Mars is the part of you that insists on Action. He's your soldier, your sword—the part of you that wants to Just Do It. So do something. Take action. We all know what it's like to literally be Too Tired To Get Mad, right? Well, that's what you need to do. That way, even if you're not 'immune' to incoming advances from The Outside World, when the transit arrives, you'll have used up too much of your Mars to be as volatile as you would have been.

PLANNING YOUR TRIP

In a nutshell, then, the idea behind working with transits is first to figure out just exactly what your current lesson is. What skills are you being nudged by The Universe to learn, right now? What do you already feel drawn toward trying next? After that, your quest is to figure out how best to learn the lesson(s), in ways that will make you happy and further your growth as a person.

Think of it as planning a cross-country trip. You have several options. You can put some gas in the tank and wing it, asking directions as you go and trusting that eventually you'll find your destination—through trial and effort. If you'd like to be a little more prepared but still want some degree of spontaneity, on the other hand, you can get a pile of maps and tourist guides and lay out the trip yourself. You can also go directly to an agency like AAA, to find the fastest or most scenic way to get you where you want to go, and get the latest information on possible delays or detours due to road construction or other Inevitables along the way. It's up to you. Regardless of the type of preparation you choose, if you point yourself in a particular direction, you'll probably get there—eventually.

Well, once you know astrology is Out There, and once you know what it can 'do,' you have the same options available to you for your life's journey. You might decide to wing it, to just go on instinct, trusting that The Universe will provide road signs and guideposts as you need them. You might opt to get a copy of your chart and learn to do astrology on your own—or you might consult someone who's an expert in the field, and get their help to lay out your trip one step at a time.

Personally, I recommend number two or three for your long-range planning, and number one at all times. Yes, The Universe will always get you where you're going somehow, and yes, you'll always need to look out for the directions it will send along that won't be found on any map—things you wouldn't know any other way than by actually Being There. (Those of you who've read The Celestine Prophecy know what I'm talking about here). But if you've got a time limit in mind, or a particular mode of travel, or if there are certain stops you'd rather not miss, it's a good idea to plan as much of the trip as you can to suit your tastes.

Now, please don't forget to use some basic common sense—along with your ephemeris—when you're planning the future. Remember that we humans are really, really good at Creative Interpretation, too, and that even if you're only seeing wonderful things in the future, you might want to consult a professional about your stock investments, your upcoming marriage, or your health, anyway. (As you spend more and more time working with astrology, by the way, you'll come to understand just what I mean about how creative we truly can be—especially at the beginning of a new relationship. I like to call that the Before and After Syndrome of Synastry and Composites—but that's another book....) Aspects Transiting Planets Make—A Primer.

THE DIFFERENCE BETWEEN 'HARD' AND 'EASY' ASPECTS

Now, whenever a planet touches one of your planets, you're going to get a variety of scenarios, both good and bad, (to use those extremely Uncool, almost-banished terms). See, different aspects made by transiting planets produce different times. In a nutshell, conjunctions are the most action-oriented transits of all, because a planet has literally barged right into both the sign and degree of your natal planet and turned it on. Your planet has been invaded by another planet who's sitting right on top of it. It has no choice but to react. Transits by trine may not bring anything at all, save for a really good feeling—you know how lazy they get. Sextiles show exciting opportunities that are now available—muscles that are just dying to be worked. Squares indicate times that may be hectic, overwhelming, or irritating, times when you'd rather be in Philadelphia. Oppositions tend to play out in our relationships, since they're 180 degrees apart, and it's often easier to project a part of ourselves on to someone else than to own it. Quincunxes bring up health concerns, and difficult no-win adjustments— either/or situations that are touch to resolve, but eminently satisfying when you do. Semi-sextiles get change underway— especially when they're exact.

To keep things simple, I've included interpretations for each of the planets as it touches each of the natal planets and points, divided into four sections.

You'll find interpretations for:

1) Overall Symptoms of a particular planet, regardless of the aspect it's making by transit.

2) Difficult or Hard aspects—traditionally, the Square, Opposition, some Conjunctions, the Quincunx, and the Semi-Square and Sesquiquadrate—vs. Easy aspects—traditionally, the Sextile, Trine, some Conjunctions, and the Semi-sextile.

3) Transits of each planet through each house.

4) A list at the beginning of each chapter of what you ought to have in your Kit—to deal with a particular transit of a particular planet. Like I said, I wanted to give you a good laugh before you looked up your transit.

AND SPEAKING OF TRANSITS THROUGH THE HOUSES...

When you notice a transiting planet about to enter a house, keep in mind that it's moving in for a visit. When Inners enter a house, our daily activities begin to revolve around those matters for a short time—but since the Inners tend to travel in "packs," that relatively short amount of time can be very, very intense. For example, the farthest Mercury can be from the Sun is 28 degrees, and Venus can only be 72 degrees away. Put the two of them in the same house as the Sun and you've got a Meeting. Add the Moon, who makes a loop once a "moonth," too, and you've got an emotional situation.

When you're attempting to interpret this type of thing, you've got to pay attention to which house a pack is transiting. If it's the fourth house, we're due to spend an awful lot of time taking care of our homes—tending to Family Values, you might say. If it's the seventh house, we're about to enter a time when our One-to-One relationships will be primary. Watch as packs move from one house to the next and your interest in the matters you handle with that side of your personality subtly shifts and moves along with them.

Now, when an Outer enters a house, the situation is quite different. Instead of just getting involved with a particular Life Department for a month or so, you've just signed up for a period of years. For example, since Uranus has an orbit of 84 years, he spends an average of 7 years in a house. This, then, is no ordinary week-end house guest—this guy's here for what's going to seem like forever. Neptune and Pluto stay even longer—up to 20 years in a house, in fact. Needless to say, while the Outer Planet is visiting, we need to make adjustments to accommodate the new circumstances circulating around us. Big Adjustments. Now, after awhile, we don't notice an Outer's presence any more, but that doesn't mean it's gone—it's just that we've gotten used to it.

It's like this: when you open the door to a flower shop, your olfactory apparatus is barraged by Flower Scents. You're over-whelmed by how wonderful the air smells. You take a deep breath, smile, and say 'Mmm, it smells soooo good in here' to the florist, who, nine times out of ten, will smile back and say, 'Does it? I don't notice much any more.' No matter what we're exposed to physically, we eventually tune it out—smells, sounds, and visuals, too. How many times have you walked by a sweater you tossed on a chair weeks ago without seeing it? Well, that's how we react to Outers in houses. We feel their presence most acutely when the planet first enters the house, and then again when it leaves and we've got to clean up after it. In a nutshell, it's like this: Outers move in and re-vamp a house to suit their purposes—they re-arrange the furniture to suit their own tastes, that is. Inners just stop by for the weekend, but if they arrive in a bus, you've got your hands full for that weekend. Either way, it's really fascinating to watch your focus change.

Well, all right, then. Let's get busy. I think that's everything I wanted to say, in a preliminary sense. Of course, if I think of anything important, I'll jump right in. By the way, I realize that this ends your period of Continued Attention, and that from this point on, you'll only be nipping in and out of the book as your transits decree. That's okay, too—just make sure you read the first part of every planet's chapter for additional info on what to expect from it in general.

CHAPTER THREE

THE SUN

Your Sun Transit Kit:

A spotlight

A press-kit

Lots of Gold—Preferably Worn In A Crown

A mirror

A date with the movie-star of your choice

A gown or tux, to wear to the Awards Banquet in your honor

A Limo

Sunglasses—to hide out from the paparazzi

A Copy of 'A Star Is Born'

An all-expense paid cruise to the warm island of your choice

The Sun—Let's Talk About You— What Do You Think Of Me?

All right. Let's go right to the top, and start with transits of The Sun—the Head Honcho. We've talked about the importance of the Sun's role in your chart, and about how that importance stems from the fact that the Sun is the very center of the Solar System—the source of heat, light, and therefore, all life on this planet. We've established, too, that the Sun is like an Executive

Director of a Corporation, a Big Boss. So how do the Sun's transits pan out?

Well, it's like this: Wherever the Sun is transiting in your chart at this moment is a place where tending to the activities symbolized by the house and planets involved will make you feel happy and fulfilled. Sun transits to a planet you own bring out what you really love about that planet. Sun transits through a house show the area of life where you especially want to be loved, appreciated, and patted on the back at the moment, and where you're most likely to gain attention and fame for performing well. Remember, the Sun is a symbolic font of creativity, so as long as you're doing what you really love to do under Sun transits, you're a shoe-in to do it well.

Sun transits are also not notoriously selfless times. Since the transiting Sun brings our natal planet or point into the spotlight, we tend to put the interests of the particular planet or point involved first. We're after recognition under Sun transits. Accept that from yourself, and take a couple of extra minutes in front of the mirror if you're having one—just in case the paparazzi catch up with you....

The Sun Through The Houses

Because the Sun's apparent orbit is so regular, it's the only planet whose travel through the houses in our chart can be used to plan out our year. For example, if we have 5 degrees of Aries rising and 7 degrees of Taurus on the second house cusp, then we know that every year from the time the Sun is at 5 Aries, (March 25th,) to the time it's at 7 Taurus, (April 27th,) the Sun will be passing through our first house. You can do the same with the rest of the houses in the chart. It's fun, in fact, to make a list of the dates the Sun will spend in each of the houses, and watch as your focus changes, literally almost overnight, as the Sun moves from room to room (house to house) through your chart.

Since the Sun acts like a flashlight of sorts, it's trek through the houses shows which side of your personality you'll be using most at that time of year, every year, and which areas of life will demand most of your creative attention. Since the Sun's transits are also famous as indicators of trigger times for Outer Planet transits, you may find that it's during May that you tend to move, during August that your major relationships begin, or during

October that you tend to switch jobs. Since Mercury is never more than 28 degrees from the Sun, and Venus never more than 48 degrees, the Sun is also, appropriately, 'attended' by these planets—as befits royalty. Once every two years, Mars will join the pack, and the Moon jumps in for 2 and a half days out of every month, too. As a result, the house the Sun is transiting is often a very busy place. Here's what you can expect, then, during each of the twelve months, as the Sun winds its way through your chart.

FIRST HOUSE—AND THE ASCENDANT

Since the Ascendant really is your Front Door, this first house is the entryway into You—it's where you keep the side of your personality anyone who meets you gets to see first. This house, then, is greatly responsible for whether or not anyone actually wants to come in and get to know you, and the planets that transit it symbolically show what type of face you'll turn to visitors—and whether you're in the mood for them at all. When the Sun and it's magical golden spotlight patrol the area, you can expect to meet new Others by the truckload.

You'll find yourself hanging out the Welcome mat and extending your hand to introduce yourself over and over. (Now, remember, if Saturn or Pluto is also transiting your first house, the plot will thicken—literally—and although this may still be the case, you may not enjoy it nearly as much....) Now, the first house represents sunrise, so it's indicative of new beginnings of many different kinds.

Don't be surprised, then, if this is the month out of every year when you regularly find yourself turning over a new leaf of some kind, quite often of the physical nature, since here is where the issue of Your Appearance and Your General Health is also found. You may diet, begin an exercise program, or change your hair or clothing styles now. Remember, however, that although this house pertains only to your surface self, whatever you do to your physical appearance really goes a lot deeper. When you change your looks, you're making as public an announcement as you possibly can—you're telling the world that you're different on the inside, too.

The Sun here inspires you to express yourself physically—it's your own creative interpretation of how you see yourself, right now. At the very least, you'll tend to dress more according to your mood than at other times of the year—clothes will be a tool for self-expression. Of course, you may even tend to be a bit of a 'show-off' now, but go for it....it's your month.

SECOND HOUSE

Get ready to meet the Banker, the Accountant, and the Check-Book Balancer in you—yes, even if you're a Sag, and you hate dealing with money. The spotlight is on finances, possessions, and material things in general—and also on whatever it is that you hold dear. This will ordinarily be the time of year when you're concerned with Stuff, when the Shopper in you will be unleashed on the world. You'll probably make most of your major purchases during this time of year, and do most of your personal financial dealings. (This transit may also coincide with a move, since moving is the one time the Universe provides us with an opportunity to pick up and examine each and every Thing we own.) Now, the way we spend our money, our attitude towards our possessions, and how we treat what we own are surface activities that really represent how we're feeling about Us at the time. So during this month out of every year, pay attention to the types of Things you're drawn to, for what you're willing to spend your days doing for money to buy them, and for your attitude about possessions and the material world in general—you'll learn a lot about what you think You're currently worth.

THIRD HOUSE

Strap on those roller-skates, kids, and hook your Walk wo/man to your fanny pack, because this is undoubtedly going to be one very busy month. This is Mercury's house, a place where communication, through speaking, writing, and third-house visits—AKA short trips, is the name of the game. During this month of the year, then, you'll find yourself doing lots of errands, making lots of phone calls, chatting on and on with neighbors, writing letters and answering correspondence. If you're into e-mail, expect your electronic mailbox to be filled to the brim with all kinds of notes—especially since this is Mercury's house, and he just loves computers.

Now, there are many ways to communicate—gestures, sign language, meaningful glances, etc.—so if you're in the mood for a class on communications of any kind, now's the time to go for it. You'll learn more quickly (depending, of course, on your natal third house condition,) and enjoy it more. Since this is also the side of you who operates on Automatic Pilot, it represents childhood, the time in your life when you learned all those functions you now take for granted. Often, the Sun's trek through this house will bring back people or experiences from childhood, visits to your old stomping grounds, lots of interchanges with your siblings, maybe even a High School reunion—formal or informal. This house also shows local government, so don't be surprised if you're more apt to become involved in community matters, now, too.

FOURTH HOUSE

This is the house that represents our home, our nest here on the planet, the Safe Place we create to return to each and every day after we've gone out there and mingled with the world. It's the physical space we share with our families, too, so when the Sun passes through this house, even if you're not ordinarily so inclined, don't be surprised if you suddenly become A Homebody, hanging out with The Family at Your Place—and really loving it. Yes, you, too, may find yourself digging in the garden, making pizza with the kids, and cleaning out the closets. (Don't be scared—it's like Christmas—it only comes once a year.)

Planets passing through this area of your chart will symbolically trigger your urge to be private, too—since this is the lowest point in the chart, representative of Midnight. So you'll probably also be in hibernation mode, Turning in Early a lot more than usual, and renting a lot more videos. Now, this is the spot in your chart where you store your memories—it's your Emotional Warehouse, as a matter of fact—so the Sun's transit of this house may bring old memories to the surface, things you hadn't thought of in years. This is traditionally the house of Real Estate, too— so if you're going to buy or sell property, now's the time you'll probably find yourself doing it.

FIFTH HOUSE

This is Leo's place, the side of you that only comes out when there's fun to be had, when work is done, and it's time to party, entertain, and be entertained. Since the Sun is most at home here, it's now officially play time, kids, a month when you'll be really hard-pressed to deal with Hafta's of any kind. This is where you keep the charming, playful, Cruise-Director side of You. The Sun's trip through this house puts the spotlight on that side of you, so prepare, then, to party, play, and Have Fun. (God/dess forbid you have to work—it'll be miserable. Save your vacation weeks and use them now.)

Your hobbies, leisure-time interests, and playmates will take Center Ring all month, and you'll find yourself amazingly creative, too. Remember, the fifth house is the side of us who creates so that we're allowed to see a bit of ourselves in those creations—it's really important that you do what you love to do now. Dance, paint, sing, or write. Spend time with your kids, or with somebody's kids—they're the best excuse any adult could ask for to regress long enough to enjoy a game of tag, a jigsaw puzzle, or a rope-swing at the lake.

By the way, this is also the house of Love Affairs, so if you're single, be on the lookout for Someone Special—(at least one)—right now. This house traditionally refers to speculation—otherwise known as gambling, so although I'm not going to encourage you to head for Vegas with your life savings, (not unless you call me first,) it's not a bad idea to check for Jupiter transits and get yourself a lottery ticket or two.

SIXTH HOUSE

All right, now. Just settle down. Yes, after all that fun you had last month, it's time to Buckle Down and Get Some Work Done. Here's the house that's associated with work, health, and slavery—(which is often how work feels.) Of course, there's also a lot to be said about the satisfaction we feel from a job well done—so the Sun's transit of this house often points to a time when we actually enjoy our work, when we're especially attentive to it, and when we're recognized or applauded on the job for our accomplishments. Now, this is also the side of us who loves to Do Unto Others. It's the service-oriented side of us, Virgo's place. So if you find yourself paying more attention than usual to Others, and being especially helpful, pat yourself on the back. You're using your Sun transit well.

Health issues often come up now—that's not to say that you're going to be sick, but more so that you'll be paying more attention than usual to how you function—both on a physical level, and at work, as we talked about earlier. Exercise, diet, and the condition of your body will be at the top of your list, now. Since pets are also traditionally a sixth-house issue, you may find yourself tending to them—and to their health—a bit more than usual.

SEVENTH HOUSE

Welcome to The Land of The Other, the month out of every year when your focus will turn to the person you become when you're relating vis-à-vis. Now, although this house is traditionally given over to marriage and business partners, it's really just the side of you who comes out when there's only one Other in the vicinity. Now, when we're involved in a marriage or business partnership, we spend a lot more time in the company of that one person—so we necessarily spend a lot more time in seventh-house mode.

Anytime we use the word 'my' to describe An Other, however, it's a good indication that they're included in our seventh houses. As a result, you can expect to do an awful lot of dealing with those folks this month, especially if you have a Significant Other or business partner. Expect to be doing an awful lot of One-to-One relating in general, too. This may mean that your work suddenly requires you to interview, work side-by-side with a partner, or train someone. Regardless, the Sun's transit through this house shows a time when the spotlight will fall on this side of your personality—so you'll have a perfect opportunity to examine the You that you become when you're with An Other, and what you're looking for in a relationship.

EIGHTH HOUSE

The eighth house is the side of you who comes out when the subject is Intimacy—which may or may not have anything to do with actual physical touching. Intimacy is what happens when we strip off everything that's extraneous to the person we really are, at our core—so we often meet up with this side of ourselves during times of Agony and Ecstasy, when we're dealing with topics like sex, death, and all manner of mergings, financial and otherwise. Now's your month to examine the issue of blending, merging, and melding with An Other, to learn the appropriate use of that power.

This may mean that you spend the month in real or imagined power-struggles with An Other, but regardless, now's when you'll find yourself suddenly playing the detective, analyst, and assassin, examining all your own motives, as well as those of others. As a result, you may find yourself involved in a crisis at this time, or with extreme circumstances of an emotional nature. Now's also when you'll find yourself craving intensity—and maybe even life-

and-death experiences, whether it's as simple as watching Cliffhanger or as involved as experimenting with skydiving or fire-walking. You'll realize the power of subtlety, and notice signals more. The Sun's trek through this house is a lesson on the delicate arts of intensity, manipulation, and power. Remember to come up for air periodically.

NINTH HOUSE

Wave Bubbeye to the fans, and climb aboard the plane, train, or hot-air balloon of your choice. The Sun's trek through this house points to a time when Adventure is the name of the game, when it's time to break routine and Go Play somewhere you've never been, in a way you've never played. This is the side of you who wants to learn through new experiences, to roam, and wander— and wonder. Now's when you'll want to Boldly Go Where No One Has Gone Before—with your trusty Sun spotlight in hand.

Foreign places are definitely one of the Places of Choice for your ninth-house side, so if you're so inclined, and you can get away, head for Europe, or Africa, or Sri Lanka. Break your routine, and allow the ninth-house side of you to bask in the warmth of the Sun's glow. This is the side of you who'll delight in learning something new, too, so now's a great time to take a class— especially if it's on a traditionally ninth-house topic, like philosophy, politics, or religion. Either way, the Sun here is just begging you for Newness. Whether it's travel or education, feed yourself something entirely different from your daily routine. This house also relates to publishing and advertising, so if you're in business or if you're in the market to see your ideas in print, now's the time to train the Sun's light on those areas.

TENTH HOUSE —AND THE MIDHEAVEN

Wondering why you've been called to the Principal's office? Well, if you're due for either a public pat on the back or a public chastisement, expect it now—and most especially on the day when the Sun actually 'hits' the door of this house—the 'Midheaven' of the chart. This is the house in our charts that's the equivalent of our own personal stage, the place where we post our accomplishments for all the world to see. The Sun's visit to this house points to a time when you're currently The Star of the Show, when all eyes are trained on You, when the spotlight is directed on What You've Done. Now, this is traditionally a time of public acclaim, when you'll be recognized, congratulated, or applauded publicly for what you've done. That's if you've done it well—the Sun up here is simply a focus on your Reputation—what you're 'reputed' to have done—so if you've done bad, that's going to come out now, too. (Especially if Saturn is here, too—in which case, it's probably time to choose a new state, and definitely time for a new identity...) Since this is the side of you who deals with Authority Figures, and with the responsibilities associated with becoming one yourself, the Sun's trek through here is also a time when your dealings with The Authorities, or your behavior as An Authority, will also become public. This is the symbolic 'roof' of your house—get used to the fact that during this month out of every year, everything about you is going to be available for public scrutiny. And make sure you're up for the challenge.

ELEVENTH HOUSE

Pull out your ballcaps and your team sweatshirts, because now's when you'll want the world to know Who You Belong With. Yes, this is the month out of the year when you'll be especially concerned with Groups—everything from your friends and associates to your favorite sports-teams, to your Causes. As a matter of fact, if you're about to join a group, choose a team, or identify yourself as part of an association, now's when you may do it. Since the Sun is very much the leader, now's when you'll also be likely to be drawn into that role with regard to the groups you already belong to. Whether it's Amnesty International, Greenpeace, or the NRA, now's when you'll want to play a starring role—or at least be recognized for your contributions to your group's efforts. You'll enjoy working with others more, now, (again, depending on the condition of your eleventh house, in general,) and see what the Team Player in you is really all about. On the job, you may also be asked to work with a union, organization, or society. Pay special attention, at this time, to the part of you that's 'fed' by the groups you're a part of—the common denominator you share with them says a lot about your goals for the future.

TWELFTH HOUSE

Pull down the shades and put some New-Age music on, because it's That Time of Year. Since this is the side of you that only comes out when you're alone, during this particular month, you'll find yourself more likely than usual to withdraw, retreat, and contemplate. The Sun's trek through this house is a time when we aren't quite as social as we might ordinarily be, when we prefer our own company to anyone else's. We want to go away to a meditation center, or we spend a lot of time simply on our own.

Now, this house also shows the side of us that comes out when it's time to deal with Secrets and Secret People, so the Sun's transit through this house may also point to a time when we're more than usually involved with behind-the-scenes adventures of one kind or another. (Use your imagination here.)

On a much deeper level, the twelfth house is where we keep the behaviors we were taught very early on to stifle, repress, or deny. The Sun's transit to planets in this house will often bring those subconscious behaviors to our attention—for better or worse. We suddenly become aware of our tendency to deny our feelings (Moon,) our anger (Mars,) or our ideas (Mercury,) for example. This is the side of ourselves we feel was subtly discouraged in our early lives. We learn to express it in alternative ways as we grow older, through acting or 'playing pretend,' for example, but also through subconscious expressions. The Sun moving through the twelfth house allows even this shy side of us to shine through.

Well, that was your personal walking tour through the houses. Now let's talk about the Sun as it joins forces with all of the other planets in your chart.

Sun/Sun Transits

FIRST, THE CONJUNCTION...

Happy Birthday! The Sun is right now just about exactly where it was on the day you were born. You're about to get a whole new Solar Return chart, which means that a whole new year is laying out right in front of you just waiting to unfold, with all its joys, sorrows, passions and adventures. (A solar return chart, by the way, is a chart calculated for the moment each year when the Sun returns to the exact degree and minute where it was when you were born—this chart is seen by many astrologers as a whole year's worth of transits. In truth, solar returns really are amazingly accurate descriptions of how your year will pan out.)

So what will you be feeling today—and how should you spend your day? Well, what do you *want* to do today? What do you really enjoy? As much as some folks consider it 'childish' to treat ourselves specially on our birthday, my advice is to do just that. Take the day off and plan a full schedule of the things you most love to do. Birthdays only come once a year, and it's your right— your privilege, in fact, as Royalty For A Day—to enjoy this 24-hour period to its fullest. So sleep late. Get a massage. Go out to dinner, too—no cooking. (Unless you're a Taurus, and you like to cook, of course.) Whatever. If you've really got to work or attend to Should's of one kind or another dues to circumstances beyond your control, just make sure you take a really good chunk out of today, come hell or high water, and spend it pampering yourself.

Look at it this way: It's *your* day, a day when you can really recharge your solar battery for the year by tending to You. You're sitting on a 'double dose' of Sun energy today—and that's pretty rich stuff. Roll around in it. And if you want to get to know yourself better, by the way, pay very special attention to however you're feeling today, because that's the way the Sun inside of you would feel all the time if you never stifled it. Remember, the Sun represents your Pride and Confidence, your Identity, and your Ego. It corresponds with gold, that rich, royal metal that adorns Kings and Queens. Give yourself a gift of some kind today— and enjoy the spotlight.

OTHER SUN/SUN TRANSITS

In addition to acting like the Spotlight of the Moment, since the Sun is the Yang or Masculine principle, Sun transits also point out times when Yang figures, such as men or authority figures, will take the spotlight in your life. When the Sun aspects itself, the nature of the aspect will describe what you can expect as to the quality of those encounters.

The Sun squaring itself, for example, can point to a time when you feel as if What You Want To Do is blocked by The Authorities. The square is representative of an 'argument,' so this transit can literally point to arguments or conflicts with authorities, but it can also be a time when you're having an inner argument with yourself—about What You Really Want. Now, squares show where you're pushed towards growth by feeling 'forced' to find a new way to handle a situation—so although circumstances might be difficult in the meantime, these transits are often the ones that signify not so much major events as times of inner tension that prompt you to reevaluate the way you deal with Responsibility. This transit can also indicate a time when you feel a bit 'tense,' too, with or without a reason, since that's the dynamic of the square, and since the Sun is representative of Your Outgoing Energy—energy that, under a square, may not find the outlet it wants.

The opposition, on the other hand, is not usually experienced so 'internally.' The Sun opposing itself is very much a tug-of-war— a symbolic 'debate' between you and The Authorities. You may feel as if superiors or higher-ups are deliberately trying to counter all your best-laid plans, or that nothing you try to do goes along without a battle. In reality, it's a debate you're having with You— you've just hired out one side of the opposition to someone else to help you see it. Since the opposition is, above all else, symbolic of Awareness, this aspect really presents us with the opportunity to see a part of ourselves we wouldn't ordinarily see, most often through our dealings with An Other. Remember, all oppositions are really just matched pairs, so whatever you're seeing in The Other that you're not fond of might be a projected part of your own personality that you need to own. The end result of all oppositions can be Balance—so learning the fine art of compromise just might be on your schedule now.

Sun trines and sextiles are just dandy. Things go along well, The Authorities are cooperative and helpful, and you're the apple of their eye. Under the trines, this is especially true, but you might not notice it so much because things are going along so well, and trines are a bit on the lazy side. If you've got to ask a favor or get the support of an authority, by the way, now's the time—if they don't just do it for you first. You can ask just about anybody for anything now, matter of fact, and expect some valid help. Under the sextiles, you're provided with opportunities to further yourself, or a 'tip' that helps you towards accomplishing something that will further your career in the future. Both the sextile and the trine are wonderfully happy and social times, too, when all's quite well in your world.

Remember that no matter which transit the transiting Sun makes to your Sun, the outer events—those involving authorities for example—are really reflections of what is going on inside. So, if you've got problems with others under a Sun/Sun square, look closely, and see if you're not expressing the energy of the square by being a bit *too* prideful—or maybe not prideful enough. If an opposition is not going along well, consider that it may be time to project your ego Out There instead of repressing yourself. This is a great time to contact others who can help you "shine"—but it's also a time to see how your creativity has affected or impacted others.

Of course, you may also be projecting a bit too much—in which case, Sun/Sun oppositions can be times when you're dealing with tension, feeling ashamed of yourself, or when you're a bit too "ego-centric." Your Sun represents your ego, remember, and under Sun/Sun transits, it's also possible to become a bit "touchy," or take things too personally.

Under the "nicer" transits, you'll feel proud of yourself too, often without anyone's pat on the back but your own. You may be seeing a creative project begin to flower, and your self-esteem begins to rise. Again, the Sun's "job" natally is to show you what you're here to accomplish, and to guide you into activity and experiences that give you joy. Don't forget that the Sun in your chart is full of the inner joy of Just Being You. Make sure that you make yourself proud then—before you turn your attention to anyone else.

SUN/MOON

When the Sun touches your Moon, the traveling spotlight is turned to home, family, Mom, women friends, and Your Feelings. Now, on an emotional level, depending on the aspect the Sun is making to your Moon, this can mean you'll be feeling particularly joyous, particularly unhappy, or just 'moody' in general. With the conjunction, it's hard to say how you'll 'feel,' but it's a given that whatever you're feeling, you'll feel it a lot—and you won't make a secret of it. The Sun is an agent on patrol for stars, and your Moon has just taken the stage. (If you've got a 12th-house Moon, or the Moon in Pisces, by the way, this transit will be a bit more of a chore for you than for others—since it's all about exposing your feelings, rather than keeping them to yourself.)

Since the Sun often brings dealings with men into our lives, the cause of your emotionality may be a man. With the squares or other 'hard' aspects, you may feel an inner tension but not quite be able to put your finger on the reason for it, or feel that authority figures are upsetting you deliberately. Family members or the women in your life may seem to be a bit on the testy side. You might also experience the challenging aspects quite literally, as emotional challenges sent your way by the Universe to make you aware of how you're feeling about a certain issue. The 'easy' aspects, like trines or sextiles, represent happy, sociable times, when the inner harmony you feel will reflect in your dealings with the world—especially with your family and your women friends. Regardless of the aspect, when the Sun shines it's light on your Moon, it's time for you to get to know yourself a little better—from the inside out.

SUN/MERCURY

Here's when you're handed the microphone and asked for your two cents. Yes, when the Sun touches Mercury, it's time for you to tell us what You think. (Needless to say, folks with Mercury in Leo just love this transit...) The spotlight is on communication, short trips, and learning. The conjunction is usually an extremely busy time—the answering machine and the mail box (and the e-mail box, too,) are jam-packed with all kinds of interesting communications. Since Mercury represents the principle of duality, you'll also often find that these are times when messages and people tend to turn up in your life in pairs—with 'odd' or 'coincidental' similarities that make you grin and feel as if someone is playing a game with you.

The squares and other tough aspects point to times when you may feel challenged by authority figures, or forced by them to defend your point—like you're giving a lecture and there's a heckler in the room who knows enough about your subject to be a bit intimidating and more than a bit annoying. These aspects also show up during hectic, busy periods—times when we feel like we're 'caught in traffic,' literally and figuratively.

Oppositions and other challenging aspects can also represent times when we're arguing with the men in our lives. Now, remember that 'hard' aspects are more likely to coincide with events than 'soft' aspects. So if you're waiting for a communication of some kind, expect it now.

The 'easy' aspects are times when it feels as if everyone automatically understands you, when it's easy to get your message across, easy to learn something new, and easy to talk to others. If you need to take a test of any kind, then, wait for the trines and sextiles. And if you need to make a statement, talk something out, or make your point, these are also good times to do it.

In all, any transit of the Sun to Mercury points to a time when your mouth or your hands are spotlighted. You're going to be able to talk the pants off the best of them, to sell yourself or your pet project with skillful word play. Anything you've got to do that employs your eye to hand coordination will also gain attention. Just make sure that you're saying and doing things that you *want* to be noticed, because now isn't a good time for secrets.

SUN/VENUS

Who and what do you love—and how do you love it? That's the subject you handle with your Venus, and that's the Topic du Jour when the Sun comes along for a visit. You find yourself handling your possessions, dealing with money matters, and relating with Others of all kinds—Significant Others, friends, and even complete strangers. (More women than men, too.) See, Venus is where we keep our supply of Behavior That's Pleasing To The Other—so when the Sun arrives, the focus is on manners, politeness, and sociability. Don't be surprised if you're the recipient of the kind of attention that brings out this side in you now.

By conjunction, expect to be dealing with relationships and money issues with tact and diplomacy. (That's if you've got the type of Venus that's well-mannered. If you've got Venus in Aries, forget the tact and diplomacy—instead, expect simply to be even more aggressive than usual with your Other. If you've got Venus in Sag, expect to overindulge in something...)

The trines and sextiles from the Sun to Venus are fun, easy times—you enjoy others, they enjoy you, shopping goes well, money matters happen along without much stress (except if you've got Venus in Sag, and you're always broke, anyway....,) and you're the giver and receiver of hugs, pecks on the cheek, and compliments.

The squares and other 'hard' aspects, at worst, mean you'll want what you want Right Now, and you'll want a whole bunch of it. Remember, Venus is how we spoil ourselves. If your Venus is at all inclined natally toward art or music, by the way, this is the time to sit down and Let It Flow. Venus is the patron saint of The Arts, and the Sun is the planet who provides the urge to create. Create beautiful things, then—and realize that it's your own inner beauty that you're bringing out into the world.

SUN/MARS

On your mark—get set—Go! Get ready to prove yourself, to show The Authorities your assertive aggressive side. This transit of the Sun to Mars points to encounters with others who, in one way or another, want to see how far they can push our personal envelopes. In the case of the conjunction, the spotlight is on How We Handle Anger—and often it's at these times that we need to decide whether an offense was intentional, then whether we need to react aggressively, or let it slide.

With the 'hard' aspects, we feel as if They've pushed us into a corner, and, Mars being Mars, we come out fighting—sword drawn, ready to defend ourselves. This can mean that we're especially willful too—for better or worse. Of course, the squares and other action-oriented aspects from the Sun also point to times of extra-inspiration, especially on the physical level, so if you've got something physical to do—and participating in sports is a particularly good use of these transits—you'll have the extra inspiration of the Sun to help. In other words, run the race now.

If you've got to start something, now is a super time to do that too. You're quite literally going to be a "ball of fire." With the easy aspects, we still feel 'pushed' by our environment in some way, but it's more inspirational than intimidating. Higher-ups in our lives provide us with healthy challenges, designed to make us 'stretch' by pushing us into Action. Either way, the Sun's transits to Mars give us the opportunity to put Rambo in the spotlight. Basically, now's when you'll establish your own personal style of handling conflict and challenge.

SUN/JUPITER

Jupiter is where we keep our ability to expand, and to laugh at ourselves. When the Sun transits Jupiter, the roar of the crowd accompanies the photographers to our most optimistic, generous and positive side. By conjunction, this is really true—these are times when the Santa Claus in you gets interviewed, in other words, anyone who meets you will go away thinking you **are** Jupiter. Since Jupiter also rules publishing, education, and long trips—the wanderer, philosopher and statesperson in you, that is—this is typically a time when ventures related to those fields take center stage in your life. It's not a bad time to begin a long trip, either.

Now, as far as the hard aspects go, remember that since Jupiter also represents the principle of excess and waste, although you may not realize it at the moment, too much of a good thing really isn't all that good. If you're having a period of excess, or overdoing something (whether it's food, drink, or an activity), when a hard aspect comes along from the Sun to Jupiter, you'll have your chance to really See the Light. If you can crawl out of bed the next day while it's still bright out, that is....

The easy aspects point to days when The Authorities either bring goodies, or expect you to provide some. You're the star of the show, and when Things In General go along remarkably well. These are also traditionally lucky times. Again, although I'm not sending you off to a casino, you might want to pick up a lottery ticket, or take a chance on that car the animal shelter is raffling off.

SUN/SATURN

Saturn's in charge of all the opposite qualities to Jupiter. Saturn builds walls, Jupiter pushes them open. Saturn rules contraction, caution, and prudence. Jupiter's the patron saint of expansion, risk, and daring. When Saturn is transited by the Sun, then, the microphone is handed over to The Authority Figure in you—the side of you who's in charge of following rules, paying dues, and Just Saying No. By conjunction, we're often simply asked to become the Authority Figure for a day or so. We're put In Charge of something, and watched to see how we'll do.

By hard aspect, the challenge is to put our money where our mouth is. Our accomplishments are examined by a team of experts, and we're expected to explain why we did it That Way. Needless to say, these are times when we receive valuable lessons on how to follow directions, keep to The Plan, and Respect our Elders.

The easier aspects are times when we're honored in some way for our accomplishments. The boss drags the visiting reps into our office so they can meet the person who came up with that great idea, technique, or plan, maybe. Sun transits to Saturn, then, regardless of the type, can be times of great personal reward and a sense of pride in what you've done.

SUN/URANUS

Even if you're convinced that you don't have a radical, rebellious, or eccentric streak, these transits will prove you wrong. Your Uranus is where you keep all those qualities—and when the Sun comes for a visit, you get to let the Mad Scientist in you out of the closet for a day or two. By conjunction, this side of you is in the spotlight, so classically these are times when you're quite willing to Be An Individual, rebel, revolt, and Challenge Authority. Others will be heard to say things like, "I never knew..." (fill in the blank,) as they raise their eyebrows and cock their heads to the side.

By hard aspect, the Sun's visits point to a day when it will be time for you to Fight City Hall, to tell the authority figures that you're not going to cooperate because their way is the wrong way. The hard aspects also push you to use the brilliance Uranus is famous for—to discover or invent a new way to handle an old problem.

The trines and sextiles are times when you're encouraged to be an individual, when Others smile and shake their heads in amusement at your 'quirks.' They're also times of increased understanding, when flashes of insight come to you. Write them down. Regardless of the nature of the transiting aspect, you'll probably surprise yourself at what you'll think, do, and say now.

SUN/NEPTUNE

Neptune's spot in our chart is a place that's pink, fuzzy, and misty. Not too brightly lit, not too exposed, it's quiet, secret, and secluded—like an ashram, a convent, or a retreat center. It's the spot where we feel safe to dream, wish, pray, and Transcend. Well. When the Sun comes along to this spot by conjunction, we may feel a bit like a mole in a cartoon who comes out into the light of day with x's over his eyes. The Sun's light brings publicity, attention, and exposure. All of a sudden, our secrets are on display—along with any tendencies we have towards withdrawal, denial, and avoidance. Of course, so are all our tendencies towards compassion, spirituality, and idealism—not bad qualities to become momentarily famous for. It's a mixed bag.

With the easier aspects, it is the nicer side of our Neptune that we show to the world—the easier aspects seem to coax Neptune out, rather than forcing her to make an appearance.

With the harder aspects, we feel 'forced' to come out of hiding in some way. Regardless of the transit, the Sun to Neptune brings us an opportunity to be amazingly creative, through uniting the two most artistic, imaginative planets in the galaxy.

SUN/PLUTO

Pluto in our charts is the place where we stash our personal power. When the Sun makes any hard aspect to Pluto, it's time to see what we're made of. Now, that can mean that we become involved in conflicts or power struggles of some kind—possibly with authority figures or with the men in our lives. It can also mean that we're faced with a situation that inspires us to handle ourselves with a degree of surety and confidence we didn't know we had. Either way, the Sun's visits to Pluto make us realize just how much we can endure, on all levels. Physically, mentally, emotionally, and spiritually. Under the conjunction, we're often faced with difficult situations or heavy power struggles that seem to force us to see the darker side of our nature—what we're capable of when we're cornered. It might feel as if authority figures are working against us, too—Pluto is where we keep our supply of Suspicion.

With the trines and sextiles, we're called upon to be very strong. If we draw from that considerable well of energy and endurance that Pluto also represents, we can rise to the occasion beautifully.

CHAPTER FOUR

TRANSITS OF THE MOON

Your Moon Kit:

Family Photos
A Box of Tissues
Your original Teddy Bear, with or without its nose
A Shopping Trip With Your Mom
A Phone Call From/To Your Sister(s)
Water—Showers, Hot Tubs, Swimming Pools
Some Quality Time at Your Place
A Nap
Pot Holders, Aprons, Wooden Spoons
Your Mom's Favorite Recipe
Nesting Supplies — (Shredded Newspaper or Batting)
Canning Jars and Casserole Dishes
Crisp, Clean Sheets, just off the clothes line
A Copy of *Terms of Endearment*
A Kitten or a Puppy (or a stuffed animal,
if you're allergic) to snuggle

Moon Transits

Back in the Introduction, we talked about the Moon and described her as the Head of the Department of Feelings. That makes her the bringer of all kinds of subtle things that are hard to put your finger on. Moods, for starters. Ever notice how the mood you're in affects your day? It's why we just love everyone when we first fall in love, and why when we're furious, everyone we meet, for some reason, is a real jerk. (No, that's not just a coincidence.) Whatever we're feeling on the inside, in other words, has an awful lot of impact on how we see the outside—the world around us, that is.

Now, Moon transits only last a matter of hours, since she weaves her way through the sky so quickly—about one degree every two and a half hours, or about two and a half days for a sign. Her transits to a planet or point reflect the emotional highs and lows we feel in a particular life department, (as symbolized by which of our planets she touches) that only last so long, and then drift away without our noticing to make way for whatever we're feeling next. The feelings that we get—our gut reactions, that is—about the situations we encounter are also brought to us courtesy of the transiting Moon. When she touches a planet in our chart, it's time to reflect, mull over, and dream about those matters—that goes for daydreams, too.

Just as Sun transits point to times of increased dealings with men, Moon transits point to times when women and feminine matters get our attention, so your Mom will often get involved, too. More than anything, remember that Moon transits are about emotions, that most unseeable yet amazingly influential part of being alive.

THE MOON THROUGH THE HOUSES...

When the Moon tiptoes her way through a house in our chart, the subject is Feelings. We tend to re-act to what life tosses at us, to internalize what happens. We become emotionally involved for that two and a half day period, too—with others who belong to the Department in our lives ruled by the house she's visiting. (The sixth house and our co-workers, for example.) Now, that's a key point to keep in mind when you're dealing with Moon transits. Think of how much more strongly we react to someone or something when we've got them in our hearts—or when they're distinctly not in our hearts. Remember, the Moon is very, very subtle, but very, very powerful. Our instinct is on High during Moon transits, too. We're more liable to sense what's going on around us than to consciously know. As she passes through a house, the Moon often symbolizes a place where we'll express or experience a gentle, mothering impulse, too. So in addition to finding ourselves nurturing or being nurtured, we may also have more interactions with our Moms regarding the matters of the house involved.

FIRST HOUSE

Wondering why you've been so darned emotional lately? Check and see if the Moon is winding her way through the first house of your chart. This, remember, is the Front Door of your chart— so any planet that passes through it is hanging out right in the entryway, and tends to greet people at the door. Whatever you're feeling, then, shows. Big Time. All types of feelings rear their little heads, matter of fact, for all to see. Needless to say, then, this transit often corresponds with what They (whoever They are) call Wearing Your Heart On Your Sleeve. Now, we all need to emote, so you might want to think of this transit as your monthly opportunity to Vent, whether that translates into laughing yourself silly, or cleansing your spirit with a good cry. However you think of it, allow yourself to express whatever the You inside is feeling during these two and a half days.

SECOND HOUSE

The second house shows What You Hold Dear—and that's a pretty wide topic. For starters, on a surface level, it's a statement about possessions—so this house is a strong indication of the types of things we choose when it's time to bring out The Shopper in us, and of how we'll tend to them once we've got them. When the Moon passes through here, notice that we find ourselves shopping for Moon-related items. Home furnishings, kitchen accessories, and, of course, food are in that grouping, as are a few of the things I listed back on the first page of this chapter where the Moon Transit Kit is located. We may also find that we're dealing with family treasures, family photos, and other family-oriented Things at this time. Expect to make purchases based on how they make us "feel" then, when the Moon is here, and even more so, watch as we select things that make us feel safe in some way—

another Moon function. Remember, too, that since the Moon rules Moods, we're going to be the type of Impulse Shopper more than one ad campaign has been built around—so it's best to keep a careful eye on the checkbook. More than anything, keep in mind that this house has everything to do with our own self-worth— with what we think of ourselves. When the Moon is here, you'll be more aware, emotionally, of how You've been treating You.

THIRD HOUSE

This third house is where the Scribe, Scriptwriter, and Secretary in you hangs out. Here's the part of you who handles all routine communications. Automatic habits, gestures, conversations with folks we see daily, and short trips around your Little World are all part of the job duties of this slice of your personality. When the Moon is passing through here, then, it's a good bet there'll be lots of short trips with or on account of Moonfolks—The Family. You may be especially busy with chauffeuring the kids around, Mom-style, running errands for other family members, etc. Now, some of the people we find in our immediate environments include our brothers and sisters, (while we're growing up,) along with our neighbors and those we see as we travel through our daily routine. The Moon's passage through here often reminds us of the strength of the emotional bonds we've formed with these folks, and with the others who live in our expanded immediate environments as we grow older—The Neighbors.

Since this side of you also has a lot to do with the way you enter into conversations with others, the Moon's presence here will show a time when there'll be lots of Emotional Words in your chats. You may also notice now that your voice will tend to reflect what you feel—whether you want it to or not. Since, (along with Mercury, the Cosmic Whiz-Kid,) this house is where we find an individual's ability to assimilate and learn, you'll find that when the Moon is here, you'll do better at either of those tasks when you're emotionally involved.

FOURTH HOUSE

Here at the very bottom of your chart is the Moon's House—her very favorite place to be. Since this is her place, then, and since she's so at home here, it's important to pay special attention to your feelings over the next couple of days as she spends time puttering around in her own room.

This quiet, private point corresponds with The Cellar in a house, and with what we keep down there. Now, everyone has a box of sentimental mementos, and lots of us keep that box tucked safely under our cellar stairs—things like letters, dried flowers, ticket stubs, and so forth. These things serve no useful purpose in our lives other than to keep us connected with the emotions we've felt in the past, and we don't drag them out and pore over them every day. Still, having that box makes us feel secure in some way—so much so that some of us might save it first in the case of an emergency that forced us to leave our possessions behind. This fourth house spot, then, is where you'll find your symbolic box of memories. It's an emotional tapestry, and woven into it is the memory of how everything that's ever happened to us felt to us.

When the Moon passes through this house, you've got a guest— The Owner. It's like a tiny little lady with glasses perched on the edge of her nose comes to visit, and heads immediately for the cellar. Think of her as your own personal Historian— whose specialty is You. She stops by monthly to rummage through the file cabinets down there, each one of them chock full of Your Memories.

Now, every time we enter into new, unfamiliar, or scary situations, where we find ourselves reacting from the gut, we're reacting with this side of ourselves. When the Moon is transiting here, we often find ourselves symbolically dashing down those cellar stairs to catch that little lady while she's in town to ask her what she thinks of all this. In other words, when the Moon is here, you may find that your decisions will be made based on how you feel rather than what you think. Your memories of How This Worked Out Last Time You Tried It will be extra-keen. In short, your past—your childhood and your past lives, if you believe in them—will have a profound effect on your reactions to Life over the next couple of days—for better or worse.

This fourth house side of you also refers to the way you were nurtured and to the parent (or person) who you felt nurtured you. When the Moon is here, it's a good bet your Mom will have a major influence over current events in your home-life—(again, for better or worse, depending on your own Moon's aspects.) You'll also see yourself dealing with your own children based on your past emotional conditioning, so this isn't a bad time to examine how your own rearing is affecting the way you raise your own kids. In the physical world, the fourth house side of you is the side you take out to choose what your home will be like. Where you live, how you live, and who you live with are described by your fourth house. When the Moon is here, you may be more in the mood to make your home truly Moon-like—safe, secure, private, cozy, and comfy.

FIFTH HOUSE

Here's the side of you who's ready to play, who's built for light-hearted fun—to enjoy life, and carry on at length. In a word, here we find what you enjoy—and what you love to do. When the Moon is here, you may find that you're happiest at home, involved in Moon-like activities such as cooking, caring for children, or doing crafts. Raising your children, in fact, is a task that's handled by the fifth-house side of you—so when the Moon is here, it's really not a task at all—it's fun. Having a birthday party for one of your own kids, then—a job ordinarily met with a groan from most parents—would be just fine with you right now. Of course, entertaining your grown-up friends at home is also a great delight right now, as would be having the whole family over for Sunday dinner.

In the fifth house we find a description of the Cruise Director in each of us, too. When the Moon is here, your idea of a day or night on the town—if you do decide to go out—will include your kids, your Mom, or your women-friends. You'll enjoy crafts-shows, family-oriented entertainment, and eating out. In a nutshell, your idea of fun will be to pile the whole family into a van and head off for a day of Quality Time together.

Since this house also refers to the side of your personality that emerges when you're involved in a love affair, it's a good bet you'll tend to mother your dates right now, spoiling them with home-baked goodies, warm drinks on cold nights, and foot rubs. Emotional situations with lovers will also be more apparent now—so don't be surprised if you find yourself making promises, setting dates that will take you out of the 5th and into the 7th, and telling your date all about how that felt.

SIXTH HOUSE

This is the place where you keep the side of you who's in charge of all the functions you perform on a daily basis—everything you do regularly to keep your lifestyle up and running. Your health, exercise, and hygiene habits are here, then, since all those things contribute to the upkeep of your body. As a result, any planet that passes through this house is important to check for its effects on your health. This is even more so with the Moon, since she rules emotions, moods, and fluctuations—so right around now, the condition of your health may very closely parallel your emotional state. Since this house shows what and where in the physical body will be most likely to break down, keep a special watch on body parts that relate to the Moon at this time—the breasts, the stomach, the ovaries and womb, and anything having to do with the regulation of body fluids. It's also a great time to tend to Moon-related physical functions—like nurturing yourself through rest, a good, nutritious meal, or a nice, long soak.

In general, this house refers to what you do regularly—so it's also a description of your job, the side of you who performs duties to earn money and keep yourself supplied with what you need to live. With the Moon visiting in this house, your job duties may, first of all, need to be performed at home—in other words, you may find yourself working at home, or you may work in homes—cleaning, cooking, care-giving, designing or decorating homes, or even selling a home, if the Moon is in an appropriate sign (like Capricorn or Virgo or Taurus.)

Since the sixth house is Virgo's neat, clean, and helpful territory, it also describes the side of us we take out when it's time to Be A Girl/Boy Scout—pure and simple—for no other reason than that. With the Moon here, our style of helping at the moment will often be to Mother those who need it.

SEVENTH HOUSE

Several houses in the chart refer to relationships. The fifth reflects the type of playmates we'll choose—our dates. The eighth house refers to those we'll select to be intimate with. This seventh house is an all-around description of the side of us that comes out when we're relating One-to-One with An Other. It's the person you become when you're in the company of One Other Person—just one. Now, this house has often been referred to as the house of marriage partners and business partners, and that's appropriate. When we take on a spouse or a business partner, we necessarily spend a great deal of time with them, so the door to the seventh house room spends an awful lot of time open. When the Moon passes through this house, your attitude towards others is a nurturing one. You may find yourself treating others as if they were your children—or you may just baby them with affection. Others may look to you for support and comfort—and you may be amazed at what they'll confide in you. Of course, all our energies work both ways, and with the Moon here, we may also be babied or taken care of by our Significant Others. The pitfall to watch out for is the possibility of becoming involved in a co-dependent situation at this time—that is, feeling as if your sense of self depends on whether or not you are needed by an Other.

Now, since the qualities we look for in An Other are also described by this house, when the Moon is in the neighborhood, you'll probably be looking for An Other with very strong emotions and the ability to express them. Be careful of attracting someone that's too moody or emotionally unstable right now, too. Remember that at these times you're specially equipped to bring the Moon's unconditional love into any relationship.

EIGHTH HOUSE

Here in the eighth house is where we stash the crisis expert in each of us, the side of us that comes out in times of Extremes, when the subject is agony or ecstasy. Here's where we experience the highest of the highs and the lowest of the lows—the peaks and black holes, the major crises and unbelievably wonderful experiences that combine to make life as full of juice as it is. This side of you is prepared for any emergency. It's the side of you that comes out when the situation is deep, heavy, or intense, when it's time to deal with the issue of death, sex, and all the other unmentionables. Whenever you let go of all else but your core self—which is the only time that intimacy can really be achieved—it's this side of you that's operating.

Now, the Moon is a very emotional lady—so when she's passing through this house, you're going to experience all those highs and lows on a very personal level. Your reaction to most crises that come up now will be a very emotional one. You'll try to help and 'take care of' the situation, to fix, soothe, or comfort whoever or whatever is in need, and you may even find yourself taking up a task that allows you to do all that for others. No matter what type of crisis or intense situation comes up when the Moon is here, you'll feel everything those involved are feeling—almost as deeply.

Of course, since the Moon is such a very personal planet, when you're having this transit, what you're wanting above all else—for yourself—is emotional intimacy. You understand how wonderful it can be to share yourself with the right person, and just how deep a cut can be delivered by trusting the wrong person. You may also find yourself in situations that exemplify what it's like to be both controlling and controlled on an emotional level. Because this house also refers to taxes, inheritances, and Joint Finances, you could also be dealing with any of those issues now with respect to your home, your family, or your Mom.

NINTH HOUSE

Ever feel like you've just got to get away from it all? Like you're badly in need of a break from the routine of your daily life? Well, that's your ninth-house side talking, the side of you who just can't take it any more, who's bored to tears and needs a distraction. When the Moon is here, you may feel that all the more so. You may be really craving something alien to your routine, anything that will create a fresh emotional perspective. See, the ninth house side of us is the side that comes out when we need to be completely and totally awake and aware of everything that's going on around us. Think of how you'd feel if I dropped you off in the middle of France with $200 and told you to find your way to Zurich by noon Saturday. You could do it, of course, but you'd have to think out every step of the process consciously. It's the opposite of your third-house Auto-Pilot side. Here, then, is the side of you that lives totally in the moment, that enjoys being in foreign places, with unfamiliar faces around you. With the Moon here, then, don't be surprised if you're In The Mood to visit another country, or just head off on a long-distance road-trip— taking your home on the road. The Moon's natural relationship to children means that you may also be exposed to or even consider for yourself the possibility of foster-parenting or adopting a child from another country at this time.

Since all mind-expanding experiences involve learning something new, usually something we set out to learn consciously, this house also rules Higher Education—college, or any classes we take because we want to learn something, rather than because they're part of the established curriculum. When the Moon is here, you'll most enjoy classes on children, families, or foreign customs. Your ninth-house philosophies on topics like politics, government, and The Big Picture will also necessarily be influenced by the Moon's presence. You'll find that all or most of your philosophies will now be emotionally driven, and many of them will take into consideration the effect of laws, government, and religion on children's rights.

TENTH HOUSE

Here at the very top of your chart is The Roof of your house. This is the Midheaven of the chart, your symbolic Bulletin Board, the place where you post all your accomplishments for all the world to see. This house is also the place where you'll keep the side of you who deals with authority figures and those above or over us. These terms, of course, refer to our higher-ups or superiors, all words that place those folks in an elevated station—which is most appropriately put, since those we give our respect to are dealt with by our tenth house personality, the side of us that lives at the top of the chart.

If the Moon is here, your relationship with those in positions of authority may be very emotional at this time. That is, you may tend to react towards your employer or other authority figures as if they were family. You may also find yourself working more at this time with women or children, or considering a career in other Moon-oriented occupations, such as catering. If you're an employer yourself, you may feel as if you're as the head of a family right now—rather than as the boss. Your style of management at this time will be to guide your employees like a parent, rather than giving them orders.

Now, this house also shows your reputation, or what folks hear about you even before they meet you. What you'll be most noted for on a public basis at this time, then, will be your emotions, your home, your family, or your relationship with your Mom—so expect to be dealing with any of those private, emotional issues in very public ways for the next couple of days.

ELEVENTH HOUSE

Remember your parents telling you not to hang around with Those Kids because if you did, you'd grow up to be just like them? Well, unfortunately, they were right. The peer group we select—at any age—has a profound effect on us. What we're really selecting is a category or classification for ourselves, so if it's the wrong group we choose, for any reason, we're still going to be associated with them in the minds of others. When the Moon is transiting this house, the groups you'll associate with will most likely be concerned with, and composed of—women or children. You may also find yourself involved with nurturing, care taking, or self-help groups—anything that helps you to deal with your emotions. Of course, group therapy is a natural draw for you with the Moon here—formal or otherwise.

Since this is the team player in you, it's also the side of you that describes how you act in group situations like meetings, club get-togethers, or even friendly gatherings. Since the Moon is so security-oriented, you're right now going to be more convinced that there's safety in numbers, and you'll also crave the emotional security of kindred spirits and the feeling of safety you have when you're with them.

TWELFTH HOUSE

This is the place where we keep our secrets, where we stash the side of ourselves we were taught not to do, not ever—and especially not in public. The messages may or may not have been direct—but the end result was that we learned to hide certain behaviors, to only do certain things when we were in places of retreat or seclusion, places where we felt safe. Our 12th house is where we stash what we feel needs to be protected about ourselves, and we stash those sides of us by hiding, denying, or carrying out those activities in secret. When the Moon transits through the 12th house, then, you may often find yourself denying emotional issues—the need for a family, for children of your own, for a relationship with your Mother. You may also apologize for your feelings at this time, by saying things like, "I hate to get emotional, but..." or "I hope you don't think I'm being a cry-baby, but" before you express them.

Since this house describes the behaviors that we need to do when we draw back and regroup, when the Moon is here, it's very important to spend time alone getting in touch with our feelings so that we can recharge or regain our strength after being out in the emotionally-draining world. Retreat of any kind—even if it's just time home alone, in fact—is one of the best ways to soothe and comfort ourselves under 12th-house Moon transits. Of course, we can't always find a great deal of time to spend alone, but it's really important for each of us to find an outlet for our 12th-house transits—so here's a tip, another suggestion. Planets that transit the 12th-house really love to play make-believe. They need secret playmates and secret places so that they can act without really acting on their own behalf—so acting is a most healthy way for any 12th-house planet to express. Let the Moon Play Pretend when she's here. Take her someplace she can be deep, mysterious, and evasive.

MOON/SUN

The Sun is the person inside each of us who's constantly out for Experience, who wants to reach, grow, and accomplish something—and to be recognized and congratulated for those accomplishments. Any transiting planet that touches the Sun provides us with a temporary additional tool of sorts—to help us achieve our life goals. When it's the Moon who's visiting, she lends us her Special Moon Tool—Instinct—which is now at our disposal to use as we see fit to further our life's goals. In other words, if you've got a decision to make that involves your future, and you've got to make it now—trust your gut.

This conjunction has also been referred to by many others as a New Moon of sorts, a time of brand-new beginnings. If you're looking for a good time to make a Brand-Spanking New Emotional Start, then, to clear the boards and begin a new life—this is it. Smile, shake hands, cut your losses, and move along.

Now, on another level, visits of the Moon to our Sun make us much more emotional in general, especially where issues of pride, ego, and our creative endeavors are concerned. This means we're a whole lot more emotional about the recognition we receive—or don't receive—at this time. In other words, if we do get our applause now, we'll be just beamin'—very happy campers. That's what typically happens when easy Moon transits to the Sun show up. Life seems just chock full o' pleasant emotional experiences. It's a great couple of days, and our Pride Department is purring. We receive not just a pat on the back, but a squeeze—a warm, emotional expression of support and love from folks who are important to us. Since the Moon is the ultimate feminine, it may especially be women who hand out our hugs, blue ribbons, kudos.

These easy transits can also point to times when children and other family members—not the least of which is our Mom—enter into our lives to support our creative goals, often just by being there for us.

Now, all that applies to us when we do get our back patted and our standing ovation. If we don't get all that, however—well, just be warned that it can get ugly. Under the tougher Moon transits to the Sun, we walk around tripping over our lower lip, looking totally dejected, and tugging on our Significant Other's sleeve saying things like, "You don't love me, huh?" The difficult Moon-to-Sun transits seem to show up as times when the tide feels as if it's running against us, rather than pushing us along. We feel unappreciated and unsupported. We sigh a lot, too. As with all Moon transits, it's comforting to know that these passing moods are just that. Still, don't lose sight of the fact that Moon transits in general are often symptoms of larger issues.

MOON/MOON

She's the side of us who operates on Instinct, the Inner Child who remembers how everything felt, right from Day One. She decides what's safe and what's not. She's the soft inner side of each of us that cries, fears, and dreams, the side who remembers everything about our childhood—how everything that ever happened to us felt, right from Day One, whether we're conscious of it or not. Needless to say, then, when the transiting Moon conjoins our own Moon, we get a double-dose of our own particular brand of Emotions—complete with all the Ups and the Downs your natal Moon's aspects indicate. Now, this moment is a very strong indicator of how the rest of the moonth is going to go for you, as is a chart set up for the exact moment when the transiting Moon returns to the exact degree and minute of our own Moon. This chart is called a Lunar Return Chart, and it corresponds with the emotional climate we'll operate from for the entire month. It's a backdrop of sorts that shows what type of personal emotional needs we'll be concentrating on until the Moon comes home again next moonth.

Now, not all emotions are pretty. There's quite a range of possible feelings we humans enjoy, in fact. When the transiting Moon touches our own by a difficult aspect, we're afforded opportunities to experience the downside of Feeling. We're cranky or testy—or we feel as if we're being faced with emotional no-win situations. A square from the transiting Moon to our own, for example, may point to a time when we're anxious, worried, or vaguely uncomfortable in some way, as if we're sensing that something is wrong without really being able to put our finger on it—and our behavior can certainly reflect that crankiness. (So next time you feel yourself sneering at your Other—without a good reason—check the position of the transiting Moon before you tell them to pack up their stuff and hit the road. This could save your relationship.)

Tough Moon transits to our own Moon are also usually in the neighborhood during times when our dealings with family members—most especially women, children, and our Moms—are a bit more challenging to handle. Still, tough Moon transits are often the inspiration behind recognizing that there are others out there whose needs are different from our own—one of the most necessary factors in relating to our dear ones. On the other hand, easy Moon aspects to our Moon turn up at times when life just seems swell. We feel peaceful, happy, and at ease, both with ourselves and with others. In a word, good Moon transits are times of contentment. Since, again, the Moon does symbolize family, if there's Stuff you know has got to be handled between you and family members, listen to the Universe, and plan it now—'tis the season.

MOON/MERCURY

Get ready to Talk It Out—whatever It is. When the Moon whispers in Mercury's ear, Feelings often tumble out of our mouths. Prepare for that strong possibility by taking a moment to reflect on how best to express those feelings. We may actually even use the phrase, "But what about my needs?" Well, it's okay to talk about our needs. Especially now. That's what we're supposed to be doing now. Just be very sure that no matter what you say or to whom you say it, you let them know that these are your feelings, and you're not blaming, condemning, or congratulating anyone. Remember, Mercury is The Messenger of the Gods. When the Moon touches yours, the Gods have an emotional issue to discuss with you—and you with the Outside World.

Tough Moon/Mercury transits can be times when we amaze even ourselves at how self-absorbed we sounded just then. Our thinking—and all our communications—is colored by what others may tell us are irrational impulses. Well, nobody ever said the Moon had to be rational, of course, but Mercury's supposed to be. As with all else, of course, the more rational we ordinarily are, the more irrational we're going to be seen by others when this transit happens along. On the other hand, easy Moon/Mercury transits are the inspiration behind heart-to-heart chats, softly spoken promises, and offers to help. In a nutshell, then, expect your feelings to color your judgment at these times. And keep in mind that the emotional nature of the Moon, regardless of the aspect she makes when she touches Mercury, is the key to true inspiration.

MOON/VENUS

These two planets are astrological girlfriends. As the two prime representatives of The Feminine among the personal planets, they back each other up, hug each other when they need it, and watch each other's pets when one of them is on vacation. When they get together, there's a whole lot of Feelin' goin' on—and a whole lot of touchin' too. This is the type of combination that produces an urge to embrace, hold, and take care of our precious ones—animal, vegetable, or mineral—since Venus shows who and what we love, and how we'll love it.

Now, the Moon shows how we'll cope when we're hurt and how we'll express our joy when we're delighted. In a nutshell, she tells us how we'll respond to what the outside world tosses in. When she touches our Venus, the Moon raises emotional issues with the loved ones in our lives which mirror how we're feeling about ourselves and what we feel we deserve—another Venus issue. The Moon's transits to Venus also point to times when we'll be especially emotional about our Things, whether we're shopping for them, or deciding what to do with them because we're moving.

Under the tougher Moon/Venus transits, the worst we can expect is to feel as if our feelings aren't reciprocated. In other words, we'll be mooning—pining over, that is—someone or something we don't feel belongs to us. (This is another of the sighing transits, by the way, and another of the dreamy, wistful, romantic transits, too—regardless of the aspect involved.) The best we can expect is that the push of the difficult aspects may also prompt us to be especially emotional about who and what we love—often with wonderful results. Maybe there's someone out there who needs a bit of TLC, for example.

Now, with easy Moon aspects, we're feeling safe, loved and satisfied. All our needs are met. We're surrounded by everyone and everything we care about, and life's good. Too bad we can't conjure this transit whenever we feel like it, hmmm?

MOON/MARS

I like to think of Mars as our own personal Rambo, the planet in each of our charts who shows what will get us riled up, ticked off, and inspired to Take Action. 'Course, he's also a good indicator of how we'll react when we're challenged—of how we'll defend ourselves when we feel it's necessary. When the emotion-toting Moon comes along to Mars, there's a couple of things that can happen—especially if the aspect is a conjunction. First off, we can find ourselves expressing our anger or asserting ourselves on behalf of ourselves in most emotional fashion. In other words, we'll Go Off. Big Time. We won't be shy about doing it with fireworks, either, and all the accompanying emotional theatrics these two planets can conjure when they're excited about something.

Now, excitement is the operative phrase here. The Moon and Mars both represent some pretty darned trigger-happy urges inside us humans: Anger and Feelings. Both of those urges rear up before we know it, albeit for different reasons. When the excitement is of the pleasant kind, it might be as simple as a really good time out with friends, where the energy level in general is high, everyone is instinctively keyed into each other, and a Great, Great Time Is Had By All. Or maybe good news arrives, and we're emotionally charged—we've just been present at the birth of a friend's child, or someone has just told us they love us, for example.

On the other hand, if the aspect is a tough one, we can definitely experience this transit as an angry time, possibly even unjustifiably so. The Moon isn't rational, remember, and Mars has never been accused of that, either, so if she's squaring or opposing him, we might also be a bit over-defensive. On the high side, the easy transits usually show up at times when we're emotionally inspired to put a great deal of personal energy into a physical project. How many races have been won by someone who was inspired to keep pushing well past the limits of their real physical strength?

MOON/JUPITER

Sometimes your heart is just plain old happy, for no apparent reason. Maybe you've just answered a question right in class, or just had a surprise hug come up from behind. Or maybe you just took a good long look around you and realized what a great planet this is. Whatever. There's a warm, full buzz that comes along with those moments that those of us who grew up in the 60's and 70's might associate with something we did inhale, and others among us might put on a par with the halfway point of that first Margarita. Euphoria, some call it. At any rate, it's Good, and it's how we feel when the transiting Moon touches Jupiter in our charts.

See, Jupiter is where we keep our Real-Good-Feel-Good stash. When a planet transits that spot, a little bit of Feel-Good gets stimulated, and leaks out. When it's the Moon, it's an emotional trigger that sets off Jupiter, and the end result is a good, warm glow. Now, when we're feeling this good, we tend to give it out to others, and whatever we give out is what we get back. These transits, then, can be just great—once again, depending on the aspect and how our own Moons are wired up natally.

On the other hand, both the conjunction and the traditionally hard aspects can also point to times when we're Doing The Jupiter on the downside of his coin—overdoing it, that is—and we might tend to get righteously overemotional about something, or maybe take something personally that wasn't intended so. Or we might just blow our feelings 'way out of proportion. Of course, regardless of the aspect the Moon is making to Jupiter, since she's the planet we associate with Home, and he's a Long-Distance kinda guy, now might be when we contemplate moving long-distance, or traveling to somewhere we've never been (expanding our horizons via taking the Home on the Road.) Since the Moon rules children and families, we might now also feel the urge to expand personally by adding to the family via An Other person. As with all difficult transits to Jupiter, the pitfall is that we can often get swept away when he's set off, and literally become Too Big For Out Britches. Fortunately, this transit will only last a few hours. You can imagine what it's like when it's Jupiter that's visiting the Moon.

MOON/SATURN

Now here's an odd combination. He rules the urge to be dutiful, responsible, and unemotional—he's where we're experts at stifling our feelings—at Just Saying No and just following orders. Needless to say, when Mr. Serious gets visited by the Moon, look out. He's about to feel something, and he doesn't like that much. Saturn's usual reaction to visits from the Moon is to turn her nurturing impulse into an opportunity to complete a duty of some kind on behalf of whoever or whatever in our lives is dependent on us. That is, he'll do a family-oriented chore or task—something Responsible, to let Them know we care. Maybe he'll suggest a visit to the bank to set up a trust fund, or a parent-teacher conference. One way or the other, now's a time when your responsibilities to your family and children will be first and foremost on your mind.

The aspect involved between the transiting Moon and Saturn will describe the type of situation to expect—a trine, for example, might produce a heart-to-heart talk that's been overdue between a parent and a child. A square might point toward an argument or a request for a large favor. Either way, you're not going to be feeling especially warm and fuzzy right now. Saturn contracts, and it's the Moon's touch that's going to symbolically stimulate that right now. You can also expect to be feeling a bit on the pessimistic side now, too, by the way—because Saturn's where you keep your supply of pessimism. Now, with the trines and sextiles, you may just be in the mood to be by yourself for awhile—to think things out, draw back, and regroup. With the squares and other tough aspects, you'll still want to be alone, but you'll feel a bit more anxious about it—and let's not forget a couple other Saturnian emotions you might experience at this time: guilt and worry. If you start to feel this way, remember—Moon transits aren't forever, and guilt and worry are what Dr. Wayne Dyer refers to as the useless emotions. Just don't tell your Saturn I said that.

MOON/URANUS

Uranus is the spot in our chart where we're at our most unpredictable, where anything can change at a moment's notice. He's the symbolic impulse behind all last-minute reversals and abrupt changes of heart. When he's touched by the Moon, although predicting exactly what might happen is out of the question, it's for sure that you're going to be feeling a bit finicky, let's say. Think of it this way: Uranus is like an On/Off switch. Whenever we feel like life has trapped us in a mold we're not happy with, that switch goes off and we either start or stop doing something suddenly—to Get Free. He's our radical, rebellious self—so visits from the Moon are going to set him off, for better or worse, via a situation of the heart.

Now, if the aspect she makes is a conjunction to Uranus, the outburst or sudden shift in direction is going to be quite notice-able. Sometimes a person steps into our lives at this time, an agent or messenger of sorts who stops us in our tracks and surprises us somehow. With the Moon involved, of course, it might possibly be our Moon—I mean, our Mom—that does the cameo appearance, but any old family member will do, and failing that, a woman in general. Regardless, expect to be surprised over this period of a few hours, and expect to change something that you're involved in—radically. The best of Moon to Uranus involves the rush of freedom we feel from expressing our individuality—no matter what. The worst is the possibility of an emotional shock that sends us into a tailspin. Either way, when you see the Moon approaching your Uranus, allow a bit of leeway in your schedule.

MOON/NEPTUNE
The transiting Moon is a subtle undercurrent that flows through us. She's like a traveling set of psychic whiskers we tentatively extend to test our environment. She rules instinct, that distant memory that every member of a species shares with every other member of that species. When she touches Neptune, the most intuitive lady out there, our antenna Engage and we're feeling everything that's happening around us, for better or worse. That includes the anger that's bouncing off the walls from the argument currently being waged in the corner, as well as the infatuation those two high-school kids are bouncing off of each other in the booth behind us.

Our Neptunes are also the place in us where we're idealistic, dreamy, and romantic. So regardless of the aspect from the Moon, it's a great time to find a place to hide out and Play Pretend. A movie theater, for example. Under the conjunction, we're often struck by a feeling of unconditional love for someone or something. The Moon represents personal emotions, but when she visits Neptune, the creator of the We Are All One theory, we become aware of the connection we share with all living creatures—and our temperaments show it. Under the sweeter aspects, we fall in love, fantasize about someone we don't know, or write a letter to Robert Redford, only half believing he won't answer. Anything's possible now—this is a team that's all about dreaming, and convincing ourselves that our dreams are real. It's also a team that's tailor-made for charity work or hopping in and helping a stranger, just because you've got an urge to commit a Random Act of Kindness for a sister or brother—be they human or critter. Oh, and since I'm a big fan of those four-legged types, let me hasten to add that since Neptune rules shelters, and the Moon rules the Act of Mommying, now's super time to get out there and adopt somebody with a tail who's behind bars but hasn't committed a crime.

Under the tougher Moon to Neptune aspects, we're confused emotionally, and unsure of where to turn. We feel vaguely worried about something, or, at worst, paranoid. Neptune does represent our fears, remember, since she's where we're aware of not having any boundaries to separate What's Out There from Us. When she's triggered in not-so-pleasant-fashion, we can also experience physical problems stemming from that lack o' boundary—bad effects from drugs or alcohol, from example, or allergies that kick up suddenly and then disappear just as suddenly, before they can even be diagnosed.

When these two planets combine, we turn into a psychic sponge. It's up to us to stay away from influences we don't want to be part of our world and get ourselves close to those we do. Of course, Neptune is also where we're at our most psychic—literally—so pay very close attention to impressions that seem to appear from nowhere during these times.

MOON/PLUTO

The subject is emotional control—and the arena is usually our closest relationships. Pluto, of course, is the spot in our charts where we're all ruthless, power-hungry little dictators. (Well, it is—sometimes.) It's also where we're equal parts detective, analyst, and assassin. Pluto is the symbolic King of Perception. In other words, he's equally able to skillfully interpret clues or plant them to create the trail of his choice. When he's stimulated, we're amazingly aware of little things—able to sniff the air and know if someone's coming, or shift a pile of papers to let Others know the meeting is over. When it's the Moon who's symbolically triggering our own Pluto, it's a time when we'll be able to either bend and manipulate emotional situations, or be manipulated by them.

Now, manipulation is a word with a heavy reputation. Somewhere along the way, it became distinctly uncool to use our Pluto to turn a scenario to our liking. This is where the matter of personal integrity comes in. If we use our Pluto to change over a situation than needs changing—to sell someone on the idea that they really can stand on their own two feet, without an abusive spouse, or to help someone end a habit that's destroying their health—well, then, these are positive ways to manipulate. With the Moon involved, we can be especially persuasive, too—she lends her instinct to our Pluto and changes the detective into a mother-figure of sorts. Under easy Moon visits, then, we can be a force for positive change in someone's life by providing them with the emotional support they need in a crisis.

Under the tougher Moon transits, our relationships take on a quality of intensity that often turns into power struggles, or we obsess on someone emotionally and sit up all night wondering What They Really Meant By That, or we become drawn into a turbulent relationship. Regardless of the aspect the Moon makes, remember that her visits are emotional times. When she's visiting Pluto, those emotions are amplified, funneled, and focused to the nth degree. Use these times well—direct your energy into an honest, worthwhile cause.

CHAPTER FIVE

MERCURY

Your Mercury Kit:

Pens

#2 Pencils

Paper

Colorful markers

Yellow Legal Pads

(Oh, hell—just raid a stationery store)

Newspapers

Postage Stamps

A Telephone—and an extra line

A Fax

A Ride In a Cab

A Walk Around The Neighborhood

Roller skates

A Secretary

Coffee

A Copy of The Paper

A Walk Wo/man

Mercury Transits:
Life In The Fast Lane...

When Mercury's in the neighborhood, the subject is communication and activity—all kinds. Letters, phone calls, short trips, errands. You name it. This guy just loves movement—both intellectual and physical. When he dashes through a house or skips quickly over one of our planets, we just can't sit still. We're chatty, interested, and ready to learn anything—but just a little of it, and it's got to be quick. The pace he keeps up doesn't allow Mercury to hang around anywhere long enough to gather more than a taste of any topic. In general, Mercury's visits are very busy times for us, most noticeably when he's stationing to go direct or retrograde and is sitting right on top of an important degree in our chart. At these times, especially, whatever the area of life Mercury is visiting, suddenly it's jam-packed with stimulus, as if the outside world is constantly sending messages to us.

Now, speaking of messages, by the way, remember that above all else, Mercury is The Messenger—so his transits most often do literally Bring Messages. A letter or phone call we've been waiting for will come, or someone stops by to tell us something. His visits also point to a good time to make a call, or mail a letter. Mercury transits are when messages can arrive via Symbolic Events, too. Lots of times, because of Mercury's love of duality and variety, we'll find that those events arrive in twos, as if Hermes, the Trickster, were having some fun with us. We're often put in the position of having to do at least two things at once under Mercury transits, too—and that's perfectly fine right now. This planet races around the Sun in record Cosmic time—he's the inspiration behind the phrase The Incredible Lightness of Being, and he brings that light and quickness along to any planet or point he touches.

Mercury Through The Houses

First of all, remember that a house is an area of life, a room where we keep that particular side of ourselves that's specially equipped to deal with those situations. A planet that's transiting house, then, is a guest staying in that room, and so, necessarily, when we take out that side of ourselves, the guest comes along. Mercury is the type of guest that nobody seems to mind much.

He's a quick-witted, fun kind of planet that stirs things up intellectually and gets us Thinking again. He loves puzzles and word games, and he delights in playing with language and symbols. When he whizzes through a house, then, that room in our charts is temporarily on 78 speed. Matters handled by that side of our personality typically rev up to at least that fast, and our interchanges with the folks who belong to that house pick up speed, too. Here's a look at how Mercury's dash through each of the houses will play out symbolically in our lives.

FIRST HOUSE

The subject is communication, and the subject of the subject is You. When Mercury raps at the Front Door of our chart, it turns into a revolving door, through which all kinds of interesting folks exit and enter, (quickly,) at all hours of the day and night, asking questions, wanting to take us for a quick ride or a day-trip, and offering up a myriad of intellectual stimulus—which is just what we're after right now. Although the actual day that Mercury crosses over from the 12th house to the Ascendant is really the busiest day of all— and will bring news or get you to finally speak about something you've been mulling over for the past few weeks—this entire transit shows up as a period of time when we've got our hands full just being us. Typically, this is also a time when we're involved with errands, letters and phone calls, but we'll probably also be excessively concerned with what's happening around us, since this house also describes our Immediate Environment.

SECOND HOUSE

Expect to be spending lots of time talking about finances when Mercury's here in the second house with his legal pad and clip board poised and ready to go. This may be a time when we negotiate and sign financial contracts, or we may be concerned with paperwork that involves the selection, care, or future arrangements for our possessions. At worst, we're overburdened with trying to juggle numbers. At best, we're signing on the dotted line, about to get what we're worth from the company. Either way, if we're not experts on financial legalese, this might be a good time to hire an accountant or other legal professional to help sift through the details. On another entirely different level, this transit can also point to a time when we're symbolically reaching some conclusions on What's Valuable to us—on what counts, in the scheme of things.

THIRD HOUSE

Mercury is right at home here in the third house—it's his kind of place, furnished with telephones, fax machines, computers perpetually On-Line and rental cars idling in the driveway, ready to zip outta here at a moment's notice. The subject is communications of all kinds, so lots of conversation, letters, writing, and short trips around the neighborhood take up our time now—at an amazingly feverish pace, too. Remember, this guy is The Messenger. When he's at home in his office, he's catching up on all the communications he was too busy to tend to while he circled the rest of the chart. (Again, remember that Mercury operates in pairs to see if we're paying attention, so expect communications to arrive in matched sets—two phone calls from two different people with the same name within just a couple of minutes, for example.) Since he's also a perpetual youth, and particularly fond of his childhood years, we can also expect to be chatting with folks that were a part of our youth—kids from The Old Neighborhood, folks we went to Elementary or High School with, and siblings. This transit is also a time when we may be amazed at our ability to whiz through puzzles, word games, crosswords, or logic problems. Mercury is powerful in this house. If you've got a paper to do, start it now.

FOURTH HOUSE

This house is our emotional warehouse, where we keep all our memories of The Past. When Mercury's here, you'll find him sitting under the stairs with the box of notes, pressed flowers, and Yearbooks—and you may find yourself sniffling and wanting to talk about Home. If we live a distance away from our birth-homes, by the way, now's the time we may choose for a Sentimental Journey to re-visit our roots and touch base with our base. That's if we've got time, of course, because when Mercury races through the 4th house, our own homes and families take up a lot of our attention. There are lots of visitors, lots of children in our lives, and lots of running in and out of the house-literally. On a deeper level, circumstances often come up now that provide us with the opportunity to talk about our past, about where we've come from and how it has affected the person we've become. This is a time when, if we pay attention, we can really catch a glimpse of Who We Are at the roots.

FIFTH HOUSE

The Cruise Director in us is activated by this transit, Big Time. All of a sudden, we're the Social Secretary of the moment, making arrangements for parties, outings, and other fun events. We're on the phone for what seems like all day, calling the caterers, discussing where to put the chairs for the garden party, or trying to let the folks at the print shop know how Jim and Sue would like their invitations printed. And we don't mind. Communication is fun right now—all kinds of communication. We're simultaneously doing a crossword with our current Other, watching a movie with the kids, and dashing off a letter to an old playmate. This is typically a time when we may also take off for a quick jaunt with the kids, or set off for the weekend with a date to do something fun, exciting, and fast-paced. All types of entertainment are favored when Mercury tap-dances his way through this house— yes, dancing included. Enjoy this transit—but eat your Wheaties. You'll need them.

SIXTH HOUSE

More than anything, the sixth house shows the rhythm of our day, the general pace we've come to expect from life. When Mercury gets here, that pace is due to accelerate and pick up considerably, so if you're feeling as if your life just got turned up to 78 speed, see if he's paying a visit to your sixth house. We can also count on both our work lives and the subject of health to come up at this time. As far as work goes, we can be awfully busy during this time, especially if we're already in the communications field. The desk may be heaped high with more paperwork than we can ever remember seeing before, and at the same time, the phone rings so much we can't seem to make a dent in it. We may be asked to do two jobs at once—remember Mercury's love of duality—if a co-worker is absent, for example. In the health department, we may be unusually concerned with health-related appointments, or with having check-ups for work-related purposes. Sometimes these transits also coincide with times when our co-workers are more than usually involved with the rest of our lives.

SEVENTH HOUSE

Classically, this transit is a time when our committed relationships take on a quality of movement and spontaneity, when we learn with and from those folks we're talking about whenever we use the word my to describe them. Well, that's all true. Mercury's trip through any room in our chart is a time when we really believe that variety is the spice of life, and we're more than willing to go off in search of that spice—with an interesting partner, or alone—since short trips are his favorite place to look. Still, this house isn't just reserved for those we know. It's really the side of us which emerges when it's time to have a One-to-One encounter of any kind, whether it's with an Other we belong to, or an Other we've just sat down next to on the bus. When a planet transits this house, it's a given we're going to be having an awful lot of vis-à-vis encounters— both with Others we consider ourselves half of, and Others we're strangers to. Mercury's trek through this room is especially interesting because of his fondness for duality. Watch as he visits this house and brings friends over with him, people who seem uncannily like others you know, both in their appearance and the way they behave.

EIGHTH HOUSE

Here's Pluto's place—Scorpio's house. Now, as you know, Pluto and Scorpio are the sign and planet given jurisdiction over such not-so-light topics as death, sex, passion, regeneration and rebirth. Needless to say, this is a pretty intense kind of place. When Mercury stops by and sets up shop, then, it turns into The House Of Intense Discussions and Urgent Communications. All of a sudden, we've having conversations about death, abortion, recycling resources, physician-assisted suicide, and other topics equally unsuitable to the dinner table: our own mortality, for example. Since this house is also where the side of us lives who's in charge of joint finances, we may find ourselves talking or negotiating with Others about joint resources, taxes, inheritances, etc. The main job of this side of our self, however, is to handle the issue of Intimacy. When Mercury's here, every encounter takes on a deep, profound, tone, every conversation becomes intense, and we think detective-like thoughts—What They Meant By That, etc.

NINTH HOUSE

This side of us is the part that only comes out when we're in unfamiliar surroundings, when we've got to be on our toes and totally aware at all times because nothing can be left to Automatic Pilot. When fleet-footed Mercury pulls into this house, it's time to Hit the proverbial Highway, to set off on a long trip, to get ourselves somewhere we've never been, to do something we've never done, with people we've never met. It's called living in the moment and, needless to say, it's a great time to go on vacation. Now, you'll know this side of you is being triggered when you have a craving to feed your mind New Stuff. Doesn't just have to be travel, either. Arm-chair travel has long been touted as a wonderful way to feed our ninth house. When Mercury's hiking through, it's time to take a look at the Big Picture—to go back to school and expand our horizons, or take off for as long as we can manage and hike the Rockies, or explore a new religion or philosophy. Whatever. Since Mercury is also a traveling spokesperson, and the ninth house is where we become conscious of What We Think about all kinds of topics, expect to be expressing those new viewpoints now, too—to anyone who'll listen.

TENTH HOUSE

The tenth house is the place where we keep the Authority Figure that lurks inside each and every one of us—(even in Sagittarians.) It's the side of us that we use when we deal with The Authorities, too—before we actually become one, that is. Mercury's visits through this house, then, can coincide with some pretty serious conversations. Picture a business meeting being held around a long polished conference table. Everyone who's sitting there has navy, gray, or pinstriped suits on, and you're about to give a Presentation. Are you ready? Prepared for a question/answer session? Got your pointer? That's the tone all our communications take on when Mercury transits this house in our charts. All of a sudden, we're doing conference calls on Sunday afternoons with 13 people from all over the country, sending out memos to everyone around us, and Being Held Accountable for our words. It's now that we learn what it's like for Others to look up to us for what we're an expert at. We may be called on to teach, or guide, or mentor Others, as well. Planets transiting the tenth house are there to symbolically test our capacity to Lead. And Mercury's no exception.

ELEVENTH HOUSE

In the eleventh house, we keep the side of us who chooses our teams, our Causes, and the associations or societies we feel an affinity with. This gives us a chance to see ourselves as part of a group of kindred spirits and to share in that good feeling—

remember, there's safety in numbers. When we take up with a band of people because of what they represent, we're underlining what we share with them with a yellow highlighter and focusing on those topics when we're with them. When a planet transits our eleventh house, it's there to pick us up, take us to group meetings or gatherings, and get us Involved. (Except if it's Saturn—then he's there to either make us the President or tell us to stay home.) When it's Mercury who's got the engine idling, we're symbolically on our way to a meeting (at least one,) all right, and we're going to be active, too. We're going to help them communicate their (our) ideals. Don't be surprised if it's now that we find ourselves volunteering to do the newsletter, revamp the pamphlets or brochures, or help out with a phone-tree to Get The Voters Out. Mercury is the Messenger. His transits through this house are times when we can really get in touch with what we stand for by listening to ourselves talk about the teams we've chosen.

TWELFTH HOUSE

Picture this: two people—the last ones up of the gang that went camping—are sitting in front of the campfire. It's very late, and they're having something warm to drink, staring into the fire, talking in muted tones. When they laugh, it's a low, quiet sound. Listening to their hushed voices from inside your tent, you can tell they're actually enjoying the silences between sentences, rather than pushing through them. You're half tempted to get up and join them, but the sound of their conversation is somehow so comforting that it has the effect of a lullaby on you. Before you know it, you're asleep. If you can feel that feeling, you can understand the high side of Mercury's transit through the 12th house.

This is the side of us who loves secrets, remember, the side of us who probably remembers when everything was dark, muted, warm, and safe—the nine months we spent inside our Moms. Those type of moments, then, are the positive side of the experiences we can expect when Mercury tiptoes through the twelfth house. This is the side of us who likes to hide and be alone, too, so don't be surprised if Mercury's trip through here is a type of natural retreat for us, a period of time when we draw back and regroup.

This transit is best used by calming our minds, or meditating, by spending some Quality Time alone with ourselves to think, write, study, etc. Whispers. Secret trips, secret letters, and secret conversations. Quiet comforting conversations, or no conversation at all. That's what we can expect when Mercury visits this house. The downside of this house has always been that it's the house of secret enemies. Well, okay, it's quite possible that folks are talking or communicating about you without your knowledge when Mercury passes through here—but they could just as easily be talking you up as talking you down.

MERCURY/SUN

Me. Me. And Me. That's how our conversations often sound when Mercury visits the Sun. We're all set up to talk about what we love, what we don't love, and what we'll never love. And what we think about everything. Remember that yellow pages commercial that shows someone holding a long cigarette holder, looking especially vain, saying, "Enough about Me, Darling—let's talk about you. What do you think of my dress?" Well, that's an exaggeration, to be sure, but you get the idea. The Sun is the side of us that's concerned with us—period. He's the Executive Director of the corporation of planets that make up each of us. When Mercury steps up to the Sun, our conversation reflects that concern.

Now, when it's a conjunction Mercury's making, you can bet that What They See is What Others Will Get from us. In other words, there's not going to be any 2-second delay before our mouth opens and says what we're really thinking. Of course, we do more with our Suns than just think about Us—we also create, play, and accomplish. With Mercury right there on top of our Sun, all those things are easier, courtesy of Mercury's lightning-fast translating abilities. What we want to express just is expressed—automatically.

With the tougher aspects, we often hear news or information that seems to work against Our Purpose (our Sun)—or that at least provides a challenge to our self-expression. With the easier aspects, we're able to communicate with others quite smoothly—we just know what to say to make them understand.

Now, Mercury's also a busy kind of guy, into zipping around and doing all kinds of things, two, three and four at a time. He brings that love of movement and variety with him, so regardless of the aspect he's making to the Sun, be ready for a few days of accelerated activity. With the harder aspects, we feel a bit stressed and/or tense—as if there's too much to do and not enough time to do it. With the easier ones, we're busy, but productive.

MERCURY/MOON

Prepare to Emote. Really. For the next day or so, whatever we feel is about to come out of our mouths, for all to hear. That includes The Good Stuff—the I Love You's and the expressions of joy—as well as the Not So Good Stuff—sadness, anger, jealousy, and resentfulness. Mercury is ordinarily known for his ability to be neutral—but when he conjoins the Moon, his voice takes on a much more emotional tone. If you've got something to tell someone that's emotional in nature, then, expect it to Come Out right now—and maybe even sooner when the aspect Mercury's making is a conjunction. We hear ourselves saying things like What about my needs?, or Let me tell you how I feel about that— no matter how reticent we usually are about verbalizing our feelings. If you're in need of the oomph to make an emotional proclamation, look to the more action-oriented aspects from Mercury to the Moon—the squares and oppositions, and the conjunction. But be prepared to hear (Mercury) things you aren't necessarily going to be all that happy about, too—things Others are saying that upset you emotionally (Moon.) With the easier aspects Mercury makes, we're able to talk about what's in our hearts, and let Others know how deeply we're affected by what's happening around us—and that's a very good thing.

MERCURY/MERCURY

We've already talked about the double-dose we get when a transiting planet comes home. Remember? How on our birthdays, for example, when the Sun returns to its original spot in our charts, we're filled with two times the usual amount of Me energy—Well, consider this: Our own Mercury is the tool we use to speak and write with. It's the planet that symbolizes our logic, and our ability to learn and communicate. It's the internal switchboard that's always jammed, the reason we're aware of anything we're ever aware of, from temperature to light to sound, to color, to odor. This, then, is one busy planet. Double that dose to see just how busy this area of our life becomes when transiting Mercury aspects our natal Mercury—regardless of the aspect.

The tempo of our dealings with Others picks up considerably, for starters, and it's a good bet that so will the speed of our driving. Mercury's the planet that consistently wins the race around the Sun, after all—the guy just can't drive 55. When transiting Mercury comes home to our natal Mercury by conjunction, then—the Mercury Return—I don't have to tell you just how quickly life begins to move. Since it's our own pace that's being doubled, however, usually these are busy, fun times, full of letters, phone calls, deliveries, and appointments.

Under the squares and other harder aspects, things can get a little hairy. We may feel as if we're running around a lot but not getting much accomplished, or that we're scattered, or distracted, or confused—it all depends on the condition of our natal Mercury. If we've got a mental task to tackle, however, now's a great time to do it. The oomph of squares and oppositions, (transiting aspects usually known as challenging) is a wonderful push that really helps motivate our minds when we need it.

The easy aspects are times when our timing seems unbeatable, when we can be lucky, organized, and together in general. We have conversations that go well for both parties concerned—that's if we have to finish our sentences at all—and most communications go along in a remarkably smooth manner. Regardless of the aspect, look now for things and people to arrive in twos, as per Mercury's love of games, tricks, and duality—and pay attention to who and what come along. The Messenger may be trying to make a symbolic point.

MERCURY/VENUS

Venus is that lovely lady inside each of us, the tool we pull out when it's time for us to behave in a manner that Others find pleasing. So when charm, poise, and cooperation are called for, we activate our Venus and begin smiling, nodding, and chatting lightly. Mercury's visits to this (ordinarily) lovely, elegant planet bring out all the manners we learned growing up. We suddenly become suave, accommodating, full of Pleases and Thank You's. In short, we're right on our polite little toes when we've got our Venuses on High. Now—add Mercury's love of conversation to Venus's Niceness, and what do you get? Poetry. Music. Sweet nothings. Purrrrrrring into The Beloved's ear. Compliments. Social Niceties. Holding hands. Not a bad transit, in other words.

Now, all that pertains to the easier transits of Mercury to Venus, and to most of the conjunctions, as well. The easier sides to this transit can range from something as light and simple as chatting about Venusian goodies like cookies and art with a good friend, to something as meaningful as saying I Love You for the very first time. Adding Mercurial movement to Venus often adds up to dance, tender caresses, or visits to a loved one, too.

Now, with the tougher of the transits, we're dealing with a whole different thing. In fact, just reverse everything you read, and consider it. If Mercury's Messages to Venus aren't good ones, what might they be? Well, they might be bad news in the relationship or money department, or hectic mental activity (AKA stress) in either department. Might also mean that the women (Venus) in our life aren't seeing eye to eye with us at the moment. If Mr. Mars gets involved, these transits could even point to an argument about money or possessions or The Relationship, or an argument with a woman. Of course, the energy that the harder aspects symbolize can also be channeled into the type of creative burst that produces the poetry, music, and sweet nothings we talked about above, too. Remember, hard aspects don't have to be bad—they're just looking for a project.

MERCURY/MARS

Take one part Mars—Mr. Feisty himself, the guy after whom expressions like Seeing Red, Hot Under The Collar, and All Fired Up were created for—and add one part transiting Mercury, the traveling mouthpiece, the Bringer of Words. What do you get? Well, it depends on how you shake them, but as a general rule, what you get for starters is a Heated Discussion. Yes, these two planets unite the concept of Action with the concept of Communication. In other words, Mercury's an expert at fanning Mars' already fiery disposition into action—and at providing him with all the verbal bullets he'd ever need to get his message across in no uncertain terms. Yes, when Mercury visits Mars, all of a sudden, it's time to Let It Out—whatever it is we're angry or excited about, that is.

Now, the key thing to keep in mind when dealing with Mr. Mars is that he's not a bad planet. He just tends to get a little bit on the cranky side when he's not used right, that's all. It's similar to having a bored guard-dog on your hands. Of course, there's nothing better than a guard-dog when it's time to defend yourself, so Mars definitely has a very valuable job to do for us. When any planet touches him, however, he jumps—he's a bit on the trigger-happy side, see. When Mercury touches him by conjunction, then, our Anger, Assertion, and Me-First impulse has its hands on the microphone.

Since Mars never was particularly concerned with what Others think of him, if you're not in a situation that you feel is appropriate for the expression of anger, you're going to have your hands full controlling him. (Warn your Saturn and see if he'll help.) Actually, if you've got something to say on your own behalf, now's a great time to say it—just understand that you're going to say it with Gusto. Mercury is at his best when he's moving quickly, and he bestows that gift on Mars when he conjoins him. Okay, sure, maybe with the conjunction and some of the hard aspects, we're talking arguments. Fine. Arguments aren't necessarily bad things, provided they're handled without any physical interchange. In other words, now's the time to yell, and Vent Your Anger, and get it out. Just don't hit anybody. And by the way, you don't necessarily have to have an argument now. If Mars-type activities are your business, (athletics, manual labor, working with heat and/or fire, etc.,) you'll just be especially busy right now.

Under the easy transits, someone's words or gestures quite literally excite us. Someone tells us we're the sexiest thing they've ever seen, or they make us a job offer we can't refuse, or we just meet someone who gets our heart rate up by providing us with a spirited discussion. Regardless of what the aspect is, now's the time to give Mars the chance to speak on our own behalf.

MERCURY/JUPITER

Jupiter's in charge of expansion—Mercury's in charge of data. When the two of them get together, The Forest meets The Trees, and we have an amazing opportunity to learn everything because we Understand. Think of Mercury's visits to Jupiter as a student visiting a teacher. All kinds of wonderful questions and answers come up, and we find it difficult to quell the urge to learn. We want to grow, to travel, to meet folks with accents and ask them about what it's like where they're from. We want to have long philosophical discussions with friends, all of us seated at the feet of The Teacher. So don't fight it. Ask questions, try to fashion answers, and take a look at how very much there is to know, learn, and experience here on Planet Number Three.

These transits are times when we're capable of amazing even ourselves at what we know that we didn't know we knew. Understand, however, that under the more difficult transits to Jupiter, our ability to, oh, let's say wax pompous will Out, and we may tend to do a bit more proselytizing than usual with a little less factual back-up than usual. In other words, we can really Go On at length when these two get together—and sometimes we're filled more with zeal than facts. Do I mean exaggeration for effect? Okay, that's a good way to think of it. That's not much of a problem, however—we just need to make sure we've got our facts straight. (If you hear yourself start saying things like 'No kidding, there I was...,' however—you may be about to tell a proverbial Fish Story—one possible symptom of this transit.)

The highest side of Mercury's visits to Jupiter will bring out our ability to laugh and see the best in ourselves and in others. Jupiter is where we keep our stash of optimism and the belief that everything will work out just as it should. He was called Jove by the Greeks, after all, and Jove is where our word jovial came from. The best of this combination brings out our wit, temporarily bestows us with a wonderful gift of gab, and guarantees a few days, (at least,) of laughter, fun, and incredibly witty exchanges. Enjoy these days—tell a few jokes, talk late into the evenings with like-minded friends, and open your eyes to the wonders of the planet.

MERCURY/SATURN

Saturn rules Statistics, that unemotional recounting of Facts— Just the Facts, ma'am. When Mercury visits Mr. Factual, then, it's a good bet we'll be talking turkey with someone. Forget embellishing the situation, forget the flowers, the flourishes, and the yellow highlighter. Just get to the point. The Bottom Line is the only way to go right now. Of course, we don't need to be told this when Saturn visits our Mercury. We're suddenly very aware of how serious a discussion can be. Under the tougher aspects, in fact, we may be feeling quite serious because Mercury could bring news of that nature—something that's got a little too much reality involved, thank you, that's not what we want to hear. In that case, the tougher side of Mercury's touches to Saturn could mean that we receive news that makes us unhappy or depressed. If that's the case, we need to remember that although Saturn often feels heavy, he also rules structure, so he's often quite literally what keeps us together when the you-know-what hits the fan.

Under any Mercury transit to Saturn, nice or not, our thinking in general becomes more disciplined, but again, under the tougher ones, there's always the possibility of running into a day or two when we experience those Saturnian mental topics, guilt and worry. We could also be put in the position of ending something for Responsible Reasons right now, like it or not, in which case this transit might mean we need to tell someone or something Good-bye. At any rate, you get the idea: now's not a great time to schedule a party—unless it's a business party.

Speaking of which, business will go along quite well under some of the nicer transits Mercury makes to Saturn. We'll find that we're able to concentrate, sit and work quietly and patiently on a project, and Be Studious. We're often on the receiving end of facts, too—Mercury's job is to bring us facts, remember. When he's visiting Saturn, he brings serious info. Data. Numbers. Statistics. So now's a great time to present what you know in factual fashion, to give a presentation or a lecture, to say or write anything that requires you to sound like you're an authority figure. Just make sure you're really prepared before you step up to the podium.

MERCURY/URANUS

Uranus is the higher octave of Mercury. In other words, what Mercury the Messenger does for personal conversation, Uranus does for the Internet. They're both concerned with communication, then, but for different reasons. Mercury wants to help us communicate with What's Out There so that we can get our needs met. Uranus, however, wants to Spread The Word to the populace—to get what he sees as our collective needs met. Remember, nobody gets as fixed in the realm of thoughts as Uranus does.

Now, Mercury is in charge of the keyboard we use to send our e-mail out—so when Mercury visits our Uranus, our urge to communicate The Cause to The Collective often comes across— Big Time. In fact, since it takes the cooperative efforts of both of these planets to learn to operate things like computers, monitors, CD-ROMs, word processing machines, and, again, the Internet, when Mercury comes along to Uranus in our charts, we may get interested or involved in these things for the first time. Of course, Uranus in our charts is also the place where we derive our greatest pleasure from coming off as completely different from everyone else—so Mercury's visits can also mean that our urge or need to be futuristic, independent, and maybe just a tad rebellious is given a voice.

This, then, under harsh or easy aspects, may be the transit that signifies our very own Independence Day. Now's the time when we tell someone No for the first time, or when we strike out on our own because we just can't contain our urge to do what we really need to do anymore. Of course, any transit to Uranus in our charts provides us with a chance to Get Ourselves Free, and this one's no different. We're just a bit more vocal about it, and a bit less concerned with what Others think. Regardless of the aspect transiting Mercury makes to Uranus, we may also receive some Uranian news—something that's shocking, surprising, or a reversal of what we previously held to be true, that is.

MERCURY/NEPTUNE

Neptune in our charts is where we keep our stash of pink dust and pink smoke, which, when we opt to do it, turns whatever we're not wanting to see realistically into whatever we'd rather have it be. In other words, our Neptune is where we can use our magic to change reality into unreality. When Mercury comes to Neptune, then, we have the temporary ability to cast a wonderfully creative spell with words—to make word magic. As with Mercury/Venus combinations, that magic might produce music, poetry, or romantic conversation—the loveliest of all possible symptoms of this transit, and the ones most likely to turn up under the easy transits. Neptune's ability to dissolve boundaries is also famous, however—so when Mercury's in the neighborhood, it's easier for us to fall into a trance, to receive psychic impressions from our environments, or to go under hypnosis. Those are the type of experiences we can expect when Mercury and Neptune get together in the easier combinations.

The harsher transits from Mercury to Neptune might bring hypnosis of another kind, however, and You're Getting Very Sleepy might pertain to being confused, not understanding the full ramifications of what's being said to us, or deliberately allowing ourselves to be deceived because we don't want to see reality at the moment. Of course, as will all transits to our Neptune, we often don't see anything—much less the truth of the situation—until after the transit's over. In other words, if you've got this transit on right now and you're wondering if you are really being deceived by someone or if they might actually be A) the reincarnation of Cleopatra, as they told you, B) with the CIA, working undercover, as they told you, C) too busy over the past 5 weeks to call you back, or, D) an extraterrestrial sent here to do research—

well, ask someone who's not having this transit at the moment, and stop back in four or five days. In the meantime, don't sign anything, don't make any promises you wouldn't want to keep to a much lesser person than you think you're dealing with right now, and avoid chapels in Las Vegas at all costs.

MERCURY/PLUTO

Pluto is the spot in our charts where we love to dig—both literally and figuratively. It's where we want to Get To The Bottom of something—everything. When Mercury taps tentatively on Pluto's door, then, we may not have a lot to say for a day or two, but we're going to be very busy internally. We'll be mulling over clues in the conversations of those around us, for starters, (since this is another of the What They Meant By That transits.)

When we do actually speak under transits to Pluto from chatty, word-wizard Mercury—Well, my goodness, talk about persuasive. This is the transit (along with Pluto to Mercury—the same thing, basically, but for much longer) when we can literally sell ice cubes to the Eskimos. We have a built-in x-ray vision of sorts where our Pluto is, a kind of radar we bounce off of whatever we're interested in Out There. That radar sends back a schematic diagram of The Subject's Inner Workings, and we then know how to approach said subject for maximum results. When Mercury comes to that highly-charged and perceptive spot, we suddenly Just Know exactly what to say so that our words will have the most convincing effect possible.

Of course, Pluto also loves investigation and research, so Mercury's easier visits are a great time to dig for information, to work in a corner without a break until we solve a problem or find an answer. This transit coincides with an ability to focus and concentrate that borders on obsession. Now, that can be good and that can be bad. It takes a type of obsession to do anything thoroughly—or even simply to finish something.

Under Mercury's tougher visits to Pluto, however, it's entirely possible to spend a couple of days at work wondering if someone is plotting against us, obsessing on what They said the last time we talked to Them, or re-running a conversation over and over in our brains, so much so that in extreme circumstances we actually can't sleep. All the while we're driving by their house, calling them to see if their line is busy, and figuring out a way to stroll casually by their office at 12:03. In a nutshell, then, regardless of the aspect from Mercury to Pluto, we're going to be able to totally fixate and concentrate on something. It's up to each of us to choose wisely. If choosing wisely doesn't work, if you're still feeling like you just can't stop thinking about something you really don't want to think about any more, well, then, read a mystery or detective novel, and feed your tired little brain what it really wants right now—Intrigue.

CHAPTER SIX

VENUS

Your Venus Kit:

Flowers
Extra Money
Pictures of Your Other
A Victoria's Secret Catalog, and
Sachet for the Drawer Where You'll Keep Your Purchases
A Bottle of Chanel/A Bottle of Polo
An original work of art
Yanni's Most Recent CD
A Beau
A Gown or Tuxedo
Rich Chocolates—Godiva will do...
Pillows
Silk Sheets, covered with rose petals
A Bottle of Dom
Crystal Champagne Glasses
A Copy of *Sleepless in Seattle*

Venus Transits

You know your good old Uncle Jupiter? The guy with the after-shave, the ceegars, and the hugs that could cure anything? Well, he's got a partner—your Aunt Venus. She smells like rose water, wears high heels everywhere, and, no matter what her age, turns heads when she walks down the street. She's attractive, that's why. God\dess knows she's got The Big Guy wrapped. He calls her his Lady Friend—even after 37 years of marriage. When she's in the neighborhood by transit, she brings that same attractiveness, sweetness, and charm to the planet she touches. Yes, even if it's Saturn. Venus transits are like a peck on the cheek from that favorite aunt—and maybe a quarter, too. They're times when the Universe often gives us a small token of warmth or affection—a well-deserved break, a compliment from someone we love, or a present.

These are, for the most part, sociable, friendly periods when we do more than our usual share of mingling and are more interested in good food and cushy conditions than anything even remotely resembling work. In fact, the only subjects we really want to concern ourselves with when Venus stops by for a visit are Creature Comforts, Relationships and Sociability. Period. We're looking for a buzz, the kind that comes from being around people, places, and things we find appealing—that make us happy to be inside our bodies. For that reason—usually—Venus transits are experienced by most of us as "good," to use that antiquated, nearly illegal astrological term. Now, since The Lady also rules money, and since money is one of the ways that we draw the objects we love to us, she's also in charge of Finances, so we do also spend a fair amount of time concentrating on our checkbooks when she's around. In a nutshell, Venus transits are all about Feelin' Groovy—whatever it takes.

Venus Through The Houses

Picture that lovely lady we just talked about tapping lightly at a chamber door, dressed wonderfully, holding a box with a big red bow on it, and smiling to herself as she thinks of how delighted you'll be with the contents. That's how Venus makes her arrival at the door of each of the houses. When she comes along, whether or not we're actually treated that way, we think we should be—we're In The Mood for All Good Things. Now, understand that we won't necessarily *get* all those things we want when Venus transits a particular house—but we'll certainly learn an awful lot about The Good Life, and what our own ideal of that is. What we usually do receive with Venus' trek through the houses are kudos, hugs, and financial boons from the folks associated with that house—regardless of which one it happens to be—especially from Others of the female persuasion. In the sixth house, for example, it may be our co-workers who rub our shoulders, give us squeezes, and buy our lunch. In the tenth house, it might be The Boss. At any rate, now's the time when the Universe brings along Venusian envoys in all shapes and forms, just to make life a little easier. Accept the gift from the lovely lady at the door. Enjoy.

FIRST HOUSE

No matter what we do, when Venus transits our first house—the Front Door of our house, that is—we're lookin' good doing it—or we know the reason why....Venus/Ascendant transits bring out the vanity in all of us, so don't be surprised if primping is a bit more important now than it usually is—even for you Leos. Now's the time we'll be more apt to do something new to our hair, shop for a whole new look, or start a diet—something to make ourselves look as good as we feel. Of course, the way we present ourselves on a social level also has a lot to do with the condition of our Ascendant, so Venus' trips through this house also seem to coincide with times when we're a lot more personable, sociable, and charming than usual—even you Libras.

Of course, in addition to making ourselves look more attractive, we also become more involved with making our surroundings more appealing to the eye—and to the aesthetics. So now's also a time when we may do a bit of redecorating or rearranging—just so things are balanced.

SECOND HOUSE

I like to think of this house as the side of us who decides who and what we hold dear — in all departments. That goes for material things, like possessions and money, and for living things, like animals and Significant Others. This house also describes the qualities we admire and respect—what we look for and value in An Other. Well, all that said, let's just consider the effect a visit from Venus will have on What We Hold Dear. Needless to say, we're going to be drawn to beautiful things, beautiful places, and cushy situations—all of which cost money to behold.

So it's pretty much a given that when Venus transits this house, in addition to quite possibly being on the receiving end of all those lovely things, we're also going to be putting out an extra dollar or two to treat a special Other to an elegant dinner, and to keep the pantry stocked and the car polished, just in case they decide to drop by. Remember, in addition to the actual selection process—Shopping, that is—which we do an awful lot of when Venus stops by—we'll also be dealing with the care of the possessions we already have.

THIRD HOUSE

The third house has everything to do with the side of us who performs on Auto Pilot, who moves through our little world—our neighborhood, community, and places we visit on a daily basis, that is. When Venus comes along, we often find ourselves a lot more busy than usual with errands, most of which will pertain to Venus-related topics like money, possessions, food, and our Other. We may be more than usually aware of the loveliness of our surroundings—or more offended than usual by ugliness around us. Now, this is also the place we look to for dealings with our siblings and our neighbors, so we can expect a certain smoothness to those encounters now, too, and a bit more Venus-type socializing, too. This third house's relationship to communication combines with a visit from Venus to produce all kinds of loving missives too: love letters, sweet nothings on the answering machine, and maybe even the ultimate sweet communication—a proposal.

FOURTH HOUSE

When Venus transits this house, we want our physical home to be beautiful, to show others how peaceful and settled we feel inside. We're in the mood to redecorate, rearrange, or just clean like crazy. Truth is, our homes in the physical world are really a reflection of however we're feeling inside. Ever notice how disorganized we feel in general when the apartment is disorganized, and how together we feel just following a cleaning binge?

Now, this house also pertains to our dealings with A Parent— whoever we feel raised us emotionally—and with our families. During Venus' visits here, our dealings with those folks are usually quite peaceful and loving. Of course, The Lady does also rule money, so on a more surface level, this transit can also refer to money negotiations within our families at this time. Since this house points to our gut reactions, packed as it is with the emotional memories of All Things Past, Venus transiting here may also point to a time when we're more nostalgic and emotional than usual about our childhood homes or even about certain events from the recent past.

FIFTH HOUSE

I just want to say this immediately: This is one of the transits relationships are started on. Really. See, wherever Venus is at any particular moment is a place where we're most apt to behave in a way that's Pleasing to the Other, to load on the grace, charm and courtesy, and keep it comin.' When Venus visits this house, most popular for its connection to Love Affairs, she inspires us to load all that Good Stuff on to Prospective Others. They respond to us in equally charming fashion, and the show is on the road. Everybody being so Nice to one another creates quite a pleasant atmosphere, and under these extra-Nice conditions, many of us have fallen in love. It's that simple.

Of course, this transit doesn't always mean we're going to begin the relationship of a lifetime, and there's no guarantee that anything that does start now will last. (That's another story-an Outer Planet story.) But this certainly is the technology behind those classic Falling in Love or Being on the Honeymoon Syndromes. At the very least, we're going to be on the receiving end of some serious flirting, and probably more than one offer to have dinner. Those of us with Others can look forward to a particularly good couple of weeks, and since this house also pertains to children, now's a great time to spend Quality Time with them—being a child ourselves.

Now, all creations of the body, mind, and spirit are our children, so with Venus here, those creative endeavors are likely to carry her stamp—beauty, grace, balance and harmony.

SIXTH HOUSE

Prepare to Overdo It, in some small way, when Ms. Realgood Feelgood transits this house. See, in the body, Venus relates to the sensory organs, the bodies' receptors. Makes sense, too—these are the spots that tell us what feels good and what doesn't. When she passes through this house, then, the one that describes our health and hygiene habits, we become a bit more generous and lavish than usual with spoiling ourselves—food and drink-wise, that is. Since she also rules beauty, this is also quite commonly the time when we adjust our schedules to provide time to beautify ourselves, or when we take up a course of diet or exercise.

Of course, this house also has everything to do with our work—with what we do on a daily basis. When Venus is here, work-related matters and relationships with employees may go along a bit more smoothly than usual—the Lady's in charge of Cooperation and Compromise, after all, and she just loves it when we all get along. We may also find that we're working more with women when Venus is here. In some cases, this transit may also coincide with adopting a new pet. This house is the one most commonly related to domestic critters.

SEVENTH HOUSE

Transiting Venus shows where—and how—we're turning on the charm when we're out to attract what we love. That applies especially to people, and especially when Venus is passing through this seventh house, already famous for Other-pleasing behavior. The Lady, it seems, is an expert at sweetly drawing Others to us—mainly because she just loves doing things with someone. She loves to be with a partner. Since she's in charge of all Behavior That Is Pleasing To The Other—light, social chit-chat, polite small-talk, smiles, hugs, and kisses—when Venus is transiting this seventh house of One-to-One relationships, we turn those Venusian methods up High to attract Others to us. We adorn ourselves to make An Other want to come closer, and practice all our best Pleases and Thank Yous. So whomever it is that we want right now becomes the lucky recipient of both our Best Behavior and our best look—all delivered in one sweet-smelling, smiling package. In other words, they don't stand a chance.

Now, as with all transits, whatever we're giving out is what we're going to be getting back from Out There, so we can expect all of our dealings with Others to be tinged with an extra order of respect, courtesy, and cooperation. For obvious reasons, then, this transit, along with outer planet transits that set the backdrop, can point to a time when we do really find Mr. or Ms. Right. If you're single, then, get out there now and look around. You can't win if you don't play.

EIGHTH HOUSE

One of my first teachers, Nancy Hastings, used to call Venus and Pluto the Queen and King of Manipulation. Pluto for obvious reasons, Venus because she can be awfully good at being sweet when she wants something. Imagine, then, what happens when Venus stops by Pluto's place in our chart and slips into one of the outfits he just happens to have hanging in the closet. Picture The Lady Venus all done up in black—the perfect attire for seduction, power, and control. All of a sudden, eighth house issues like Sex and Intimacy magically turn into Lovemaking. In a nutshell, when Venus is here, all of our intimate encounters—and we're drawn to them more so than ever right now—will take on a quality of loving tenderness. There'll be much more intensity, depth, and true sharing now, too.

Of course, this house also relates to matters of joint finances, and since Venus does also rule money and possessions, we may be dealing with negotiations pertaining to those topics right now. When we're looking for indications of good or bad times to deal with joint finances, by the way, this transit, with Outer planet transits supporting it, can point to a time when we magnetize or attract money or possessions to us. In other words, if we're looking for a good time to apply for a loan—someone else's money— or to buy jointly on credit—someone else's things—now's the time.

NINTH HOUSE

When Venus enters the ninth house, she's got her matching luggage, her travel-size cosmetics and her best travel-dress on. She's prepared to hit the road, to take off on a long trip with a dear one, whether that be a woman friend or a lover, to see something she's never seen before. Of course, she's looking for a place of incredible beauty to soothe her aesthetic little soul. If we're planning a trip to somewhere that's famous for its sunsets, its expansive ocean views, or its mountain tops, then, this is definitely the time to do it. If that trip happens to also be a business trip, to buy goods, perhaps, or to deal with the importing or exporting of possessions, so much the better.

And let's not forget about Venus' fondness for finding Others for us to Share the Experience With wherever she goes. When she's traveling through this house, she's primed to inspire us to begin a relationship with an Out-Of-Towner—maybe even someone with an accent, maybe even someone we meet On The Road.

Now, when you're not having dinner with that gorgeous Frenchman or exotic Spanish senorita, remember that since The Lady also rules money, and this house rules foreign places, this might not be a bad time to invest a dollar or two in a foreign lottery. Check out the Irish Sweepstakes, for example. (Especially if Venus' main man, Jupiter, is also involved.) Above all else, remember that you're going to be attracted to—and attracted by—new experiences of beauty—on all levels.

TENTH HOUSE

Planets that make an appearance in our tenth house either bring out the Authority figure in us or step up our contacts with authority figures. When it's Venus that's here, there are several situations that might come up: First off, since the Lady is sooooo charming, it's a good bet that we'll be on the receiving end of Good Stuff from authority figures. At best, they give us a raise, tell us we did good, and invite us out to the summer cabin (a ten-room chalet) for dinner. While we're at dinner, they realize just how darned personable we are, and they begin to think about what else they might be able to use our pleasant little selves for. In the process, the wheels begin to turn towards a promotion or an increase in our professional dealings. Even though we may not know it, something has been started.

Now, we may also become an Authority Figure at this time, and if that's the case, lucky them. We're extremely benevolent wherever Venus happens to be at the moment, and when she's in this house, we may become the benevolent dictator. Of course, her connection with money may also mean that Venus' trip through this house puts us in touch with a new career, one that involves business finances or even individual money matters. We may also take up counseling others on their relationships, or begin working at a career with a partner. Or we may simply invest money in a new career start. Whatever the symptom, know that with Venus here, we're not automatically guaranteed success, but we're off to a darned good start.

ELEVENTH HOUSE

Since this house has everything to do with the groups with whom we ally ourselves, and since The Lady Venus is such a sociable kind of gal, when she's passing through this already quite sociable house, we undoubtedly find ourselves more involved than we ordinarily are with groups—and probably quite pleasantly. The eleventh house is the place that holds our understanding of just how good The Group Experience can be. Camaraderie. Kindred spirits. Friendships based on a common denominator. Take all that warm and fuzzy potential, add a dose of Venus, and you've got a party. At least one, and maybe several. Watch as the invitations start coming in. Reunions. Weddings. Parties. You name it. (And by the way, if you'd like to have a party yourself, now's a great time to do it.) Since Venus rules women, expect an awful lot of the attendees to be her representatives, too.

Now, since The Lady is in charge of Money and Things, our group experiences now could also involve dealings with financial organizations or group associations we're part of at the time because we're working on a financial venture for a common cause. Benefits and fund raisers, for example. Whatever your Cause is, then, expect to be more caught up in it. Remember, Venus by transit points to where we're currently forming and caring for our bonds with Others.

TWELFTH HOUSE

When Venus passes through the dreamy twelfth house, she's in the mood for secrets—for fantasy, unreality, and The Unobtainable. Now, being Venus, the Lady who loves to be in love, this may just correspond with the beginning (or heightening) of a secret love affair—since all those terms certainly do apply when you're in love but unable to be public about it, for whatever reason. At the very least, many of us realize that we have a secret admirer out there when Venus transits this house, or that we've been quietly admiring someone ourselves—without consciously knowing it.

Of course, Venus is also the Lady with the purse-strings, so this transit can also indicate the possibility of behind-the-scenes money dealings or secret negotiations over possessions. Since Venus rules the women in our lives, this transit may also mean that the women around us are up to something—doing things that will affect us without our knowledge, that is. Now, although this house has a terrible reputation, keep in mind that secrets aren't always bad. We may have a guardian angel or two working for us at this time, winging around behind the scenes and taking care of us without our knowledge. Regardless of the symptoms in the physical world, this transit is all about romantic dreaming. Allow yourself to Play Pretend—and hold off on any major decisions on any Venusian topics until after she crosses the Ascendant and gets a clearer perspective.

VENUS/SUN

When The Lady Venus visits with the Sun in our charts, it undoubtedly puts us in the mood to Feel Pretty—or Handsome, whichever applies. The Sun is our sense of self, the way we see ourselves, our core self. That includes our physical self. When Venus stops by to see the Sun, regardless of the aspect, it's time to decorate. OurSelves, that is. The hard aspects, of course, (and that may include the conjunction, if the natal Sun is aspected harshly by other planets,) seem to be in the neighborhood when more drastic changes take place—a new haircut, maybe, or the beginning of a strict diet. Hard aspects can also point to times when Others see us as self-centered, selfish, or self-absorbed—and they could be right. The Sun is where we keep our stash of Ego, Vanity, and Self-Centeredness, all of which can be wonderful if kept in check, and awful if they get away from us. Remember, the Sun is our literal and figurative source of heat and warmth, but it can scorch, too.

The hard aspects from Venus can also point to times when money or possessions come to us—or we give them away. With the softer aspects, it's easier for us to be seen simply as charming, suave, and appealing to Others. We're in the mood to Get Gussied Up and have someone tell us how good we look all gussied up. That's the skin-deep part of the transit.

On an inner level, the reason we're In The Mood to look mahvelous is usually because we're feeling mahvelous. Falling in love, of course, is Reason Number One that we humans most often Feel Mahvelous, so any transit from Venus to the Sun can correspond with the start of A Relationship. There are all kinds of possibilities. We may get our Venus visit via a raise, a pat on the back from a superior, or simply seeing our art framed or our name in print.

VENUS/MOON

Venus transits to the Moon are usually warm, fuzzy times when we're often the spoiled recipient of all kinds of expressions of love, affection, and appreciation. Now, most of the squeezes at this time will be delivered by the women in our life, but we can also expect a wink and a Hershey's kiss from our dear ones in general. Maybe we receive a housewarming gift, or just a token of affection. Whatever we receive, it's delivered sweetly, and usually followed by a hug. Basically, these are more FeelGood transits. In other words, if times are already good, they're going to be even better now. If, on the other hand, times aren't good—if we're in the middle of some uncomfortable outer planet transits, for example— well, then, Venus/Moon transits often show a break in the action, a time when we catch a brief respite from the troubles of the world.

Since Venus is in charge of money, we may also be on the receiving end of a monetary gift from a woman, maybe even from the Ultimate Moon Rep in our lives, Mom, or from someone we think of as a Mother. Remember, no matter which planet she touches, Venus transits describe times when we're much more social, when being pleasant and practicing Random Acts of Kindness with our natal planet are the order of the day. When it's the Moon she's visiting, we're so content on the inside we want to show it on the outside.

Take a look at a contented cat, lying in the Sun, purring. That's Venus to the Moon. Usually, no matter which aspect Venus makes to the Moon, a benevolent mood seems to infiltrate the day. At worst, we could be a bit overemotional—needy, or depressed. We may also feel as if we can't have what we really want right now, or that it isn't good for us.

VENUS/MERCURY

Mercury lends his voice to any planet that's visiting him. He's a celestial microphone, remember? When Venus dashes by Mercury's place, then, Love, Money, and Possessions are going to be the topics of the hour. Of course, when Venus speaks, it's politely, so under the conjunction and the softer aspects, we can expect our conversation to be very, very courteous—especially if we're shopping for a new Other. In general, the trines and sextiles are wonderful times when we express our feelings easily for our loved ones—and they express right back at us. You know the warmth that spreads across your chest when you're looking across the room at your Significant Other, asleep in the Sun? The same feeling you get when you back away from the new car you just bought? You know how warm and happy you feel when someone leaves an "I Love You" message on the answering machine? Those are positive Mercury/Venus combinations.

If we're chatting about a financial deal, however, another Mercury/Venus topic, the plot's going to thicken right around now. We'll be voicing what we think we deserve—so the more convinced we are that we ought to be on the receiving end of something wonderful, the more determined our negotiations will be— especially with the harder aspects. In general, with all Mercury/ Venus contacts, the subject is how we think about ourselves and what we're worth. It's a great time to listen to our own words and get to know ourselves a little better.

VENUS/VENUS

Feelin' Groovy—that's what Venus/Venus transits are all about. Whatever it is that we just love, whatever makes us feel spoiled and happy just because it's near us—and that goes for animal, vegetable, mineral, or human—when Venus comes home, we'll find it elegantly gift-wrapped and waiting. Our Venus, remember, is our magnet. She's the piece of each of us that's expert at Attracting what we love to us. When she's visited by transiting Venus, there's an awful lot of Nice in the neighborhood, and we're on both the giving and the receiving end. Now, this is going to be especially evident when the aspect she makes is a conjunction— the ultimate double-dose of any planet—but all the other aspects Venus makes to herself are going to produce similar results.

Of course, with the easy aspects Venus makes to herself, we may not notice anything happening at all. No news, as they say, is good news, and Things do go along remarkably peaceably, for the most part, with Two Times Venus. She's also not what you'd call a regular ball of fire in the ambition department. The Lady just loves presents, candy, and cushy conditions, so it's only natural that when she happens along, especially by easy aspect, our natal planet won't be much in the mood for work. Good company, good food, and good times will be more like it—and with the harder aspects, we can expect to overdo at least one of those things, and probably all of them.

In general, the hard aspects from Venus to Venus are the only ones with enough Ooomph to signify when money will come our way—or gifts, or boons, or other sweet blessings. With the easy aspects, we're usually much better at spending than at earning or receiving, because it's time to spoil ourselves.

VENUS/MARS

Venus softens Mars and makes him chivalrous, courteous, and polite—but still brave and daring, and very sexy—much like the romanticized notions we hold of the Knights of the Round Table. Instead of charging off, ready to kill whoever or whatever gets in the way, then, we find ourselves with a Mars (self-assertion) impulse that's a bit more tempered than usual. This Knight, in other words, will allow his opponent to rest before he begins his next assault—to be fair. Translated into human terms, this means that no matter how angry we may ordinarily get when we're pushed, no matter what type of temper we've got, right now we're a lot less likely to get revved and Go Off on an unsuspecting victim.

Fact is, regardless of the aspect, when lovely Venus touches feisty Mars, he's much more in the mood for making love than making war. Venus rules love, but Mars rules heat and fire. This, then, is a combination that's tailor-made for passion. So if we're feeling especially romantic—or should I say arduous—during this transit, that's a good thing. One of the healthiest uses for Mars energy, in fact, is Getting Physical with a consenting Other. (And if they're also having a Venus or Mars transit, so much the better....) Don't be afraid of the squares and oppositions between the two, either. This is one combination where a 'harsh' aspect often turns out to be the one that's action-oriented enough to start something wonderful.

Now, in every silver cloud there's a dark lining, so I really need to also mention that this combo could also point to arguments with your Other, but only if there are other indications present. It could also point to arguments over money—again, if other factors suggest it. In general, however, since She likes to attract, and He likes to pursue, when these two planets team up, we've got the impetus and the charm to go after what we want and get it, too.

VENUS/JUPITER

Whenever we're pleased, satisfied, or content enough to purr, it's a pretty good bet that Venus is in the neighborhood. When she visits Jupiter, her very favorite guy, get ready to have a wish come true—at least one. Think of it this way: our Jupiter is where we keep our ability to be optimistic, outgoing, and lucky. When Venus transits him, she brings along A Little Something to make The Big Guy even happier, luckier, and more positive than he usually is. Which puts us in such a good mood, folks just feel good being around us. So if we're already pretty darned Santa-like wherever our Jupiter is, now's the time when we'll be giving out presents and being amazingly generous. Whatever it takes to make everyone around us feel as good as we do—and that's how it is with all the aspects Venus makes to Jupiter.

Of course, Venus is a very sensory kind of planet. She's the Head of the Department of Nice—all kinds of nice things. Getting you your favorite people, places, and things is her job. Whether it's chocolate, music, flannel sheets, or the person at work you've got a mad crash on, if you want it, it's Venus that tells you how to attract it to you. All that good stuff can be pushed 'way past the boundaries of what's good for us when Jupiter's involved, however, so now may be a time (and this applies especially when Venus is making one of the hard aspects to Jupiter) when we overdo whatever we do to such an extent that we're gluttonous, wasteful, or totally hedonistic. In other words, we could actually make ourselves sick from being so excessive with food or drink

Also in the case of the hard aspects, since Venus rules money and possessions, too, now may be the time when we win money, (hard aspects are definitely more prone to inspiring activity, remember,) or lose money, or receive gifts. As with all transits, of course, we may also be the giver of money or gifts when this transit is on—and if that's the case, there's a good chance we'll be generous to a fault now. Under the nicer transits of Venus to Jupiter, our relationships with our dear ones, especially the ladies in our lives, are particularly good.

All that said, understand that since these two benefics (to use an olde-time word) get along soooo well, these days may not be particularly noteworthy—we may just feel as if we're on vacation, that all our wishes, at least for today, have come true, and all's well with the world. That's fine, of course, but be on the lookout for taking that good feeling to the nth degree, overdoing everything, and then being sorry when Saturn shows up and sees what you've done.

VENUS/SATURN

Venus is the most sociable planet out there. She loves to chat, mingle, and schmooze. Saturn, on the other hand, does not. Saturn doesn't like to chat, because it's a waste of time. He doesn't

like to mingle because he doesn't let his walls down easily enough
to enjoy it, and he's not much on schmoozing because he doesn't
want anyone to think he's Looking For Anything from them. He
wants to get everything the Old-Fashioned Way—by earning it.
Needless to say, he could use a little softening around the edges.
When Venus comes along, that's just what happens to our charts.
In that one spot where we're ordinarily rigid and awkward at
worst, and cautious and reserved at best, we suddenly feel a bit
more mellow—as if a weight is lifted, and we can grin a little.
Yes, Venus does softens Saturn up a little. She makes him feel a
little more social, a bit less cautious, and a lot more apt to have a
conversation that's not based strictly on statistical findings—
especially if she arrives in a hard aspect with enough push to get
him to loosen up a little. Of course, it's got to be on his terms,
because he's definitely The Boss, no matter what, so although
now's the time when we're definitely more likely to Just Let Go in
the area of life where our Saturn happens to be, it's going to be a
rather tentative type of letting go.

In other words, if Saturn lives in our second house, when
Venus visits we may suddenly be in the mood to part with a dollar
or two—provided it was to make a good deal. A well thought-out
and well-researched deal. If natal Saturn is in our seventh house,
we may actually start a relationship now, too—but chances are
good it's going to be with someone who's either a lot older or a lot
younger than ourselves, someone that we see as an authority
figure, or someone that sees us as an authority figure. Saturn/
Venus combinations are like that. They're what Spring/Fall
relationships and employee/supervisor relationships are all about.
On the other hand, a hard aspect between these two can make us
feel 'starved' in some way, as if we can't have what we want and
we need it badly.

Regardless of the aspect, now's when we'll be especially close
to older/younger folks, and probably also on the giving or
receiving end of loving advice. Under the easier aspects, we feel
more secure financially, have more willpower with food or
shopping than we usually do, receive a commitment we've been
waiting for from a loved one, or become aware that the Universe
has provided exactly what we were just now needing. One thing's
for sure, however. Even if it is Venus, the present-giver that's the
reason for the season—Saturn allows us only to have what we
Need—nothing more, and nothing less.

VENUS/URANUS

Suddenly we look up and see someone that's unlike anyone else we've ever known. They're taller, shorter, older, of a different ethnic background, maybe even a different gender. Who knows? Regardless of the differences between us—and most likely, because of them—we're immediately In Love. Yes, the only thing we can truly count on with Uranus, regardless of which planet comes to visit and thereby activates our rebellious, radical side, is that we're going to surprise even ourselves with what we'll do.

See, Uranus in our charts is the spot where we're out to prove how very unique we are—it's the place where we make darned sure that everyone knows it, too. Any transiting planet is simply an excuse for us to Be Different, and the Uranian part of each of us just loves that. (At least, with Venus activating this spot, it's Interesting..... Wait till we get to Mars.....) Anyway. Next time this happens, next time you fall for someone that's ridiculously unlike you, check the ephemeris and see if it's not a Venus/ Uranus combination. If it is, realize that this person is a perfect example of how independently we see ourselves. Then decide if you want to continue.

Now, money situations can also come up suddenly when Venus visits Uranus—and I did say Suddenly. Be prepared, then, for the car to break down, the kids to need $97 for the field trip today that they forgot to mention when it was planned 6 months ago, and your number to finally come up in the state lottery— whether or not you bought the ticket. As with all transits, the conjunctions seem more potent than some of the other transits— especially the softer ones. Now, with the hard aspects, all these symptoms of relationship and financial change might not come along under the best circumstances—then again, since the hard aspects are the ones that signify activity, if we're looking to change our situation suddenly, by proposing marriage to someone we just know is The Right One, winning something, changing jobs, or declaring bankruptcy, now's the time to do it.

With the softer aspects, we may experience a rather pleasant surprise in the money department, or we may just declare our independence from a situation that made us feel constricted or repressed. Regardless of the aspect, when Uranus gets going, it's best to simply expect the unexpected and go along for the ride.

VENUS/NEPTUNE

Isn't love grand? And isn't it amazing that you've just found the person of your dreams, right there under your nose? And even more amazing that he/she is just perfect — everything you've ever wanted? Yes, if ever a transit was built for romance—it's Venus/Neptune combinations. When Venus visits any planet, she arrives with a dose of sweetness—even Mars and Saturn are nicer when she's around. Needless to say, then, when she visits dreamy, romantic Neptune, who's already the spot in our chart where we want Things to be wonderful—things Get Wonderful. Fast. Especially under the conjunction. That's when we're open to magic, when one moment can truly make a difference in Forever.

Now, Things don't necessarily stay that magical way forever, so even if we've just met the person of our dreams, it's best not to dash off to a chapel in Reno—at least, not until the pink smoke clears a little and this amazing new Other has a chance to be what they really are. Same goes for money and possessions. When Venus transits Neptune in our charts, she brings along a gift — (or at least, it seems like a gift, to our Neptunes)—that's just exactly what we wanted. Now, under the hard aspects, we're more likely to experience illusion, delusion, and eventual disappointment—if we fall too hard for the spell these two cast, and forget to open our eyes as soon as possible after the transit is over. Venus/Neptune hard aspects can also point to a time when we're more prone than usual to overindulge in Substances—whatever Substance you use to escape, that is. Alcohol, drugs, sleep, meditation, prayer, devotions, even television.

With the softer aspects from Venus to Neptune, we're often feeling just wonderful—a bit spacey, maybe, but wonderful. We can also be wonderfully creative under Venus trips to Neptune— the Lady does inspire so well, and Neptune is a creative well that never runs dry.

Now, monetarily speaking, Venus' trips to Neptune can arrive with something that strongly resembles a Get Rich Quick scheme. In other words, it's not a great idea to sign any financial contracts right now, especially under the harder aspects, especially under the opposition, when An Other may be pulling the pink wool over your little eyes. In general, these two planets combine to produce a beautiful inspiration—they inspire us to wish, dream, and sigh. Enjoy them, but don't forget—it may only be a movie.

VENUS/PLUTO

Venus and Pluto are a mighty combination. First off, wherever Pluto is in our chart is a spot where we're perpetually in All Or Nothing phase. It's a place where we're out for intensity, passion, depth, soul-searching, and heavy, deep encounters. Needless to say, when Venus comes along to this spot, especially by conjunction, she's definitely not looking for a one-night stand. She's after a long-term soul mate, someone who will sit up with her all night long and talk about passion, true love, and just how close two people can be. Someone who will love her completely. When she visits, then, she may just bring you someone like that.

Now, this doesn't mean it's going to be easy, necessarily. The type of depth and intensity our Plutos are after in An Other isn't to be taken lightly. Under the harder aspects, we may even get the wrong type of intense Other hovering around us, and end up involved in a major power struggle within a new or existing relationship, or feeling as if someone is trying to take over our lives. Like I said, with Pluto it's All or Nothing.

Since Venus also rules money and possessions, these aspects can also indicate those type of dealings with Others—for better or worse, depending on the aspect. The harder aspects can show struggles over inherited money or possessions or joint resources. Under the easier aspects, we may simply become more intensely emotional with An Other than we ever thought we could be. At any rate, now's when we'll be aware of how deeply we're capable of caring for An Other.

CHAPTER SEVEN

MR. FEISTY GOES TO THE GYM

Your Mars Kit:

Health Insurance—for you and for your victims
Car insurance—   ”   ”
Workout gloves, and a Weight Belt
A Trainer That Looks Like Arnoldt
Red Anything
An Hour In A Shooting Range
A Huge Truck
A Blowtorch
A Sword
A Shield
An Attitude Adjustment
A Copy of *Rambo*
A Chip For Your Shoulder
A Swiss Army Knife

Mars Transits: Don't Step On My Blue Suede Shoes

Okay. Listen up, and listen good. The subject, under Mars transits, is Assertion—and these are pushy times, kids. Visits from Rambo The Warrior Planet mean that it's time for us to start Looking Out For Number One—Time to Stop Taking You-Know-What from You-Know-Who. Yes, indeed...under Mars transits, our spunkiness factor goes right up to a plus fifteen—on a scale of one to ten. Yes, this even goes for those of us with Libra planets who are ordinarily quite cooperative, compromising souls. When Mr. Feisty is in the neighborhood, there's just no getting around it—Everybody finds it more difficult to think of Others. (Except possibly as The Opponents.) But that's okay. Every transit has a purpose—and the purpose of Mars transits has nothing to do with Others. Mars transits are all about Me, Me, Me, What I Want—Right Now—and Me, Me, Me. Period. Mars adds an urgency to the spot he's transiting—and when we're feeling that anxious, it's hard to be patient and think of Others.

It is time to find out what we're made of, time to get in touch with that survival instinct we humans don't use much anymore, now that we're not living in caves. It's time to defend ourselves, and that means we can't worry about anybody else. In a nutshell, kids, when Mars is around, we don't take kindly to anyone stepping on our blue suede shoes—in any way. That includes anyone foolish enough to utter the 'N' word in our direction— "No," that is—which, when we're under Mars transits, sounds an awful lot like a dare.

Now, with all that feisty red stuff circulating, it's understandable that we may not notice the effects of our behavior on Others. However—there are several clues even those of us who are firmly enmeshed in Mars transits can be taught to recognize, several hints that, with time, will send up a Red flag in our hot little heads to alert us to the fact that we just might be acting in hot-headed fashion: Here's what to look for: First of all, suddenly everyone has An Attitude—and we're absolutely convinced it's not us. Can't be—we're Right. The boss is out to get us, our Significant Other is deliberately trying to make us mad, and all the folks you deal with at work are acting like total jerks. If you notice any of these Symptoms popping up in your life, reflect for a moment. See if it might not be that there's a bit of unused Mad in there somewhere, some anger that was summoned but never delivered to the proper address. See, the hardest thing to do under Mars transits—especially if you were born female—is to deliver your anger to its rightful owner. Especially if you happen to discover that the true owner is The Boss, the person who signs the paychecks, or Your Other, the person with whom you share most of your waking hours. This is where Self-Assertion comes in—because it's entirely possible to let Mars out of his cage without alienating the Powers That Be at the office, or making your Other so mad they spend the night on the couch.

In actuality, finding that the owner of our anger happens to be our Boss is one of the better discoveries we might make under a Mars transit. Sometimes it's much tougher—for example, when the owner of the anger is ourselves, and we don't know that's it, much less what to do about it. In fact, inner tension or anxiety for what seems like no good reason is another Symptom of Mars In The Neighborhood. Picture Rambo standing behind you, arms crossed, tapping his foot impatiently, waiting for the guy in front of you in the check-out lane to find his check-book, get his license out, and sign the damned thing. If you're already late for work, it's enough to send even the most mild-mannered among us over the edge.

Mars transits also have a funny way of making everyone around us seem rather testy, which might be due to the fact that even if we get angry and don't show it, Mars is still around. So if we don't get all the anger out immediately at the person who owns it, Mars will happily keep digging at everyone. Doesn't matter to him if we yell back at one person and are done with it, or if we direct it at 100 people, a little bit at a time. He's just not leaving until he has his say.

So—what can we do to placate this pushy ball of fire that's suddenly rolling off of us in waves? Well—the best thing to do under Mars transits, if we're feeling as if we want to lash out at anyone who's handy, is to figure out who we're angry with, and tell them about it. If that's just not possible—for example, if the offense was unintentional, or if the summoner of our anger doesn't deserve to meet up with it—the next best thing is to have mercy on those innocent Others we encounter during the day by giving Mars a strenuous project to work on—to keep him busy. Something that's appropriate to the nature of the planet he's visiting is nice—which is the purpose of this chapter.

Remember, when Mars is in town, our energy level is running high. We feel "hot," charged, revved up—and sometimes even feverish, physically. We're stronger, more restless, and amazingly active. We've got to give him something to do, then— so we're not sitting on all that energy, stewing—and more than a tad on the cranky, irritable, impatient side. If these symptoms show up, no matter what type of Mars transit you're having, it's time to exercise, exercise, and exercise. Run. Work it out. Get Tired. If it's your own Mars that transiting Mars is visiting with, working out with weights is a great solution. Mars is the side of us that wants to win—and every time we use transiting Mars to complete a repetition, we win. Remember, Mars rules muscles, iron, the color red, and anger—but, most of all, Mars is into expending one great big push of energy. It's up to us to choose our method consciously. Now read on—before I get mad.

Mars Through The Houses

We've already established that this is one feisty planet—the kind of guy who brings excitement, adrenaline, and a sense of Code Red urgency with him when he barges through any door. So it's not surprising to find that our lives are suddenly busier—a lot busier—when Mars is around. We're in the mood to Just Do It, and a lot more apt to take a stand on our own behalf than we usually are.

Sometimes that's a good thing. Sometimes our relationships with the Others who live in the house Mars is visiting have gotten to a point where we need to Say Something or Do Something, to let them know we've had it, we're mad as hell, and we're not going to take it anymore. Sometimes, however, we get, oh….let's say a bit overzealous in our defense of ourselves— over-defensive and over-aggressive. See, when we're under Martian rule, we're symbolically reacting to what we perceive as Challenges. As a result, we often tend (albeit unconsciously) to treat the Others in our lives as if they're those Opponents we talked about earlier—rather than Loved Ones.

When Mars visits a house, then, it's time to pay special attention to the quality of our relationships with the Others who are ruled by that house—to make sure that we aren't either A) victimizing them unnecessarily because we're angry at ourselves, B) beating ourselves up and stressing out over insignificant things rather than letting someone know when we're mad at them, or C) stirring things up just for the challenge we're craving. Regardless of what happens in the world around us, Mars' visits are energetic, active times. The best thing we can do when we see him approaching is to find him a job—something strenuous to do—that will allow us to use the considerably high physical energy level we'll be packing.

FIRST HOUSE

Here's the situation: after two months of tsking and pouting and carrying on in quite a sullen fashion while Mars transited the twelfth house, one day we wake up and suddenly decide enough is enough. We've had it. Just step aside so you won't get hurt. This, friends, is traditionally the way we feel when Mars crosses the Ascendant. He arrives right at the Front Door of our charts, all done up in red (and quite noticeable, even to the untrained eye,) with trouble on his mind and a sword in his hand. He's a Dude with an Attitude—an attitude he's been keeping in check for two months—no easy task for the planet who rules spontaneity, Just Doing It, and adrenaline.

Needless to say, since this house has a lot to do with how we present ourselves to Others, chances are good that we're going to be in a pretty darned feisty state of mind for the duration of his stay. So what's the best thing to do with him when he's here on our Ascendant, and in our first house? Well, first off, we've got to find a project that will require us to be personally assertive—something that will let us announce to the world that we're a force to be reckoned with. Since this house rules the physical body, now's an absolutely super time to start an exercise program. (Wearing red to the gym is a good idea under any transit, by the way—it's Mars' favorite color, and it's a great energy rev.)

Most importantly, when Mars hits the Ascendant, we need to recognize that we are now entering Warrior Mode, a condition that will last for about the next two months. Armed as we are at this time, then, it's important to consciously direct ourselves toward an appropriate target when we know we're about ready to Go Off—and just as important to be very careful.

SECOND HOUSE

First, two facts. One: Mr. Mars just loves to stir things up—he's famous for it. Two: This is the house of Money and Possessions. So when Mars approaches the door of this house, just for the heck of it, it might be best to think about setting aside a couple of bucks—before he barges in, rather than after—and maybe even have that rattle under the hood checked out before any extended trips. See, this leg of Mars' trip through the houses has always been associated with sudden expenses—sudden automotive expenses in particular. And justifiably so. Mars has a lot to do with autos, since they're made of his metals, steel and iron, and since they're one of the tools we use to assert What We Want over an obstacle provided by our environment—distance.

In addition to dealing with finances in an extremely Martian fashion, then—and that includes Impulse Spending, arguing over money and possessions, and being more assertive about What's Ours in general—we may also find ourselves dealing more than usual with Martian objects. Vehicles, for starters, but also tools and weapons. That's what to expect on the physical plane.

On an inner level, this transit symbolizes an urge to display our self-worth. That can show up on the outside through taking charge of our financial situation and our possessions, or getting a new job that puts us in a position of greater financial independence. Since this house also shows How We Earn Our Money, this transit may symbolize a time when we start a Mars-related job of some kind.

THIRD HOUSE

Issues like self-assertion, anger, and Taking Immediate Action are on High when Mars comes along, no matter where he happens to be, and the third house is the side of us that shows how we make our way through our everyday environment, both by navigation and communication. With Mars here, our two-month quest is to learn to deal with Mars issues on a daily basis—almost without noticing his presence. (Ha!) Needless to say, it's best to be prepared for the tempo and the tone of our communications to take on the type of urgency that only Mars possesses. We may just become much more assertive than usual in our conversations, tucking a couple of extra "I's" into every sentence—but we might also find ourselves dealing with Martian topics more than we ordinarily would. Anger, confrontation, competition.

On the other hand, since all transits can arrive via a third party, an angry, confrontational, or competitive person may also enter our daily routine—someone we can't seem to avoid or appease, who continually provokes us. No matter what disguise

The Red Planet is wearing when he shows up, then, remember that this house is where we keep the side of us who emerges when we're on Auto-Pilot, cruising around inside the comfortable circle of our third-house Little World—home, work, school, the grocery store, and anywhere else we visit on a routine basis. Although this transit could simply indicate a time when we're doing a lot more running around in that circle, on a much more hectic schedule, it's also a pretty good bet we'll find ourselves storming out of the house, being short with a neighbor, or slamming down the receiver on a third-house sibling at least once while Mars is here. Regardless of how we experience this transit, one of the lessons we're learning is about the power of words as weapons—and every weapon needs to be used wisely.

And here's a tip: since this house also relates to short trips around the neighborhood, it's not a bad idea to avoid driving while angry. Mars represents Point A To Point B energy—he's never been known for his ability to slow down and look both ways.

FOURTH HOUSE

Since this house relates to our Nest in the physical world—our Home—and since Mars is such a feisty, fiery kinda guy, this transit has been declared by The Fatalists to bring along a danger of fire in the home. Well, that's certainly a possibility—and it's a good idea to be especially careful of smoking materials, fireplaces, and stoves, especially on the days when Mars is closest to the fourth house cusp, and therefore angular, a condition that turns up the volume on any planet's visit, or if he happens to stop for an extended stay—a station—here. But there's a lot more to it than that. Even if we confine ourselves to thinking of the fourth house as our home, this transit doesn't necessarily mean we're going to have a fire break out.

We might be really busy in the home, expending a lot of energy doing Martian work with tools—laboring in the home, knocking down walls or ceilings, or even taking the Martian initiative and breaking ground to begin building a home. Our relationships with family members may also take on an urgency, or a parent may need us to help them in an emergency situation. But this house is the very core of our Selves, the gut we react from instinctually, the place where we keep our emotional stash of all those memories, right from Day One (and before that, if you're a believer in reincarnation,) that Color Our World. It's also the place that describes the tone of our childhood home. When Mars passes through here, then, we may find ourselves revved up about an emotional issue—and often, it's an old one. It might be old anger we're experiencing, or just a need for more definite action with regard to our home or our family. There could be an argument raging within our homes, too.

No matter how it shows up, we're learning to deal with a very deep-seated type of anger here—the type that directs our actions from an invisible place, almost without our knowing—which is what the IC is all about. If we take a moment to get in touch with the root of the anger, we're up for some constructive healing. Remember, Mars loves to initiate action. His transit through this house, (and through any water house, in fact,) is a great time to begin therapy.

FIFTH HOUSE

Here's the place where we keep the Cruise Director that's hidden inside each of us, the side that comes out when it's time to fall in love, play with the kids, party, and just generally be Young At Heart. When Mars takes off through this house, all those activities take on a more active, energetic quality than usual. And it can happen in a number of ways. Maybe we fall suddenly in love—quite passionately, too. If that's the case, you can bet they'll be someone who's very Martian—an athlete, someone who works with metal, heat, or tools, or even a police officer or enforcer of some kind. (My Venus in Capricorn, always an admirer of A Man In A Uniform, made me mention that.....)

Transiting Mars also shows where a lot of our energy is going at the moment—when he's transiting House Number Five, we're often expending a lot of energy on playing. We're out late, in constant motion, and up early—burning the candle at both ends. You get the picture. We may also take up a sport ourselves at this time, and become an athlete, rather than date one. Since Mars is such a feisty kind of guy, and since this house refers to The Kids, we may also spend a lot of time at their athletic events, and find ourselves totally involved in their lives. Then, too, we may have rather feisty experiences because of The Kids now—in other words, arguments with them, about them, or on their behalf. Since this house works with Leo and the Sun, it's a fiery place already. Don't be afraid to pick up the pace a bit when Mars is trekking through here—live a little.

SIXTH HOUSE

In the body, this headstrong planet corresponds to the head, as well as to the blood and the muscles. The sixth house describes our health, our work, and all the other duties we necessarily need to tend to so we can continue living comfortably inside these bodies. Now, any planet that transits this house brings its qualities along for a visit. When it's red-hot Mars that's transiting, then, there's a good possibility that we'll be dealing with Martian health issues—fevers, burns, infections, irritations, or anything that makes our body literally feel hot to the touch. We could also find ourselves needing to come to terms with stress, tension, or anger—especially if they begin to affect our physical health. With all that red energy behind us, however, this is a perfect time to take charge of our health: initiate an exercise program, start working out, or take up a sport.

Since this house also describes what we Do at work, anything that happens to us as a result of an impulsive Mars-like inattention to caution on the job are also a possibility at this time. Think of it this way: the metals that correspond with Mars are Iron and Steel—both of which are used to make weapons, tools, machinery, and automobiles, all the things we use to enforce our will over that of An Other or over our environment. When Mars storms through the sixth house of work, there's a good chance we'll use these instruments at work—even if we never have before.

On another level, we may also be involved in disputes or arguments with co-workers at this time. Or we may be much, much busier than usual, with an overly large workload to tend to, or a shorter amount of time available than usual to complete a job. Regardless of the symptoms, Mars trekking through this house will turn up the volume on work and health issues. Remember that Mars rules the muscles, and the sixth house rules health. If you're looking for an antidote, then, Get Thee To The Gym.

SEVENTH HOUSE

Here's the house that describes the way we relate, One-to-One, with An Other. It's the side of us that comes out a lot more, of course, when we're involved in a serious relationship, or a business partnership, since we tend to spend a lot more time alone with those folks once we've committed to them. Well, now. Just imagine how those Others are going to see us when Mr. Mars comes for a visit to this house, armed-up and ready for battle.

All of a sudden, we're ultra-confrontational, with a capital C. We're ready to defend ourselves, let loose and Have At whoever seems to be bullying, badgering, or pushing us a bit too far. Fact is, now's when we'll tell 'em off—when we'll let Others know In No Uncertain Terms that we're not going to be shoved around any more. Needless to say, oftentimes the folks around us are a bit surprised at our reactions to them now—especially if we turn from Clark Kent into SuperMars overnight.

Seriously, however, look at it this way—that quality of Red that Mars brings into a house always revs things up. It never fails. So if we're already involved in a relationship, chances are good we're either going to get more fiery and passionate with that Other, or angrier. If it seems to be anger or violence your Other is putting out, use Mars' cutting abilities —and the guts he bestows— to cut an unhealthy situation out of your life. Of course, this transit isn't only about endings. Mars loves to initiate, too— so don't be surprised if it's now that an especially passionate Other enters the picture.

EIGHTH HOUSE

Sex. Passion. Arguments over insurance, inheritances, or taxes. Power struggles. A tremendous physical intimacy—or tremendous fighting with an intimate partner. All these are possible symptoms of Mars' transit through the eighth house. Now, the sex and passion parts aren't usually too tough for most folks to take—a bit of Mars' heat in the Intimacy Department is a wonderful thing. But that same heat can also be the heat of an argument or dispute over joint resources, another eighth house topic. Maybe you and your Other decided to split the sheets when Mars was in the seventh house, and now it's time to divvy up The Stuff. Maybe it's an inheritance you and your family members are arguing over. Or maybe it's the IRS who's got you riled— taxes are also possible topics for arguments at this time. Since the eighth house holds the side of us who deals with situations we have absolutely no control over, Mars' trek through this house can also coincide with an emergency.

Regardless of what happens in our world to challenge us, now's the time when our ability to handle sudden urgent situations is tested. Remember, this is the side of us that remains when all else is gone—it's us at the very core of ourSelves. It's where we keep our survival instinct. When Mars passes through here, it's

time for a crash course on what we're really like at that core—
what we're really capable of. Fasten your seat belt, then, and get
ready to experience sudden highs and sudden lows. This house is
a bottomless well of strength. If we pay attention to how we react
to what life tosses at us now, we'll learn an awful lot about What
We're Made Of—and how much we're capable of handling when it
comes right down to it.

NINTH HOUSE

Travel. Education. Brand-spanking new experiences. All those
things are considered Food by the ninth-house slice of us. This is
the house that holds the side of our personality we take out when
we're on completely unfamiliar territory, when we have no choice
but to be totally aware of our surroundings, wide awake and
thinking on our feet. It's the side of us who can stand anything
but being bored, who loves to be in new places because they
require us to have a new perspective—a bigger perspective. When
Mars enters this house, then, with his I Want It Now attitude in
tow, we're struck with an immediate craving for New Stuff. Talk
about getting bit by the travel bug. We're ready to hit the road,
Right Now. We're ready to see something we've never seen, ASAP.

If we're not in the mood to leave home, we may suddenly
decide that's it's time to take a class on something we've always
wanted to learn—and chances are good that it will be a crash
course or an intensive. We want to learn, but we want to learn it
now—not in three or four months. We may also take a course on a
rather Martian topic—athletics, muscles, working with iron or
steel, self-defense, or job-assertiveness.

If all else fails, we might just meet someone sexy from Far
Away, (maybe even with an accent,) who's willing to tell about
what it's like There. If other factors support it, we may even
decide it's time to move long-distance—and do it overnight. At
any rate, this house and this planet are all about Just Doing It—
only thing is, the It has to be brand-new.

TENTH HOUSE

Nobody loves to start New Stuff like Mars does. He's the kind of
guy who thrives on stress, which is really just our body's reaction
to new circumstances. He's also the kind of guy who doesn't like
to be told what to do. He's much better at pointing his finger at
what needs to be done and telling someone to do it. When he storms

into this tenth house of career and public reputation, then, it's shouldn't come as much of a surprise to hear that we often start thinking about what it might be like to make some changes in our career—quickly. Maybe we're suddenly at odds with The Boss, or maybe we're presented with an opportunity to start up our own business—but we've got to do it now. Truth is, this planet is nothing if not The Executive Prototype—he's a take-charge kind of guy, a leader who gives orders and expects them to be carried out immediately—so it might not be a bad idea to consider any offers we receive now very carefully.

We may also be involved in some type of dispute or argument with the Powers That Be at this time—our boss is the most likely candidate, but any authority figure will do. We may also be drawn to a very Mars-oriented career right now—a career in the Armed Forces, or with the Police or Fire Department, or another enforcer occupation. Mars' trek through this house, more than all else, is about taking charge of our life purpose, and taking action to make what we see as our life-goal come true.

ELEVENTH HOUSE
First of all, I want to say that just because Mars likes to mix it up doesn't necessarily mean that we're going to take on a whole gang of Others when he's here. It doesn't have to be that way. Although Mars certainly is a spunky kind of planet, he's really just looking for a place to put his energy—which is considerable. So if we're already a member of a group of Mars-like individuals who spend their time together in Mars activities—i.e. athletics, martial arts, hard physical work, or anything that involves the use of fire, cutting tools, weapons, or machinery—chances are his trek through this house will just get us much more involved with this group. In fact, we may even find ourselves at the steering wheel for a while. Regardless of the type of groups we're a part of, matter of fact, Mars will definitely heat things up to a fever pitch for us when he gets to this house.

So if we're not involved with a Mars-oriented group—and even if we are, if other factors are involved—there's a chance we may experience the other side of Mars—the contentious side. Suddenly we're arguing with the folks at our Thursday night dance class about how we think things ought to go. Or we discover that the peer group we had considered ourselves part of isn't as perfect as we may have thought it was. Or we find ourselves up against a whole gang of Others who seem to be opposing us and/or our ideals.

Fortunately, there's a remedy: if we've got Mars banging around in there, we can give the guy a project—offering to take a leading role within our group, for example, and putting all our energy towards the group's purpose. (Just make sure you keep the group's interests in mind, or you'll end up arguing, anyway.) Our best bet under Mars transits through this house is to answer his challenge and Lead. Even if it means we're leading the Others in the group into battle, as long as it's for a collective Cause, Mr. Feisty can be an ally.

TWELFTH HOUSE

The twelfth house has everything to do with the behavior we exhibit when we're all alone. It's where we hide the shy side of us, the side who's afraid to come out into the light of day. We're convinced that no one wants to see this part of us—and that they wouldn't understand, anyway. Well. Needless to say, combining the nature of this house with the nature of this very red, very active, as-far-away-from-shy-as-you-can-get kind of planet takes a bit of work.

The high side of it all is that if we do need to express something that we don't ordinarily allow ourselves to express, now's the time we'll Out With It. It's pretty tough to keep Mars quiet, no matter where he is. I like to think of this house as the closet just behind the front door. Now, picture Rambo trying to 'hide' in there. First of all, he wouldn't like it, and second, he wouldn't do it well. He's a noisy, rambunctious, assertive kind of guy, and closets aren't his preferred place to hang around. So even if he's in there, he's going to make his presence known.

As a result, unless we can give Mars a holy cause to champion, (as per the spiritual nature of this house,) his trek through this last house may typically present itself through what I call Tsk Syndrome. That is, for about as long as Mars bumps around in here, whether or not we know it consciously, we're silently seething about something. Well, okay—mostly we're silent. We don't talk, that is. We do an awful lot of tsking, harrumphing, slamming doors, stomping our feet, and wearing sullen looks, however. Needless to say, it's obvious to everyone around us that we're furious—everyone but us, because we're not yet ready to talk about it. Meanwhile, when someone dares to ask what's wrong, we bark out "Nothing!" and toss them a horrible look. Talk about a good time.

The good news is that all this only lasts for a month and a half or two months. At that point, Mars crosses our Ascendant, and whatever we've been silently boiling over charges through our Front Door—in quite striking style. The better news is that if you've got a strenuous or demanding project to attend to alone, now's the perfect time to sequester that Mars energy and yourself and get it done.

MARS/SUN

Well, now—here's the two most fiery, most masculine planets out there. One represents our will to accomplish, achieve, and be recognized. The other is in charge of the assertiveness it takes to get there. Needless to say, then, when Mr. Assertiveness visits with Mr. Star-of-the-Show, we're due for a jump-start in the Recognition Department. Yes, when Mars touches the Sun, we become more charged up than ever about Finding Our Bliss— no matter what it takes.

Now, there's a positive and a negative side to that type of Me-oriented energy. The positive side, which we'll most often see under the easy aspects of transiting Mars to the Sun, will show itself in a number of ego-affirming, healthy, positive activities— everything from doing aerobics (to literally raise the heart rate, a very Mars/Sun thing,) to defending ourselves against an adversary, (particularly the kind that threatens or insults our pride or sense of Self,) to introducing ourselves to an important contact in a business situation. Now's when we're at our most confident, most energetic best. If outer planet transits support it, matter of fact, we're pretty darned unbeatable under positive Mars/Sun transits.

Now, under the conjunction, our Sun symbolically takes on the characteristics of Mars. Basically, we feel as if we've become Rambo For A Day—so if someone should attempt to step on our blue suede shoes, figuratively or literally, they're in for quite a surprise. When Rambo's on duty, all opponents are history. Dead. Outta here. Immediately, too. Mars isn't the kind of guy who sits down and thinks things out rationally. He shoots first and asks questions later—maybe. When he's touching the Sun by hard transit, we may have a bit of a chip on our shoulders—the size of a Redwood, that is. We may find ourselves overreacting to

Others, (authority figures, especially,) and taking what they say extremely personally, too. Of course, as with all hard aspects from a transiting planet, this is the time we're going to feel either charged up enough or uncomfortable enough to Make Changes. If we can channel all this fire, then—regardless of the aspect involved—we stand to make tremendous personal gains.

MARS/MOON

If there's any time we'll be more likely than usual to Vent, this is it. See, Mars has one particular specialty—heat—which he symbolically bestows on whatever planet he visits. Add a dose of this heat to the planet of emotions, and a number of things happen. First off, we're going to be Excited—with a capital E. The nature of the aspect will tell us whether we'll be excited for better or worse.

In general, with the conjunction, it's tough to say which way things will go. It all depends on the condition of the Moon in our chart. If we're the proud owner of a Moon who tends towards the overemotional, there's a good chance we're due for an extremely emotional moment or two when Mars arrives. If we're the equally proud owner of a Moon that's more on the mellow side, we may just get some great news that makes our heart beat a little faster— anything from an I Love You to a proposal to a birth announcement. Regardless of the Moon's natal condition, when Mr. Mars stomps up to this tender lady in a square or opposition, we may feel emotionally threatened, confrontational, or just angry at ourselves. The Moon has everything to do with our emotional safety.

Another possibility with the hard aspects, of course, since the Moon rules women, kids, and our Mom, and Mars rules anger, is that when Mars comes along to the Moon, we'll be involved in a dispute or argument of some kind with one of those folks. Our home can also be an issue at this time—we may move suddenly, argue with someone in the home, or just have a great party. And speaking of parties, when Mars touches the Moon by sextile or trine, we'll be the life of the party.

MARS/MERCURY

My girlfriend, Diana, has the Ultimate Mars/Mercury bumper sticker on her (red) Blazer—it says "Get in, sit down, shut up, hold on." Now, although that one phrase says just about all you'll ever need to know about Mars and Mercury, I feel obligated to explain this duo a bit further. For starters, realize that you're going to be rather short-tempered, to say the least, right around now—so don't sign up for a course on How To Be Polite, Patient, and Cooperative, because it's not going to work. See, when Mars stomps up to our Mercury, we speak first and think later—maybe. Makes sense, too. These two planets, in any combination, are a quick, potent pair.

Mercury's already at least as fast as the speed of light—he whips around the Sun in 88 days, and in our charts, he represents the urge or need we've all got to Communicate with one another and with What's Out There. Mars loves to heat things up—and you know what happens when you heat air. The molecules start to speed up, and eventually they bounce off of whatever happens to be around them. In astrological terms, that means that What We Think Is What We Say—which can be a wonderful thing. Suppose, for example, that we need to debate an issue, and we need to do it quickly—or that we're a contestant on a game-show—or that we need to run a race, or just plain old Hurry Up. In those cases, the warmth Mars adds that symbolically speeds Mercury up would be a wonderful thing—and those are often the type of situations that come along when the aspect Mars makes is an easy one—a trine or sextile or easy conjunction.

In addition, now's when we're going to be amazed at our ability to do several tasks at once—even if we ordinarily feel scattered when we try multiple projects. Under the hard aspects, (and the square most especially, due to its connection to internal tension,) we often feel as if Things have speeded up past what we can comfortably handle. We're caught in traffic, left with too many things to do and not enough time to do them, or feeling pressured by outside influences to move faster in some way. Of course, since Mercury is also the Head of our Communication Department, when Mars prods him into action, we may also have an angry word or two with someone who we feel is putting us under pressure.

Regardless of the aspect Mars makes to Mercury, now's when our minds will be extremely competitive—when we'll think in terms of Winning, in conversations, especially. Remember, Mars loves to Do Battle. Put him together with Mercury, and you've got quite a spirited debate on your hands.

MARS/VENUS

Venus is the planet we use to attract who and what we love. As far as possessions and finances go, she's a regular magnet, a lure, the carrot we dangle from the stick when it's time to catch the attention of someone we're attracted to. Ordinarily, unless she's in especially feisty condition natally (in aspect to Mars, or in Aries, for example,) our Venus is where we tend to be on the mellow side, where we prefer peaceful situations, pretty music, good food, and hanging out with Others. However. When Mr. Mars comes along, all of a sudden, the Lady has an Attitude. We decide it's time to Pursue what we want, to go out and Get Him, Her, or It, rather than waiting for them to find us or notice that we're watching them and smiling. Instead, we find ourselves asking them to dinner, making the first move for a kiss, or telling someone to back off, because He, She, or It belongs to Us. Period. That's what it's like when Mars visits Venus. At least, that's part of it—and we'll notice ourselves doing these things most often when Mars is making a conjunction to our Venus.

Since the Lady is also in charge of Money and Things, however, with the conjunction and with some of the more difficult aspects, we could also find ourselves involved in disputes inspired by this Martian kind of feeling. With the squares, problems might include arguments or face-offs about money, or arguments within our primary relationships—or both, since, according to every survey out there, money is what we most argue about with our Others. Of course, the oomph of the square can also mean that we become inspired to put in some serious overtime at work to stack up a pile of money for vacation, too. With the opposition, most often, the cause of any relationship problems or financial problems will be, in our opinion, an Other. Another interesting side of difficult Mars/Venus contacts is the classic If You Loved Me You Would Syndrome it inspires. We want to take action on behalf of The Beloved, to prove our love to them in daring, exciting fashion—and no challenge or quest is too much to ask. With the easier aspects, we're inspired to initiate new partnerships, to pump a bit of passion into existing relationships, to take on an extra job or project, or start a new job. No matter what the aspect Mars makes to Venus, whatever and whoever we love will take on a most active role in our lives.

MARS/MARS TRANSITS—THE TERRIBLE TWO'S

All of a sudden, we're stomping around the office, angry for what seems like no apparent reason. We're feeling like we want to hit something, and we have zero tolerance for lines, busy signals, and people doing 45—okay, 55—in the left-hand lane. What's up with that? Well, check around the chart and see if Mr. Mars isn't aspecting himself, because those are all the symptoms of a Mars/Mars transit.

These are times when our energy level runs on High, times that are all about taking action. We're stronger, restless, and much more active, at best, and cranky, angry, accident-prone or violent, at worst. Transiting Mars aspecting our own Mars is a double-dose of Don't You Dare energy, directed Out There at whoever seems to be standing in our way. The conjunction, of course, is the most potent aspect he makes to himself. It happens every two years, as per the fact that Mars takes two years to complete an orbit and return to Home Base in our chart—which sure does make The Terrible Twos eminently more understandable. Yes, every two years we all get the urge to Just Say No, No, No, to assert ourselves in no uncertain terms, to Have At anyone who opposes us. Mars, remember, is our own personal sword, the Rambo in fatigues who lives inside each of us that's ready, willing, and able for the next battle, competition, or conquest— doesn't matter if we're two or seventy-two.

Now that we're all grown-ups, then, when we see a hard aspect coming, instead of just sitting there arguing with everybody, we can give the guy a break and feed him. Challenge him. Use him to push past the limit, physically. Raise those weights five pounds at the gym, or run an extra mile. Hard aspects are built for hard work—or exercise, or any strenuous activity (feel free to use your imagination here, gang...) that will use up his considerable red energy so we're too tired to be mad. Don't make him go puttering around Out There, searching for an outlet—that's when things get ugly. A bored Mars is like a hungry watch-dog. Instead, then, initiate something that requires a hard push of energy—these transits are often times of birth, remember, and beginnings are Mr. Mars' specialty.

Under the easy aspects, we've still got all kinds of energy, so they're perfect times for us to try something entirely new, to put ourselves in circumstances where we've got to be brave. (Not in danger, now—just brave.) Any old alien territory will do. Remember, our Mars is out whenever we "do" anything for the very first time, and always there when we try something we've never done before, because who knows how it will turn out or what we should expect? It's his job to defend us at all times, and he takes it quite seriously—especially when he transits himself.

MARS/JUPITER

Our Jupiter is where we're at our optimistic, expansive best, where we're more likely to overdo whatever we do, regardless of the topic. Add a little Mars to that Jupiter, and you've got a great, big enthusiastic burst of energy—that's in need of a constructive direction. See, no matter what the aspect is that Mars makes when he contacts Jupiter, the very best thing to do during his visit is to find an outlet for that big burst of energy. Exercise, or run— or compete in some way, even if it's a spelling bee—those are our very best bets. Of course, the more strenuous the competition, the better—Mars just loves to Be Physical.

Of course, Jupiter is also where we're at our most optimistic best. A little bit of Mars added to Jupiter can also mean we take a gamble, and win, or that our timing is right on. This is known as one of the luckier transits, since if you translate it literally, it means fortunate actions. That applies especially with the easier transits, but also when Mars comes along and touches Jupiter by conjunction, since that's when our own Jupiter takes on a more spontaneous, impulsive tone. Now, if it's a hard aspect Mars makes, it's quite possible that we may become a bit over-optimistic right now—and maybe take a risk or two, as well. The harder aspects, as action-oriented as they are, often correspond with times when we over stretch our bounds but don't realize that they're over stretched. We feel as if we're simply on a roll, and we don't want to stop what we're doing. With the easier aspects, we've got tons of energy, we're ready to take on physical tasks, and our sense of humor is primed and ready to go.

By the way, regardless of the aspect Mars makes to Jupiter, now's a great time to be careful while traveling, especially long distance. So if you're in France when Mars knocks on Jupiter's door, look both ways before crossing the Rue.

MARS/SATURN

Sir, Yes Sir. Right away, Sir. Ever watch the way a drill sergeant works the troops? Especially after they've known him for awhile? No matter what that man bellows, everybody scrambles to get it done—quickly, efficiently, and to the best of their abilities. They're not scared of him, exactly. They just have no doubt in their minds that he's in charge, and they're not. Their duty is to follow orders, and get the job done. Well, that's what it's like in our lives when Mars stomps up to our Saturns. He's the planet that rules Accomplishment, after all—so his spot in our chart is a place where we realize, on some level, that we've got Things we need to do, Things that will accomplish our purposes. That's what we innately understand with our Saturn. Mars adds his fire to that already ambitious planet, and the show is officially on the road.

We start giving ourselves (and others) orders—or should I say instructions—on what to do, how to do it, and when to have it done by—at the latest. We suddenly Become Organized, too—even if it's not in our nature to do that ordinarily. We've got A Plan, a mission, and it's an entirely realistic one. If we already have our acts pretty well together and we're organized enough to live by lists, anyway, well, now's when we're about to tear into those lists with an eye to finishing up quick.

Basically, these two planets are partners in military strategy. When they get together in our lives, it's time to do just that—to make a plan that will eventually accomplish a difficult or time-consuming goal. Now, under the conjunction, this seems to come naturally. We move a bit more quickly in our Saturn department—which is a great help at times, since our Saturn is a spot where we can often get stuck in procrastination due to Fear of Failure. (We may also lose our sense of humor for a few days as we focus in on the accomplishment of tasks. If this happens to you, explain to your Other that it's just a phase you're going through, it's going to pass soon, and not to worry.) Under the harder aspects Mars makes to Saturn, the opposite can happen— that is, we feel as if we want to get going, and we see what needs to be done, but unless we drum up a serious amount of self-discipline, we can't seem to get moving. Under the easier aspects, we're able to mete out our energy in doses, saving what we need for later and getting everything we need to do accomplished in an orderly fashion. No matter what the aspect, the subject is Getting It Together, and the time is Now.

MARS/URANUS

If you've even been involved in a tornado, or if you've seen *Twister*, or if you've ever been stuck in a serious thunderstorm, then you're quite familiar with the concept of Mars and Uranus in partnership. This, friends, is what I think of as the most volatile combo Upstairs—not just from the weather point of view, of course, but also in our lives. The two really do have an awful lot to do with thunder and lightning. Uranus is an electric kind of guy—in fact, he rules electricity—and Mars just loves to get him going—suddenly. If we think about how suddenly a flash of light changes the room when that switch is flipped, then, it's easy to get a fix on what this partnership is all about. And actually, it can be summed up in two words: sudden action.

Now, it's sudden action that's responsible for all liberations. So when Mars touches our already rebellious Uranus, we may suddenly Go Off and decide that not only are we Mad As Hell and not about to take It anymore, we're not going to live in the same town where It happened, either. Or we're not going to work at that job anymore, and we tell the boss to take this job, and um,... find another fool to do it. Or we tell our unfaithful lover to take a hike. These are just a sampling of the situations that might come up under this transit, but you get the idea. Whatever we've been tolerating, plodding through, or putting up with, it's about to change, right now, when Mars comes up to our Uranus and pokes him in the side—and the more restricted we were, the more radical the change will seem to Others who may not understand that this has been building inside us on a mental level for quite some time.

The conjunction adds an even more immediate element to this aspect, which may mean we act even more suddenly when it's the conjunction Mars makes to Uranus. Of course, a planet being transited by a planet symbolically takes on the characteristics of the visitor, so we may also quite literally become suddenly angry—which, of course, could lead to any of the changes we talked about. Under the harder aspects, that sudden action often feels as if it's happening to us—which can be....well, unsettling, to say the least. Or we may suddenly jump up and decide it's time to do what we've been talking about doing for some time, since the hard aspects are also known to be action-oriented.

With any of the transits, we're also quite capable of literally or figuratively changing directions—another favorite activity of Uranus. Under the easier transits, we act spontaneously, change our minds, or make a decision we've been withholding judgment on for some time, and all goes well. Any combination can show up as a new, brilliant idea, invention, or suggestion, or the ability to break through an impasse. All of these combinations should be handled with care—again, these are the two most volatile planets Upstairs.

MARS/NEPTUNE

Mars is the most physical planet out there. He Initiates Action and Gets The Show On The Road. He fires first and thinks later. He loves to Get Physical, to Just Do It. Neptune, on the other hand, is the spot in our chart where we don't want to act, get physical, or even wake up, until we're convinced that Things are just exactly the way we want them to be Out There. Our Neptune is where we're quite happy to just let things go on as they have been, even if there hasn't been any activity in months—as long as we can keep our dreams.

When Mars comes to Neptune, then, this most ethereal, dreamiest part of us, the part that operates mostly on intuition, is suddenly jump-started. We feel as if circumstances at this time push us into action—ready or not. It's like being awakened from a sound sleep by a gunshot, and it can make us feel as if we're operating while only half-awake. Needless to say, our sense of direction can be a bit off at this time, so it's important for us to watch out for the possibility of acting too quickly without looking where we're going—literally and figuratively. That applies to any transit of Mars to Neptune.

With the conjunction, we may also experience a fired-up kind of feeling to this most spiritual part of us—which could translate into a spiritual or holy zeal. Our Neptune becomes Martian, like it or not, and we could even become furious without being able to put our finger on what it was that set us off. With the harder aspects, we feel stuck in circumstances that defeat us, confuse us, or throw us off our path—or we're inspired to go one step further towards accomplishing a spiritual goal. We could also feel victimized by someone or something under the harder aspects, and since we don't have any boundaries where our Neptunes are, to start with, it's probably not a good idea to take chances with our health or safety right now. With the softer aspects, we act on our intuition, and it pans out quite well, or we put our energies into a spiritual cause, taking it on and championing it, and we accomplish something for our cause and for ourselves. Remember, no matter what the aspect, Neptune is the side of us that understands that We Are All One. When Mars visits her, she's touched by the heat of a sacred fire, inspired to fight for the underdog. Our best bet at these times is to direct our energies toward something that we feel will benefit the whole planet rather than ourselves.

MARS/PLUTO

Our natal Pluto is a veritable powder keg. It's a spot where we're extremely thorough, extremely fixed, and, in a word, extremely Extreme. It's where we keep an amazing store of energy—the kind that's bottomless. In fact, our Pluto is where we keep our survival instinct, the thing that gets us through Life-Or-Death situations. Our Pluto is also where we're familiar with the concept of Rage— of just purely Losing It. Ordinarily, of course, we don't Just Lose It. It's not socially acceptable, and it doesn't get us anywhere in life—with the possible exception of jail. When Mr. Mars comes along, however, that task becomes a bit more challenging. Mars is a real spark-plug. He loves Urgent Situations, and feeds on stress—so if there isn't any tension or conflict brewing at the moment, he's only too happy to start some up, just for kicks—and the adrenaline rush.

When he gets to Pluto, then, by conjunction, it's a verrrrrry potent combination that's formed. It's impossible to label the experience of the conjunction as either good or bad, but it's a sure bet we'll be feeling like veritable balls of fire—or nuclear weapons that someone just triggered. Needless to say, it's good to have a really strenuous project on the fire (if you'll pardon the pun) when the two of them get together.

Now, when Mars comes along by hard aspect, that ability we suddenly feel endowed with to Do Anything may turn us into something that resembles a bully. We find ourselves bulldozing over weaker creatures, literally and figuratively, with no regard for them. We can become obsessed where our Pluto is, remember—when Mars adds his fire to the situation, then, we can become obsessed and either angry or passionate. Now, this combination is quite helpful if we're under siege from others, or under the gun to finish a project or accomplish a long, arduous task—Mars is the added strength of will that's pushed more than one athlete across the finish line, and there's nothing Pluto likes more than Finishing.

By softer aspect, then, we become capable of focusing our energy, of setting our sights on a topic and following through to completion. Pluto is our funnel—it's where we can pour an awful lot of our physical and/or mental and/or emotional energy on to one specific person, place, or thing. Mars is a traveling spark-plug, a burst of inspiration to Act. There's really not much we can't do when these two are cooperating.

CHAPTER EIGHT

JUPITER

Your Jupiter Kit:

A Big Dog
A Horse
Maps of Africa, Europe, and Sri Lanka
An Accent
A Mountain To Climb
A Europass
A Summer Off, and A Round-Trip Air Ticket to Anywhere
A Set of clothing a size larger than you usually Wear
A Wallet Full of Money—and no bills to pay
A Pizza With Everything On It
Gas Credit Cards, and Someone to Pay Them Off
Something to Spout About and Try To Convince Someone Of

Jupiter Transits: Up, Up and Away...

The subject is risk, growth, and New Stuff. These are *Star Trek* transits, real door-openers. When Jupiter touches us, we wake up one day and suddenly become aware that we're bored. We want to break our routine and Do Something. Anything we've never even considered in the past will do just fine. We're in the mood to Boldly Go Where No Wo/Man Has Gone Before, whether it's by traveling long distance, taking a class, or learning something new from a visitor from Far Away. The house or planet Jupiter visits wants All New Stuff, in other words. We're struck with an irresistible urge to seek out new places, new people, and new ways of tackling old problems.

Regardless of which of those methods we choose, our perspective widens and we grow under Jupiter transits. Our sense of adventure grows, too. We're so into this New Stuff that whether or not we're natally a dare-devil at heart, right now we're bold enough to try all kinds of things we thought we'd never do. Oh, and as long as no other transits suggest danger, now's definitely the time to take a chance, by the way, and risk a shot at the title of your choice. Now, that doesn't mean you should take foolish chances, of course, so no jumping out of the plane without a parachute, okay? (Even you daredevil Aries types.) Regardless of what New Adventure you decide to undertake, be aware that Santa's on your side right now—but don't get crazy. Saturn hasn't gone anywhere.

Anyway. In general, Jupiter transits are times when we're luckier, bolder, and a lot more likely to succeed. These are also times when the Big Guy *provides opportunities*—be sure and take him up on them.

Now, speaking of growth and expansion, it's also a fact that we sometimes grow physically under Jupiter transits. Weight-wise, that is. Since Jupiter rules the principle of exaggeration, our ego can get a bit inflated, too. We get to thinking that we can do anything, anything at all. Our natal planet becomes so confident and so swelled up that we feel downright euphoric. Manic, even. Jupiter transits are like that. But, damn, they feel good. Real good. Addicting, even—and I don't know anybody who wouldn't trade a good Jupiter transit for a tough Saturn transit.

Now, the Big Guy tends to be a bit on the philosophical side, what with that great ability he has for seeing Everything—so we often find ourselves pondering The Big Questions when he's in the neighborhood, too. No matter what he's doing in our charts, now's when we're symbolically being allowed to Take One Giant Step.

Jupiter Through the Houses

One of the best ways of trying to figure out what might be coming up is by looking back at what happened last time this happened. Jupiter is especially helpful for doing this type of hindsight, since his 12-year orbit is long enough to show process, yet short enough for us to remember. He spends about a year in each house, calling attention to us, making us bigger in some way, and expanding our horizons. Remember, a house is really just a side of ourselves that comes out in a particular life situation. When Jupiter enters a house, we become interested in learning all about the life situations handled by The Side Of Us who lives there. Regardless of the house he visits, and therefore the side of us he symbolically activates, Jupiter provides opportunities for each of the twelve slices of our personality to expand—that's his job. We learn new ways of coping with familiar situations, often because we're removed from our immediate environments in one way or another—by travel, education, or meeting someone who opens our eyes to new ways of doing things. In other words, he stretches us by sparking our curiosity—because no matter where we find the answers to our questions, we grow when we learn.

Now, Jupiter has always been called The Greater Benefic—and that's a reputation he richly deserves. Although it's become quite chic lately, here in Astrology-Land, to trash generous Jupiter and talk nice about strict old Saturn, neither of those attitudes is fair—especially since we supposedly know now that no planet is bad or good, and that we've got an awful lot to say about what to do with all of them. (Yes, even Pluto.) So we really can't blame Jupiter when we don't use the opportunities he brings, any more than we can blame Saturn when he comes along and presents us with a test we flunk because we didn't study the lesson.

Think of Jupiter as your favorite uncle, the guy who's too loud, too fresh, excessive in every way, and never appropriate under any circumstances—but wonderfully generous. Think of him as Santa Claus. Think of him as Jove, a generous, benevolent King. Think of him any way you like, but remember to use him. The house where he's transiting for you right now is Chock Full O'opportunities. Whatever you pursue in this area of life right now has a much better than average chance of success. Things will never be easier—again, all it takes is a bit of effort on your part. This is truly a great planet, kids. Check out where Jupiter is in your chart right now and start stretching.

FIRST HOUSE

Jupiter has been called "The Greater Benefic" since time began. He's also the Head of the Department of Expansion, Growth, and Incorporation, so when he transits this house—the house of physical appearance and first impressions (among other things)—we certainly might expect to Do The Expansion Thing and gain some weight. Of course, having Santa Claus hanging out at the Front Door of the chart can also mean that we grow in another way—in popularity. Yes, when Jupiter's in our first house, we're The Star Of The Show. Enter and sign in, please... Now, having a crowd around your Front Door—for a year—can be good or bad. Depends. If you're looking to become famous, it's great. If you're involved in behind-the-scenes ventures or secret activities you'd rather not have out in the open, stop it right now. Secrets don't stay secret for long with Jupiter hanging around passing out publicity flyers.

Now's also when we'll attract all kinds of new and interesting people into our lives—because we're so New and Interesting ourselves. Our mood is so buoyant and positive, how could anyone not want to hang around with us? In general, Life Is Good when Jupiter crosses the Ascendant, and we often find all the Great Big Dreams we dreamed over the past year (as he made his way through the woozy twelfth house) coming true.

Interestingly, since the first house is attached to the seventh house via the Ascendant/Descendant axis, when Jupiter positions his rather hefty self on the Ascendant, we often begin new one-to-one relationships—or find that our dealings with our current Other go along quite smoothly. Then again, if there are other transits that suggest the end of a relationship situation, now will be when we declare our Jupiterian urge for Freedom, and tell our Other to Hop On The Bus, Gus.

Jupiter here may also point to the possibility of extended travel or education. Our first house reflects where we are, so rather than just expanding our physical selves, The Big Guy might opt to expand the world around us, by taking us on a journey to Alien Lands. Regardless of the mode of personality growth we choose, our Front Door has just been re-fitted with a much larger window. Our entire outlook on life is about to widen.

SECOND HOUSE

Jupiter is the guy who expands things and makes them bigger— so you'd think his transit through this second house of finances might expand our checking accounts, huh? Well, that's quite possible—in a manner of speaking. Uncle J. certainly does bring goodies for the kids whenever he's in the neighborhood, and when he's in the second house, we certainly should expect Presents. But for a whole year? Well, yes. It's a year's worth of Doing The Expansion Thing, financially, which sure could mean that our income blossoms and we find ourselves with more play money at the end of every week.

Of course, there are other ways to expand in second-house ways. We may also become a bit too optimistic about our financial future, and literally overextend ourselves financially—well past the boundaries of what's prudent at this juncture. Now, again, which side of the coin you'll get—if you'll pardon the pun—has everything to do with the condition of your second house natally. If you're used to being financially comfortable, and you adhere to the belief that we all live in a benevolent Universe that's only too happy to provide all the abundance anyone could ever need in the Money Department, well, then, get ready to experience even more abundance. If, however, your life's script doesn't describe wealth beyond imagination—or even being comfortable financially—then watch very carefully for a tendency to over-commit yourself monetarily. As with all transits, you've got to look to the natal chart to see what to expect—but it's never too late to start reciting affirmations to your subconscious so any negative expectations can slide over to positive ones.

On a deeper level, since this house also reflects What We Hold Dear about ourselves, we may begin to see a new value in ourselves. In other words, we may start to have a higher opinion of our personal self-worth—which would play out both financially and personally. The idea behind astrology is to get the very best out of our lives by realizing the highest potential in our charts— and Jupiter transits are the best times to get that positive mind-set going.

THIRD HOUSE

You'll be absolutely amazed at how much running around you're going to do this year. With Jupiter expanding the boundaries of this house, short trips, (both time-wise and mileage-wise) will absolutely fill your life. Zimbabwe on Thursday, and Australia on Sunday? Sure. Why not? Jupiter's always packed and ready to hop in the car—or plane—when he's in the third house. You're going to learn an awful lot, too, about your small world—your third-house Immediate Environment. Jupiter whets our appetite for learning, no matter where he happens to be visiting at the moment, so his transit through the third house—where learning begins—often makes us aware that there's more to this forest than just the trees in the backyard. (Yes, this even goes for Virgos....)

Now, whenever we learn, we grow, and when we grow, we're no longer satisfied with small quarters. This goes for small mind-sets and small neighborhoods, too. Jupiter also represents The Conscious Mind, the side of us that's totally aware—not at all on auto-pilot, as our third-house selves ordinarily are. So, since moving our home gives us a brand-new, unfamiliar environment it's impossible to shuffle through without paying attention, this transit also often coincides with a change of residence—perhaps even a long-distance one. If we do somehow manage to stay put, the Big Guy's trek through this house will bring lots of folks from out-of-town (or overseas) into our lives on a regular basis. New neighbors, maybe, or new folks popping up at any of the stops we make on our daily trips Around Town.

Since the third house also refers to siblings, we may opt to take a long-distance trip with a brother or sister—or they may decide to travel or relocate themselves. Regardless of what actually happens now, you're going to be wide-awake and totally aware of the world around you—every moment of every day—so you won't be able to tolerate Routine. And if there's something you've always wanted to study, sign up for the class now. Learning New Stuff is never easier than when Jupiter passes through the third or ninth house of the chart.

FOURTH HOUSE

If you've been thinking about adding on or improving your home in some way, this is the transit that classically signifies the time when you'll do it. Maybe your family situation has grown to the point where there's simply not enough room for everyone who's still living in The Nest to move around comfortably, and you decide to build on a room or two. Maybe you're just tired of looking at those cabinets, and now's when you invest in a whole new kitchen. Doesn't matter how it shows up in the physical world—when Uncle Jupiter transits the fourth house, your home is about to become brand new, bigger, or happier.

Happier? Well, sure—Jupiter's visits are times of optimism, and in addition to representing the place where we actually sleep, the fourth house is where we stash the emotional side of ourselves. What makes us emotionally happier? Well, everybody loves babies, and the fourth house reflects our family situation—so some folks might decide that now's the time to have a child. We may also open our homes by adopting someone (or something) and making our family bigger. We may also decide to 'add on' to the size of our family by getting married, or deciding to co-habitate. Naturally, with the Big Guy putting us in the mood to take a chance in the Home and Emotions Department, now's also when we may be struck by the urge to move far away—perhaps even to another country.

Since this house also refers to whoever it was that nurtured us in childhood, it's a good bet that we'll become much more involved with one or both parents now. Expect all kinds of memories from the past to come up now, too. The fourth house is where we keep our emotional warehouse of memories—how everything that's ever happened to us felt. Remember, Jupiter doesn't just visit a house—he kicks the door open and ushers in an entourage. When he treks through the fourth, our homes, emotional foundations and family lives are due for a great big growth spurt.

FIFTH HOUSE

Feel lucky? Well, if you don't now, you'll have to wait until Jupiter visits your Sun, because Jupiter/5th house and Jupiter/Sun transits are classically known for being very "lucky" years. See, the 5th house is the Department of Speculation, which means it's going to be pretty darned hard for you not to be lucky in all your ventures. The 5th house is the Express Yourself, Don't Repress Yourself Department. You're already quite willing to do what it takes to Get Noticed. Add generous Jupiter to the mix, and you've added more than a little luck, coupled with a great sense of timing and the urge to take risks. Your Uncle Jupiter's ability to put you in the right place at the right moment to meet just the right person who can help you realize your dreams is what this transit is all about.

Since this is also the house of Love Affairs, even if you're not a gambler, you may decide to take a chance on a relationship. And, by the way, if a Mr. or Ms. Right does jet into your life right now, chances are good they're either going to be from distant shores, or equipped with an accent, a stack of maps tucked under their arm and a plane ticket in their hand. There may also be more than one of them—Jupiter never could settle for 'just a slice' of anything. (Tough transit, huh?) Regardless of where they're from, your new Others will come in with a Lesson Plan—ready to either teach or be taught by you during this year—in one way or another. And think of how much fun it's going to be to learn and teach this person. Jupiter reps are classically the type of folks who give us joy by their very presence, teach us to laugh from our bellies, and seem to be able to lead us to smiling fortune, all at once. Easiest lesson you'll ever learn. Get ready for lots of field trips, and enjoy the amusement park ride.

And speaking of amusement parks, remember that this house refers to the behavior we exhibit when it's time to play. So don't be surprised if now's when you take up a new sport or hobby. Remember, too, that this is the house of child-rearing, since kids are the critters that often force adults to enjoy life. So you might also expect to spend much more time in the company of youngsters than you have in quite some time. Since Jupiter loves folks from out of town, and because you'll be feeling the urge to expand in this childlike house, you may also decide to adopt a foreign child, take on a creative venture with a playmate from across the oceans, or fall in love with someone who lives on another continent.

A word of caution, however: remember that with all Jupiter transits, the tendency to be a bit more optimistic than is genuinely called for is a real possibility. Watch yourself in the gambling department, and if you have to, let someone with a strong Saturn hold on to your checkbook when you're feeling especially reckless.

SIXTH HOUSE

Since this is the house of health and work, when Jupiter passes through the sixth, expect those issues to be larger than life over the next year. That may mean that we should expect a year's worth of focusing on our health and the condition of our physical body—

in the form of a new, bold health regime. On the other side of the same coin, however, remember that Jupiter is also what you're using when you find yourself overdoing, being extravagant, or blowing something out of proportion. Now, imagine what could happen if The Big Guy is feeling a bit lazy when he arrives. Think of what might happen to your waistline when he travels through this house with an overly-optimistic attitude. Might be time to expand your exercise routine, rather than watch him expand your dress size.

Now, the real side of us that's covered by the sixth house is the side that's concerned with Functioning—and Taking Care Of Business. Our health has everything to do with the way our bodies function, but we also need to have a function here on the planet—a daily list of Things We Do. This brings us to the subject of our jobs. Now, first of all, don't confuse the sixth house of work with the tenth house of career. Our career is what we feel we're here to become, in the eyes of the world. The sixth is a bit more mundane. It focuses on what we actually do for eight hours a day, five days a week, to earn a living. With Jupiter in the sixth, our job duties may expand, literally, and we may be swamped with work. Or we may be the recipient of Goodies on the job—raises, bonuses, or just kudos. Maybe Jupiter's liberating attitude will prompt us to change jobs, to something that allows us to work outdoors, or travel long-distance. Maybe he inspires us to get involved in an import/export business of some kind, or to try our hand in the advertising profession. Or maybe we'll just find ourselves dealing with a lot more out-of-towners at our present job. Regardless of the form this urge to expand takes in the work department, it's going to take us, either symbolically or literally, to uncharted shores. Enjoy the trip.

SEVENTH HOUSE

Okay, now—here's a really tough transit to wrap up neatly into one pat paragraph. See, when Jupiter transits the 7th house, the subject is Expansion and the department is Relationships—which can be a mixed bag. So let's start from a really basic level, and talk about Jupiter transits in general for a minute. First off, you remember what I said about how your Uncle Jupiter arrives with an entourage in tow, (admirers, benefactors, etc.) no matter where he goes? You remember how I also said that we tend to 'grow' in Jupiter's transiting spot—for better or worse? Finally, you know how much Jupiter just loves Freedom? Well, if we apply all those particulars to the basic way you're going to relate to everyone you have a One-to-One encounter with—for an entire year, remember—it can mean several things.

First of all, chances are good that you're going to have one heckuva good time with Others while Mr. Personality is around. You'll meet and establish relationships/partnerships with folks who'll further your life in some way, who'll promote you and get you introduced around. You may find yourself in the company of folks with rather large check-books, too—or world-travelers.

On a personal level, consider that when we choose a partner, we spend most of our time in their company alone. This is where the seventh house's reputation for being the house of The Significant Other comes from. So, needless to say, you may find yourself involved in a relationship that takes up a large amount of your time, or in a One-to-One arrangement with someone who lives overseas, or on the opposite coast. Maybe you'll find yourself dating a teacher, or being strongly influenced by a relationship that develops between you and someone who's especially religious or political. Or famous. Or infamous. Jupiter's not picky about how we come by our fame.

More than anything, remember that the seventh house is simply the place where we keep the side of us that comes out only when we are in the company of one other person. Now's when all our dealings with One Other stand to be based on joviality, generosity, and benevolence. And although we certainly do stand to be the recipient of goodies from more than one Jupiterian individual, we'll also be in a position to be Santa Claus to everyone we come into contact with. Give magnanimously, then, of yourself, without expecting anything for it, and you'll be amazed at what comes your way in return.

EIGHTH HOUSE

So. If the eighth house is the side of us who deals with extremes, with topics like Sex, and Death, and Power, and Control, and Jupiter is the lotsa planet—what happens when we put them together? What do we get? Lots of death? Well, no, not necessarily—although since this is the house of Inheritances, that may be a possibility. Someone does have to leave the planet in order to bequeath their life's fortune to us. On the other hand, no one has to leave the planet for us to be the recipient of other Joint Blessings, like inheriting the family business, getting a huge tax refund (since taxes are another 8th house issue,) or getting the nod from a bank or financial institution on a great big loan. The eighth house has everything to do with Other People's Stuff—and when Jupiter's here, they're going to be feeling generous about sending that Stuff our way.

So how might we experience The Death Thing, and Jupiter's lotsa tendencies, if it's not through actual physical deaths? After all, it's impossible to experience our own deaths more than once. Well, with the planet who so loves taking risks in this house, it's not impossible to imagine that now might be when we'd be especially craving death-defying experiences. Fire walking. Skydiving. Taking off with a Storm-Chasers group to follow tornadoes for a week in Kansas. In short, if it's an experience that brings you right to the edge, if it's something that makes you realize just how precious life is by showing you how close to the border we live at all times—well, now's when you'll take off after it.

Now, as I said, Sex is also a topic that's covered here, but only since sex is the way most of us choose to Become Intimate with An Other. Although spending more time in bed with our partner is certainly a possibility, (Yes, this is another tough transit) we can expect all our dealings with others to be characterized by an intense intimacy, even in those of us who've had real problems with sharing of ourselves in the past. We may find that we're suddenly much more open to letting An Other see the real Us, the person that's inside, at the very core of our selves, when everything that's extraneous is stripped off.

On a deeper level, this transit may also be when we find the courage to explore The Unknown, to take a peek behind that curtain. Or, since this is the side of us that comes out when we're facing urgent times, or emergencies, we may also find ourselves responding to those times with a strength of character we didn't know we had.

In a nutshell, this is a year when we'll become braver—less afraid to know ourselves as we really are, to show others the deeper side of our nature, and far less afraid to investigate The Mysteries. Just be careful not to tempt fate *too* much, hmmmm?

NINTH HOUSE

This house holds the side of you that will probably have terminal "Grass-is-Greener" Syndrome, the side of you that will never be satisfied with what you've got, always wondering what's over that next mountain, or just beyond that next exit. Jupiter prompts you to travel, take classes, and meet new people—because he wants you to grow. The ninth house is his very own place—Sag's house, the place where you break routine in search of New Experiences. Needless to say, with Jupiter feeling extra-comfortable and verrrrry able to Be Himself, you're going to be feeling a bit more optimistic, a bit bolder, and a bit more apt to take risks than usual. See, on his trek through the ninth house, Jupiter passes along a message: that growth is necessary, and that growth through new experiences is the best way to do it. Makes sense, too. After all, there are schools, safaris, and teachers everywhere—and you're due to experience all that and more when The Big Guy comes to visit.

So make sure your passport is up to date, and get ready to travel, take classes, and be just craving new experiences—enough to get out there in the world after them. Ever been to Europe? Now's the time. Always wanted to study World History, but never got the time? Sign right here. See, Jupiter's of the opinion that Earth is just one giant playground/classroom—so when he passes through this house, you'll be after knowledge—and game to do whatever it takes to come by it.

Since this is also the house of politics and philosophy— the big Picture, that is—you might also expect to be particularly opinionated about your own world-view right about now. You'll be especially involved in the national elections, and much more concerned about those Social Issues you've always felt strongly about, anyway. You even may find yourself involved in politics, or leading the discussion at the local chapter of Greenpeace's meeting. Then, too, since Jupiter loves religion, and this is the house that holds the side of us that comes out when religion is the topic, you may feel your faith rekindled, and attend church for the first time—or go back again after a long absence. Whatever happens, know that you're going to be divinely inspired—and maybe a bit too overzealous about talking others into wearing your team's colors. Remember, not everyone has to agree with you.

TENTH HOUSE

Well, now, here's the house that holds your Public Self, the side of you that's equal parts Agent and Leader of The Minions. With

Jupiter here, you're about to get noticed, for better or worse, in a very public sense. Why for better or worse? Well, publicity can be a good thing, and it can be a bad thing. If you want to Get Famous, or Get Known, Publicity is a great thing. It opens doors, gets you introduced around, and allows folks to see what you're selling—literally and figuratively. If you're not in the mood for it, however, it's not so great. And if you're not wanting people to see what you're up to, it's downright awful. So remember not to 'do' anything you don't want the entire world to know about when Jupiter's here, because whatever you're up to, it's going to be damned near impossible to keep a lid on it now. The Big Guy never was famous for his secret-keeping abilities, and he's *always* been famous for kicking the door open wide when he enters a house.

On the positive side, if you've been working very hard to try to Make A Name for yourself, or you're trying to gain some type of professional advancement, Uncle Jupiter will see to it. Lots of folks get raises, promotions, and fantastic job offers with Jupiter in this house—and this applies especially if you've got a positive Saturn transit on at the same time. You may also take on a career in a Jupiterian field, such as travel, advertising, publicity, teaching, writing, or publishing. Then again, since Jupiter expands things so well, and since this is the house that deals with what people hear about you, (even folks that have never met you,) you may make yourself bigger in the eyes of Others by becoming part of a public couple—in other words, you may decide to marry now, or start a family.

With authority figures also a focus of this side of you, keep in mind that now's a time when all your dealings with them will most likely go quite well. If you're looking for help from powerful, influential people, then, to start or enlarge on a business, or just to get your work seen by the world—ask The Powers That Be now, and you'll be golden. In all, Uncle Jupiter is about to become the archetypal representative of Authority—The Benevolent Dictator— in your life. If you're ready to make a Social Leap, and you need help, now's when The Universe will aid you in your efforts.

ELEVENTH HOUSE

Jupiter always has been a big fan of networking. This is the planet who loves to Make The Circle Bigger—to incorporate, rather than segregate. So wherever he happens to be in your chart at the moment is a place where you'll have an extensive network of friends and associates—folks you can visit, count on, and learn from. The eleventh house side of you is the slice of your personality that comes out when you're in group situations, reveling in the feeling we humans get when we're in the company of a whole pack of other humans who believe in the same things we do. With Jupiter in this house, then, expect to become involved with groups on a very big scale. That may mean you become a leader of a group, or that you become famous within your group. Jupiter is the King, after all, and it's hard to ignore royalty. At any rate, those folks who you consider Kindred Spirits will certainly be aware of your presence—Big Time—right now.

Now, this is also the house in a chart that shows your Causes—the organizations (and their goals) that you feel strongly enough about to join forces with. So don't be surprised if you become very Cause-Oriented right about now. That might mean that you join the PTA, become more involved with a political party, or start actively participating in a group's activities. And with Jupiter here, the original Cheerleader, that may mean doing door-to-door soliciting for The Nature Conservancy, picketing against animal testing, or leading a Letter-Writing campaign to push a local ordinance through.

This is another of the Social Houses—so regardless of what else happens, your social life is about to expand in leaps and bounds. You'll meet all kinds of interesting, knowledgeable people, and probably keep many of them as friends long after Jupiter's made his way into the quiet of your twelfth house. You'll discover who you are by seeing which causes you align yourself with. Most importantly, you'll find your peer group—the humans with whom you share a common bond based on ideals.

TWELFTH HOUSE

The twelfth house is a very quiet, very private place. It's Neptune's house, complete with pink smoke, soft music, and candlelight. It's the place where we keep the side of us who only comes out when we're totally alone, or in the company of someone we trust implicitly, even with our secrets. Traditionally, this has always been known as The House Of Our Greatest Undoing, which sounds pretty scary. Undoing ourselves may mean that we're working against ourselves, that all our best efforts are having the opposite effect that we're working towards. On the other hand, the twelfth house is opposite from the sixth—the house of doing—so in reality, it's just a sanctuary, a place of retreat, where we un-do and stop functioning—to relax, alone, and recharge our psychic batteries. Not so scary when you think of it that way, huh?

Now picture Uncle Jupiter arriving into this ordinarily very peaceful place, with his plaid suit, loud voice, and a complete entourage in tow. Does this mean that there won't be anywhere to run to be alone for a whole year? Well, not necessarily. Although it's true that this may be a year when we just don't have a lot of time alone—and we're craving it—remember that Jupiter is also the planet in charge of Religion, and Higher Beliefs. He used to be Pisces' patron saint (before we found Neptune,) and this is Pisces' place. So he's familiar with the territory. All that said, how might this transit work?

Well, picture Uncle Jupiter changing out of his suit and into a monk's garb—he sure loves to philosophize, after all. Picture him as a teacher, and a perpetual student, always craving new knowledge and experiences. Now add the spiritual side of the twelfth house. What do you get? Well, you may end up with a year of meditation classes, or an extended visit to an ashram. You may also keep your present lifestyle as is—but find yourself with a craving to get to know your own secrets—through therapy, being counseled, or finding a spiritual advisor. Jupiter in this house will undoubtedly bring you spiritual mentors, folks who'll act as equal parts Guardian Angel and Guru. That's not so bad, is it?

On the other hand, since Secret People are also under this house's jurisdiction, you may also find yourself involved with lots of them. You may become involved in a secret affair, or find that you're simply working behind the scenes for a spiritual cause. Maybe you'll just play Secret Santa a lot, give a lot of money anonymously to your favorite charity, or spend some time donating your time to an animal shelter or a homeless folks' soup kitchen. Regardless of what else you do with this time, do make time for You. Sit quietly and use Jupiter's ability to see The Big Picture to help you understand your own personal Religion.

JUPITER/SUN

Jupiter transits are great fun—usually. If you think of Jupiter as that favorite uncle we talked about, who wears too much after-shave, talks too loud, laughs like a horse, smokes obnoxious cigars, but never, ever forgets a birthday, always picks up the check at the family gatherings, and still owns the pot-holder you made for him at Brownies 21 years ago, how could you not love this guy? You'd have to be dead. Still, he is tough to take in anything but tiny doses—and sometimes we are too, under Jupiter/Sun transits. We bring that Benevolent but Overwhelming Favorite Uncle everywhere, and although we're just having a splendid time, look around—everyone else might not be.

The truth of the matter is, when Jupiter is conjunct to the Sun, as with the transits of all planets by conjunction to the Sun, we become The Big Guy. We've suddenly got everything that we want, and life's going along just peachy, (again, the disclaimer: make sure your natal Sun isn't barraged by Pluto or Saturn squares before you decide to sue me.) We're traveling, learning, and having a great time, enjoying this wonderful planet we're living on. We're feeling so good, we often turn it all outward, and buy the bar a round, or pick up the dinner tab, or give someone a ridiculously long ride to and from the airport. Needless to say, everyone loves us when Jupiter's around. It's been my experience (for Other People, too, not just us Sags,) that this transit—and Jupiter's trines and sextiles to itself, too—are among the best times in our lives.

Now, Jupiter does come with a disclaimer of his own: you've got to consciously use him when he's trining your Sun. Otherwise, you'll just sit around on the couch, eating bonbons, feeling just great but not getting an awful lot done, and experiencing Jupiter's growth on the physical plane. The sextiles are a little less likely to show a lazy streak, but just remember under easy Jupiter/Sun transits, now's the time to publicize, advertise, and Get Yourself Introduced Around—even if you feel more like just taking it easy. Take advantage of The Big Guy's propensity to make a Big Thing out of everything he touches—including, right now, You.

The downside? Well, with the squares and oppositions Jupiter makes to the Sun, you'll find that you tend to be a bit on the pompous side. After all, if the Sun is your ego, Jupiter is the principle of expansion, and squares and oppositions cause growth-inspiring conflict of some kind, you've got the perfect makings here for a balloon that's going to be blown up almost to the breaking point. (Since the Sun—along with the Ascendant—also has a lot to do with our physical forms, remember that this may also be a time when we expand physically.)

You're also going to be 'way overloaded in the area of life (house) where the Sun lives. You'll have too much to do, and not enough time to do it—you think. In reality, even though you'll probably overextend yourself mightily, promising much more than even you think you can deliver, if you use your Jupiter transit instead of letting the good feeling use you, you'll be able to accomplish what you said you'd do, and more.

This, by the way, is the type of transit that Taking Your Act On The Road was named after. If you've got a quest (your Sun) or some bliss to follow (your Sun,) get thee hence, right now, when the Universe is smilin' and start creating. When Jupiter brings his camera crew, publicists, and agents along to the Sun, you stand every chance of Getting Recognized.

JUPITER/MOON
The Moon is the person on the inside who dreams, feels, sighs and wishes. She's our inner tide, in charge of our moods, and she has everything to do with how we cope and how we react to what the world tosses at us. In a nutshell, Jupiter is the planet in charge of expansion, in charge of making everything much, much bigger. So regardless of what the subject of the moment turns out to be, Jupiter's visit to the Moon is sure to mean that we're going to feel everything at least ten times more than we normally would. If we're already happy when he arrives, we're going to be overjoyed. By the same token, if we're already depressed or melancholy, a visit from Uncle Jupiter could mean that we become completely overwhelmed by our unhappiness—which might mean that it will be even harder to convince ourselves that this, too, will pass. It depends on the condition of our natal Moon, and with how we've trained ourselves to take care of our emotional needs up to this point in our lives.

All this is especially true in the case of Jupiter's conjunction to the Moon, when our feelings simply expand—as I said before, for better or worse. Of course, since the Moon also refers to our Mom, our kids, and our homes, there are several ways this transit might manifest in our outer lives, too. With Jupiter visiting, we may opt to expand our home, by adding on a room, a second floor, or a brand-new deck. Maybe we move across the country—or across the ocean. We may find ourselves suddenly quite involved in the lives of our family—or maybe we decide to take a Jupiterian long-distance vacation with Mom, or one of the kids. And speaking of travel, Jupiter's transits to the Moon do, in fact, often indicate that we're going to be setting up our Moon-shop elsewhere. With The Big Guy's famous optimism in the neighborhood of our Moon, then, needless to say, now's a great time to plan a trip.

Under the easy aspects of Jupiter to the Moon, (even if we're laboring under difficult Saturn or Pluto transits at the same time,) we're often surprised at how optimistic we're feeling. Times may be tough, but with Jupiter touching the Moon, we can find something to keep us going, something that will make us feel that no matter what, everything will turn out all right. In other words, that the Sun will come out tomorrow. That's what an easy Jupiter/Moon transit can feel like. It's an inner buoyancy, an emotional flotation device that's built into even the toughest of times. After all, if anyone can keep us going with our chins up, it's Mr. Optimism. Remember, The Big Guy is the main purveyor of laughter, benevolence, and wisdom, and when Jupiter visits by easy aspect, as with the trines or sextiles, all of those qualities are just an optimistic arm's reach away.

Now, under the squares and oppositions to the Moon, we may find ourselves going overboard in the Emotions Department—for better or worse. The hard aspects indicate times of activity, you see—so with Jupiter pushing the Moon, we may simply feel more—either for someone or about something—than we ordinarily would. Again, if we're already depressed, The Great Expander may make those feelings even huger. But keep in mind, especially with Jupiter around, there's a silver lining in every cloud.

JUPITER/MERCURY

This, friends, is a powerful combination. Jupiter rules The Higher Mind, and Mercury rules our ability to learn. Stick the two of them in the blender, and what do we get? The urge to know everything. Everything. All of a sudden, we have an amazing craving for education, travel, learning, and new experiences—whatever it takes to grow intellectually. Lots of us combine these two by learning new languages—a very Mercury/Jupiter combination—but going back to school or starting work on a degree is also a possibility. Anything that allows us to use both our ability to learn

(Mercury) and our ability to assimilate New Stuff into our lives through seeing the Big Picture (Jupiter) will do just fine.

Both of these planets are also quite good at moving around, too. Mercury in our charts (unless it's already in Jupiter's sign, Sag, or in an aspect to our natal Jupiter,) much prefers short trips and/or short distances to extended stays, but with a bit of Jupiterian prodding, we might be talked into visiting a foreign land, or taking off for two weeks—or two months—instead of two days.

Now, we also become very good at Telling Tall Tales and Making Big Plans when these two get together. (Remember that expression, you and your Big Ideas? Guess where it came from?) His gift for expansion and for making the details larger than life means that Jupiter is the King of Exaggeration—and Mercury is The Word Wizard. So story-telling, both figuratively and literally, is going to be one of our favorite things to do now. We'll entertain the gang at a party with a great joke, find the bravery to tell a story at a gathering, or finally conjure the oomph to set down that short story that's been circling in our minds forever. Remember, also, that words like too, very, and most, are the property of Jupiter, as are more and better. When Jupiter visits Mercury, you'll probably find them tucked into every sentence you utter.

When the Big Guy is visiting by conjunction, our Mercury becomes Jupiter—we Think Big, in other words. This can range anywhere from simply having a positive mental attitude to making plans to build that castle we've always wanted to live in. Again, this can also mean that our Mercury gets the urge to become Jupiter, won't settle for just routine anymore, and is ready to explore the pyramids.

Easier aspects from Jupiter to Mercury will also substantially pick up the pace in our daily lives. We find ourselves traveling outside of our usual small circle—both literally and figuratively. These two are The Great Networkers, and they love interesting people. Be prepared to meet all kinds of folks, both from Far Away, and from different mind-sets. Above all else, with Jupiter and Mercury, be prepared to learn.

Under the difficult aspects from Jupiter to Mercury, we might expect to feel as if we've got too much to do, and too little time to do it. We have all kinds of errands to run, phone calls to return, letters to write, and people to talk with—and not nearly enough waking hours to handle the overload. When Jupiter aspects Mercury in an uncomfortable fashion, we may also talk too much, too loudly, or too often. In other words, now's a great time to Watch Your Mouth. Watch, especially, what you say you'll do under this transit. Remember, sooner or later, Saturn will also aspect your Mercury, and then it will be time to make good on all those promises.

JUPITER/VENUS

Money, money, money, money—money.....Remember that song? That's part of what happens during a Jupiter/Venus transit. Jupiter's gift for expansion blows The Money Thing 'way up and out of proportion. When Jupiter touches Venus, it's like The Big Guy has decided to expand our concern over money and what it buys. Needless to say, this can be good, and this can be bad—for a couple of reasons. Maybe we win the lottery—a very Good thing which is one way of expanding our pocketbooks. On the other hand, we might also simply find ourselves with a huge list of bills. Or maybe we turn Jupiter's famous generosity into Giving—and make a large donation to the political, philosophical, or religious group we're most akin to.

Love, too, of course, is under The Lady Venus' jurisdiction, and God/dess knows, we humans don't need help to get overly involved with Others. So when Jupiter touches Venus, we may 'go overboard' in a relationship, and find ourselves completely infatuated with An Other—for better or worse. We might also end up combining Venus' rulership of Love and Money and Jupiter's fondness for folks from Far Away by ending up in a relationship with someone who lives in another state, or another country—in which case, we're going to have lots of travel and long-distance phone expenses to keep the relationship going. On the other hand, we may have too many people lining up with flowers and candy—and have absolutely no idea which one to settle down with.

In general, this planet just loves to Make Things Bigger. All kinds of things. So this is another of those transits that may indicate an expansion in our waistline—our Venus, after all, is How We Spoil Ourselves, and Jupiter's never been good at having just a slice of anything. He's also not known for being able to Just Say No to anything he wants, so this transit is probably where the expression, When the going gets tough, the tough go shopping came from. Yep. New Stuff. That'll help.

Now, under the conjunction, Venus issues become everything. We become Jupiter in our Venus Department. So a little bit of anything we love just won't do it. We overspend, overeat, and burn the candle at both ends. We're so darned generous, outgoing and charming, (remember, our Venus is also our ability to socialize, and when Jupiter's here, we know just exactly the right thing to say and do) at the same time, however, that Others can't help but love us—maybe too much. Since our Venus also refers to How We Adorn Ourselves, Jupiter's influence on The Lady may mean we're extremely concerned with Venus-type things—jewelry, clothing, etc.—and that money is not an issue.

When Jupiter touches Venus by difficult aspect (and it's hard to think of these two as being difficult, in any combination,) that means action—and that, again, may mean overdoing it, financially, by writing a check that isn't quite covered, backed only by that Jupiterian optimism that The Universe Will Provide. These tough aspects can also mean that we're in love with someone who's above us socially, or out of our reach somehow, due to geographical distance, philosophical differences, etc. In general, under this transit, Nothing Exceeds Like Excess can well become our motto.

Jupiter's easy aspects to Venus are like Manna From Heaven. We win the football pool, pick up a scratch-ticket and find $1000 there, or hit all the right slot machines in Vegas. Maybe we suddenly get a raise or a bonus. Or maybe we're the recipient of a huge amount of money, or a great big gift. Maybe someone we're ever so fond of finally says I Love You, Too. Regardless of what happens, these transits are among The Best Of Times. Enjoy— but watch your calories...

JUPITER/MARS

And the winner is...whoever's got the Jupiter/Mars transit. Here's the aspect that Acceleration is made of. Talk about energy. Jupiter/ Mars transits are times when we're jam-packed with the stuff — so this is the transit that gets the runner across the finish line when he or she is absolutely positive there's not one more ounce of Ooomph left in their bodies. Mars is the spot where we keep our Power Pack, where we have a built-in love of urgency, the ability to be daring, and a great big dose of courage. Add Jupiter, and you've got the makings of an Olympic Champion—or the Energizer™ Bunny, at the very least. Now, that's just what you need to win a race, but it's also quite helpful if you're trying to pull off a major business coup, or if you've suddenly found yourself with more to accomplish in a day than you think you're capable of doing in a week. All this is especially true under the conjunction transit, when our Mars becomes Jupiter-ized—bigger than life, that is. Remember, The Big Guy adds a touch of luck, optimism, and Feelin' Risky to whoever he visits.

Now, being in charge of our Energy Level also makes Mars one tough planet. In ancient times, after all, he was the God of War. So in addition to being the side of you in charge of initiating action of any kind, he's also the Head of the Department of Self-Defense, Aggression, and Just Doing It. He's your sword, your warrior who fights for you when you feel attacked in any way. Think of him as Rambo, or your own personal swat-team. Needless to say, this is the side of you that can be downright fearless, because Mars describes how you act when you're acting purely on your own behalf. In general, your Mars is where you're not concerned with anyone or anything but You. And unless he's tempered in your natal chart by being in a sign that's cautious, (like Capricorn, or Virgo,) or shrewd, (like Scorpio,) or in aspect to especially-cautious Saturn, he's not likely to consider the size or strength of whoever or whatever you're up against when he gets the nudge.

Now, with all that red energy just waiting to Go Off, it's a given that this is also a spot where we may get ourselves into trouble when Jupiter comes along, with his famous gift for overestimating our abilities. So it's also possible that when these two get together, it might lead to us taking on an opponent who's a bit stronger or faster than we think we are—at the moment. That's pretty much what it's like for us when Jupiter makes a challenging or difficult aspect to our Mars. In a nutshell, we often find ourselves pitched against an opponent who requires us to Get Tough.

Now, when Jupiter makes an easy aspect to our Mars, we find ourselves with an endless supply of energy, and luck, too. Assemble Jupiter and Mars into sentence-form, and you've got fortunate actions. Or lucky actions. If you've got a huge project to accomplish, then, this transit will certainly help. Again, this applies especially to physical projects, since Mars rules the muscles, and our adrenaline-supply. Think of how powerful we can be physically when Jupiter ups the adrenaline-level in our bodies, or makes our muscles perform to the fullest. Think of how daring we can be when Jupiter makes a nice aspect to Mars and encourages us to take a chance. Think of the built-in blessing any activity has when you start it with Mars, the initiator, being touched by an easy aspect from your Uncle Jupiter.

As with all Jupiter transits, and all transits to Mars, however, a word of warning is in order. These are also times when we may act too quickly, without considering the consequences, so we might be a bit accident-prone under this combination. The very best use for this transit is to find a project to pour all Jupiter's enthusiasm and all Mars' energy into in a constructive fashion. Use them wisely, and you're unstoppable.

JUPITER/JUPITER TRANSITS

You remember your favorite Uncle Jupiter? The guy in the Santa Claus suit with your Wish-List in his hand and a Gold Visa Card he's just dying to max out? You know how you got a double-dose of Me energy under Sun transits, and a double-dose of Assertion energy under Mars/Mars transits? Well, when Jupiter makes an aspect to himself, these are times when you'll be the recipient of double doses of More. More of everything. In fact, that old expression be careful what you wish for, because you just might get it has got to be something that someone learned under a double Jupiter transit.

See, Jupiter's job isn't details. He's not discriminating, and he's not here to judge—so if you want it, you'll probably get it now. Only thing is, you may get so much of it, you'll wonder how to get rid of it afterwards. You may also overextend yourself financially under Jupiter transits, with all that optimism you'll be feeling about the future, so, hard as it may seem, it's best to try not to overspend under these transits. All these things apply under all Jupiter aspects by transit, but the conjunction, as usual, is the most potent of all. So be warned—and trust me on this. I'm a Sag, and nobody's better at overdoing than we are—even when Jupiter's not around.

Of course, there's absolutely no use in my trying to warn you about overspending, overeating, or anything else you might be prone to overdo when Jupiter's In The Building. When we're under Jupiter/Jupiter transits, we just know that all warnings apply only to Others—we couldn't possibly be the recipient of any Pay-Back, at any time. Life is good, and it's going to stay that way. Right?

Well, no. Unfortunately, Jupiter transits don't last forever. Jupiter does eventually Leave The Building, and the Goodie Machine dries up. And if Saturn is the next planet to arrive for a visit, and we've been very, very bad—excessive, that is, with no regard for the future—we just might find ourselves in deep You-Know-What. So regardless of which aspect he makes to himself, and how excessive we get as a result, it's best to try to only be excessive for the moment, and not to push matters to the point where we end up spending a great deal of time in the future trying to catch up. Again, trust me on this.....especially under the squares and oppositions Jupiter makes to himself, when we're especially good at pushing past the boundaries.

Of course, all warnings aside, all Jupiter transits are wonderful, wonderful times, when life, in general is Good, and the Universe seems to be tossing goodies your way just for the heck of it. The trines and sextiles are the best, and seem to coincide with times when, with little or no investment on your part, you're golden. You win $1000 on a $1 scratch-ticket, bump into a celebrity (since Jupiter also rules famous folks), and find helpful guardian angels everywhere. Here's an example: Back in May of 1997, I was en route to a conference, and, for once, a day early. At that time, Jupiter was on my Ascendant, trine my own Jupiter in Libra, and sextile my Mercury in Sag. As I approached the ticket counter to check in, the flight attendant picked up the microphone and announced that the flight was overbooked, and they were looking for someone who could take a later flight, in return for a $300 flight coupon. I glanced upward, handed my ticket to her, and said, That would be me. To make a long story short, they bumped me three times that day, gave me $900 in free flight tickets, $50 in food vouchers, and a night's stay at the airport Hilton. Basically, my Uncle Jupiter handed me a trip for two to Europe, lunch, dinner, and snacks on him, and an evening in a very nice hotel to boot.

As if all that weren't enough, on my return flight home after the conference, Jupiter himself showed up. I took my seat, and a few minutes later, a great big man with white hair and a white beard (who was a Sag) eased his rather large form into the seat next to me and, laughing loudly, said "I'll bet you didn't expect to sit next to Santa Claus, did you?" (As a matter of fact, I did.) He spent the entire flight teaching me about his unusual vocation— bee-keeping, and had me laughing from take-off to landing. That's what good Jupiter transits are like, and we all get them. Long-distance travel, education, gifties, laughter, blessings, and advancements in your field. Remember, however, that Jupiter presents opportunities, and in order to be lucky, we've got to be game to do something new. So when he knocks, answer smiling, and get ready to take off—for exciting Parts Unknown.

JUPITER/SATURN

You know how you've always wanted to: A) dance, B) speak in front of an audience, C) walk into a club or restaurant by yourself, or, D) insert your own Favorite Fear? You know how you've always been afraid to try that particular activity? Well, all that's over when Jupiter comes to your natal Saturn by conjunction. Your Saturn is a spot in your chart where you're used to feeling a tad awkward, inadequate, and unprepared—and, generally, a bit afraid to do something. This same Saturn is also a symbolic repository for all those things you dearly, dearly wish you could do—because you really want to be good at them.

Well, when Uncle Jupiter arrives, he brings with him a chance for you to Get Over It—your fears, apprehensions, and hesitations, that is. He barges through the door of the house where your Saturn lives, walks right up to him, and tells him to stand back and be quiet, because you're going to try It now—whatever It is—and you're going to do it well, too. Suddenly, you find yourself dancing, giving speeches, walking into all kinds of places alone, and D) (whatever else you've been terrified to do.) Not only that—you're loving it. You're proud of yourself for finally working up the guts to face your greatest fear/love/ ambition head-on, and you find yourself smiling as you engage in The Chosen Activity. Oh, and once you find you really can have your heart's desire, you're probably going to do whatever makes it sing over and over and over again. They don't call Jupiter Mr. Excess for nothing, and your Saturn is a spot where you've wanted to Get Over It for awhile, anyway. All this is especially true under the conjunction, when Uncle Jupiter visits your stern, unsmiling Saturn, and The Old Naysayer finds himself laughing at a few corny jokes despite himself—and cutting you some slack in the process.

Now, with the trines and sextiles, this is also true, but instead of just allowing you to conquer your fears, Jupiter's visits to Saturn arrive with recognition and rewards. See, your Saturn is the spot where you'll probably work quite hard to become someone. He's a very career-oriented planet, very concerned with your public reputation and with Building A Name For Yourself. When Jupiter arrives at Saturn's door, your gifties arrive, too— in the form of blessings you've earned, and a little extra on the side. After all, success is usually composed of two things: mastering a skill and catching a lucky break. So if you've been very good and used your Saturn well, by following the rules, learning from your mistakes, and paying your dues, now's the time when Higher-Ups will notice, and reward you accordingly. Classically, the trines and sextiles are wonderful for career advancement, since, again, it takes both hard work and being in the right place at the right time to make it in any chosen field. Easy Jupiter transits to Saturn bring diplomas, promotions, and better job offers, among other things, and usually also indicate that you and The Higher Ups get along just swimmingly.

With the more challenging aspects, you'll find some similar symptoms—wanting to break through an age-old fear to do something you'd really love to do, putting in your name for a promotion you know you've earned, etc.—but it's going to be a bit tougher. Instead of being handed the Good Stuff on a silver platter, circumstances may come up that make you feel as if you're being forced to encounter your fears, head on. Or you may have to complete more work before you earn your better-paying position, or more classes before you earn enough credits for your diploma. Remember, however, that Uncle Jupiter's presence assures you that if you try, you'll most likely succeed. Under the tougher transits, we may also feel as if we've promised too much—and now it's coming due. In fact, Jupiter may make your Saturn feel a bit overburdened, as if your work-load has just increased by 200%. No matter. Regardless of which planet it is that transits your Saturn, your best bet is to respond by working hard. Jupiter just makes it fun.

Remember that while Jupiter encourages growth, Saturn wants us to stay right where we are. Although that may sound like a bit of a battle, any Jupiter/Saturn combination has the potential to produce controlled growth. These transits give us an opportunity to set down new personal rules, to make new decisions about who we want to be when we grow up. Jupiter doesn't do anything, remember—like any other planet, he has a job, and his is to provide jump-starts. If you're needing a jump in the Get It Together Department, then, you're in luck.

JUPITER/URANUS

Well, now. Think of what it would be like if your Uncle Jupiter were to team up with a Mad Professor. With Uncle J being oh, so fond of doing everything to the absolute nth degree, and the Mad Professor as unpredictable as he is, it wouldn't be boring—that's for sure. Now, imagine what might happen when they decide to meet up in your chart. Because you really can't. In truth, no one knows what's going to happen when these two join forces—but it's going to be something you'd never expect, and it's going to happen in a *verrry* Big Way. Take these two Wild and Crazy Guys, put them together, and One Never Knows what might happen.

Traditionally, this combination is known to produce sudden windfalls—especially in the monetary sense, and that's quite possible. But there's more to it than that. Sure, you might win the lottery, quit your job, and move to Beverly Hills. But your natal Uranus is also a place where you're very involved in Your Cause, so you also might decide to take off for Zimbabwe to join the Peace Corps. Maybe it's a more personal issue that arises—you decide to quit smoking, cold turkey, join a health club, and start body-building. Again, whatever it is that does happen, it's going to be Big, it's going to be Sudden, and it's going to allow you to truly be You—regardless of what the neighbors say.

See, your Uranus is a spot where you're already a loose cannon on the deck, where you'd always much prefer to Amaze and Shock The Masses. The house where Uranus lives in your chart is a place where you're nothing if not unpredictable, where you absolutely insist on being independent, free as a bird, and making sure everyone knows that. It's also a place where you're most prone to changing your mind at the last minute, changing your destination after you've already arrived at the airport, or quitting your job on the way to work. Add the influence of Mr. More, and you've got an expanded urge to do all that, and more. Needless to say, these transits are tailor-made for expressing yourself, to the max.

So how do you handle life on a Jupiter/Uranus roller-coaster? Well, first off, if you're the type of human that likes to keep to a schedule, you'd better leave a lot of room for, um..., well, let's say, flexibility in it, at the very least. And to be honest, you'd be best off to expect lots of days when you can just forget about keeping to a schedule at all. Under the conjunction, your Uranus becomes Jupiter-ized. Which means you're not only apt to encounter sudden changes, you're game. These are the two most freedom-oriented planets out there, after all, and neither was ever famous for playing by the rules. You're going to feel rebellious, and you won't care at all about Yesterday. Right Now will be all that matters, so whatever you're involved with will completely absorb you—regardless of what you have to do to free up time to spend at it.

Now, under the square from Jupiter to Uranus, we have all those same feelings about wanting to be free, but they tend to remain internal, until an inner planet transit of some kind comes along and kicks us into action. We find ourselves reacting to a situation as we never have before, burning all kinds of bridges without a single glance over our shoulders, and discovering something about ourselves in the process. Even if the circumstances are difficult, the squares are especially liberating. Under the oppositions, we often find these two representing sudden changes in our relationships. We're cooking dinner Friday night, and packing Saturday morning—or our Significant Other cooks dinner on Friday, and announces on Saturday that they're moving out. Remember, we can all be expert at projecting one side or the other of an opposition onto An Other when we'd rather not take responsibility for it ourselves. So if Others seem to be acting erratically and causing huge changes in our lives when Jupiter opposes Uranus, we're usually not entirely innocent. How many of us have subtly provoked our partners into leaving us when we're the one who's ready to leave, or pushed a boss into firing us when we really want out of a job we hate?

Under the sextiles and trines, the roller-coaster is still rolling—but circumstances seem to be a bit more to our liking. Opportunities arrive to change our lives completely, and we jump on them, happily, throwing caution to the wind, confident that whatever the future holds, at least it's New. And more than anything else, when Jupiter's Grass-Is-Greener attitude touches Uranus' thirst for Change, New is always better.

Regardless of the aspect, Jupiter's visits to Uranus will offer you chances to change. You'll be brave and optimistic enough to break away from whoever or whatever has been keeping you from truly being You. Oh, and since these two are so darned inspiring to the imagination, make sure you keep a pen and paper handy to record their missives—all the great flashes of insight you'll be channeling right around now.

JUPITER/NEPTUNE

Whenever I think of Jupiter and Neptune, I think of the Las Vegas strip—the place that's the ultimate in Jupiterian excess and Neptunian illusion. Nothing is real—it's all facades. But everything seems to be real—Excalibur's Castle, the Luxor's Great Pyramid, the Sphinx and Treasure Island's pirate ship included. Even the NYC skyline of New York, New York looks real enough—at night, at least. In fact, just about everything you'll see has been engineered to look like something it's really not—and no expense is spared to keep the illusion going. It's a place that inspires fantasy and greed, a place that lures you in by hypnotizing you with its bright lights and glamour. It's a place that headlines Celebrities and Magicians—very Jupiter/Neptune types. If you walk the strip and marvel at the imagination that went into creating each casino, you're enjoying the best of it. If you pour your hard-earned pesos into a slot-machine, you'll experience the worst of it—the disappointment that accompanies realizing a dream was only a dream.

Now, imagine that combination coming alive in your life. Your Neptune is already a spot where you don't want to see reality, anyway. It's a place where you're equipped with a magic smoke machine and a bucket of pink dust, where you're always ready to flip the switch, grab a handful of dust, and change Milwaukee with a used-car salesman into Camelot with Sir Lancelot. Needless to say, when Jupiter arrives, expanding that urge way, way, way out of proportion, it's easy to be swept away by illusion, romance, and dreams—and even fraud. Yes, when Jupiter visits our Neptune, we're in the mood to Dream. Big Dreams. And we don't want our feet to touch the ground, not for a second. So it's especially easy for us to believe those dreams are real, and to act accordingly. So be verrrry, verrrry careful of folks presenting deals that seem to be too good to be true—because they just might be.

Under the conjunction, our Neptune's urge to create perfection and turn away the harshness of reality is blown up, up, and away. On the positive side, this really is a place where we have the potential to realize our loftiest dreams, to actually turn stark reality into something much more magical—that's why it's so hypnotic. And Jupiter does provide enough Ooomph to inspire us to reach for the brass ring. So Big Dreams can certainly come true, magically, when these transits are in effect As I said, if we've got our feet pretty well-rooted to start with, this can mean that opportunities arise, to bring the perfection we seek into our lives. If we're already prone to ignore what we don't want to see, however, now's when we may experience the other side. We could be set up by someone who's conning us—or set ourselves up. Neptune is where we already believe that life is just exactly the way we want it to be. When Jupiter comes along, we're out of control. Of course, Neptune is also where we're at our most spiritual, and Jupiter is a big fan of Getting Us Religion. So it's also quite possible that we may turn inwards towards a more spiritual side of life now, whether that means taking up meditation, going to a church or meeting someone who becomes our spiritual guru.

When Jupiter touches Neptune by square or opposition, the situation is a bit touchier. We find ourselves pulled towards what seems to be a more perfect way of life, but we may be moving too fast. If our Big Dreams aren't based on reality, we're often set up for even Bigger Disappointment after the pink smoke clears—and that can be absolutely crushing. These symptoms may show up especially in our One-to-One relationships, where it's now especially easy for us to buy a car from a less than reputable salesperson, invest our life's savings in an oil-well in Texas that isn't really there, or believe that he or she really is totally misunderstood by their spouse, and just waiting for the right time to leave. If you've ever taken pain medications, in fact, you're already quite familiar with Jupiter/Neptune difficult transits. Pop one or two in your mouth, and the toothache is gone. Not only that, but all of life is great—and rosy as all get-out. After the pill wears off, however, the pain returns. Under these tougher transits, then, it's best to remember that we shouldn't operate anything important while we're under the influence—so don't sign away the house to the nice man at the door who's collecting for charity.

The trines and sextiles are usually wonderful times when our sensitivity to the environment and to the Others in it is piqued. Neptune's ability to allow us to feel everything is expanded by Jupiter's urge to make us Understand how all this fits into The

Big Picture, and we suddenly realize that we truly are All One. That type of thinking leads to imagination and creativity, and is certainly the stuff that great art and beautiful music, (two of Neptune's favorite things,) are made of. In fact, if you add in a good Mercury transit, these two could also coincide with writing some wonderful poetry or fiction. Just be careful, no matter what the aspect, that you're not going to wake up with a hangover.

JUPITER/PLUTO

Take Pluto, The Obsessor, and add Jupiter, Mr. More. Can you hear the two of them? You know you want this, and you know you can have it. What are you waiting for? Needless to say, these transits are times when we're amazingly powerful, not especially concerned with what anyone thinks of us, and quite capable of getting whatever we want. See, Pluto is the spot where you're already pretty darned intense, where you're quite driven by What You Desire. When Jupiter visits, that drive is expanded, and you're a force to be reckoned with. The problem is, or can be, that we don't think in terms of what we're leaving behind. See, Pluto loves to burn bridges. It's his job in your natal chart to help you with Drastic Change, and wherever he lives natally is a house where you'd just as soon trash a situation, rather than try to fix it. When Jupiter visits, and they put their heads together, the urge to change everything, Big Time, is what you'll experience, and the house where Pluto lives is where the changes will start. All this boils down to the possibility of you literally transforming into a completely new person—for better or worse—depending on what you do with the tremendous boom of energy you're feeling.

See, Pluto isn't the type of planet that settles for just a bit of anything, and neither is Jupiter. Pluto is ravenous. He wants it *all*—in fact, he's the All Or Nothing planet. When he's activated by Jupiter, who also can't stand to ever have just a little of anything, you're not about to settle, either—for less than Everything. Pluto is all about issues of control, you see, and Issue Number One is taking control of our own lives. Jupiter is only too happy to encourage us to Get Free in the process, so typically, under these transits, we turn our whole lives around. We want change, and we're inspired by Jupiter to take risks, future be damned. Which means we may end up leaving the job, getting a divorce, and moving to San Francisco. We may also transform our lives through education, travel, or political success at this time.

Now, with the conjunction, our Pluto—our drives, our desires, and our urge to be Omnipotent—becomes absolutely huge. Needless to say, this can mean we're power-hungry on the downside, and just In The Mood to start a new life on the upside. It's all up to us. This is certainly the combination that inspires a God-complex of sorts, no matter where we decide to direct it, so when Jupiter conjoins your Pluto, make sure you're pouring all that force into a healthy, positive project.

With the squares and oppositions, it's not uncommon for us to meet resistance, to find ourselves in a huge fight to the figurative death with The Forces That Be. Again, the squares tend to play out more internally, so we often feel an inner friction that won't be resolved unless we give it all up. We feel as if we're just dying to shake off whoever or whatever has been making us feel as if we're being controlled. Often, this means that we lose something in the process, but with Uncle Jupiter on our side, regardless of how difficult the loss is, there's something better waiting down the road. The opposition, as always, tends to play out in our relationships with others, so power struggles are quite common now, too.

Under the easier transits, we feel as if we're being assisted by The Universe in our quest for Total Change, as if life just opens up doors to help us escape from whatever we've felt imprisoned by. Since Pluto also has a lot to do with inheritances, and Jupiter is the lotsa planet, we can also be the recipient of large amounts of money now, or the key to the family business.

Regardless of which aspect it is that Jupiter makes to Pluto, keep in mind that you're in an accelerated evolutionary phase right now, and absolutely unstoppable. But wisdom is the better part of valor, and if you know you've got a bigger gun than your opponent, and that they're only defending their turf, go easy. Don't abuse this power, or it could actually turn on you. Use it well and you'll be amazed at the positive change you can bring to so many lives.

CHAPTER NINE

SATURN

Your Saturn Kit:

A Copy of the Ten Commandments—(with all the 'Thou Shalt Not's' underlined)

A Pocket watch

A *Daytimer*

Yellow Legal Pads

Robert's Rules of Order

A Clipboard, A Pocket-protector, and A Calculator

A Certificate or Diploma

Official Documents

A Uniform

A Yardstick

A Compass and A Straightedge

A Pin-striped Suit

A Briefcase with your initials on it

Wire-rimmed glasses

Lead

Saturn Transits: What Goes Around, Comes Around...

The subject is Reality. Just the facts, ma'am. When Saturn comes along, it's time to Wake Up And Smell the Coffee, to see things as they really are. Now, although these transits are not notoriously Rollickin' Good Times—and I'd be lying to you if I said they were—they're not notoriously Bad times, either. It all depends on you, and on how you've handled the affairs of the planet or house that's about to be Tested. You either receive kudos from your world, or you get pushed back to Go without the $200 bucks. Either way, you Learn A Valuable Lesson—which is how Saturn earned his nickname, "The Cosmic SchoolMaster."

At best, these are personally satisfying, validating times, when you get your "A's," and a buck for each one, too. At worst, you'll still get the report card, but you'll see your shortcomings show up and feel Unworthy, Undeserving, and Inadequate—via "D's, F's," and not so much as a quarter for showing up. If this is the case, don't despair. It's much the same technique that's used in the military—make 'em feel bad about what they did wrong and they'll try harder next time. And keep in mind that remedies for whatever ails you also find their way into your life under Saturn transits. When the Reality Light goes on, after all, even the toughest of solutions suddenly become quite obvious. Saturn transits teach us that sometimes the easiest thing to do isn't the best thing to do.

Basically, Saturn transits indicate periods when we're tested and graded. Saturn inspects the house or planet he touches to see if the structure is steady and will hold up through a storm. If we pass, we receive a symbolic certificate—a newfound confidence that's unshakable. Sometimes the certificates are real—like diplomas and contracts. If we don't pass, we get a Reality Check that can make us feel as if we haven't accomplished much of anything—which can be quite a humbling experience. Saturn is the Head of Quality Control in our Universe. When he happens along, it's time to Get It Together and Firm Things Up. If you can handle that part of it, Saturn transits don't have to hurt.

A final note: don't expect to be the life of the party when Saturn is in the neighborhood of one of your planets. You're going to be a lot more serious, practical, and cautious—and maybe even a bit testy. Hey, look at it this way: you may not be in the mood to party 'till dawn, but you'll get a lot accomplished. Then, when Jupiter arrives, and you do want to stay up all night, you'll be able to afford it.

Saturn Through The Houses

If a house in a birth-chart is really like a room in a house, then picture Saturn moving into one of the room's in your home and setting up shop. First off, he looks and acts like Icobod Crane: very gaunt, very practical, and very serious. He's definitely not one to waste words or smile much, because he didn't come over for a party. He's here to Straighten Things Up, and get your affairs in order. He doesn't need much to get to work. A number two pencil, a yellow legal pad or two, and a place to keep his clock and magnifying glass will do just fine. He'll want you to have the lights out by nine-thirty at the latest, and be ready to get back to work by 6 AM sharp—which doesn't leave a lot of time for entertaining, and discourages anyone but only the most business-oriented visitors from stopping by. Oh, and he'll be around for two and a half years, by the way, so it's not like you can just ignore him.

Needless to say, before he arrives for a visit, you'll want to Prepare. Scour the room, make sure it's ultra-organized, and get rid of everything that's superfluous that might make him scowl. In fact, preparation before he gets into town is really the best thing you can do with a Saturn transit. When you glance at your chart and see that he's about to change houses, get in there and Get Ready, and the old Nay-Sayer may just decide to bestow honors on you, instead of slapping your hand.

FIRST HOUSE

Picture this: Saturn, Mr. Lead, arrives at the Ascendant, your symbolic Front Door. He chases your friends away, pulls down all the shades, and turns off the television. All of a sudden, you're dreadfully somber, and your sense of humor seems to have dried up and left. You wonder what's wrong with you, and if it will ever change. Well, yes, it will, but not right away. See, when Saturn's at the Front Door, it's time to Get Serious and make repairs—and there's no time for being a social butterfly. So you might also expect to spend a lot of time home alone for awhile.

Most often, you get two symptoms with this transit, in this order: first, you feel as if you're being crushed, literally. You feel heavy, tired, and overburdened. It seems that Life has decided to make you The Honorary Principal wherever you go, (when you do manage to get out), that you're always In Charge, and that there will be no vacations until Everything Is In Order. To top it off, you're quite dissatisfied with your appearance, and you may even experience a shyness you don't ordinarily possess. At some point, since you're spending so much time alone, bringing order to your life and reflecting, you begin to take stock of how the face you present to the world, the way you dress and conduct yourself, and the condition of your body is affecting what happens to you. Eventually, you decide that it's time to lose weight, dress more like a grown-up, or quit smoking. In other words, you begin to realize that this is the only body you've got, and you owe it to yourself to be happy with your appearance. You begin to Restructure You, and then Stage Two sets in.

After awhile, the changes you make allow you to see some of the good things about You, instead of just your shortcomings. You begin to feel more and more confident with the New You that you've created, and your interactions with others begin to reflect this newfound groundedness. (Think of how much more confidently you extend your hand in introduction when you haven't been caught in your sweat-pants, and you'll understand what I mean here.) Eventually, after Saturn's been around for awhile, the changes become much more internalized, and you decide you have a perfect right to be here on the planet, whether you're being entertaining, serious, or sad. You start to see your friends again, but probably not all of them. This transit has a way of weeding out the Quality people in your life from the fair-weather friends. Although you may be surprised at who falls into each category, when Saturn leaves this house en route for the second, you'll know for sure who your real friends are—and you'll be able to count yourself among them.

SECOND HOUSE

Well, kids, get ready to live on a shoestring—or to have your income regulated for the first time in years. It all depends on you. If you've been excessive in the financial department over the past few years or so, well, then, fasten your seat belt, because The Auditor is about to arrive, quite possibly with a past-due bill, payable in full. You'll have two and a half years to pay up, but you will pay up—or your financial reputation will suffer. This warning applies especially to those of you in the listening audience with less than amazing willpower: the fire signs, for example, those with Venus in a fire sign, a fire-sign on the second house cusp, Venus in aspect to Jupiter, or anyone who's just been through a whopper of a Jupiter transit. In other words, those of you who, either natally or recently, have had less than amazing willpower with your checkbooks. If that's the case, start looking for a second job, or make a list of credit reorganization institutions. No kidding.

Now, if you've got a lot of nice, solid earth signs, a strong Saturn, or the self-discipline to have avoided overdoing it, despite a visit from Jupiter, you've got nothing to worry about. The Auditor will still show up, but he'll have something wonderful under his arm: a raise, a promotion, or a Regular Income—maybe for the first time in years. Regardless of which symptom you experience, it's not a bad idea to get yourself on a budget, open a savings account, or invest—cautiously, of course—over the next couple of years.

That's the financial news. But the second house has other meanings, too. It's an indication of What We Hold Dear, and how we take care of it. So Saturn's visit can also mean it's time to clean out the closets, literally and figuratively, en route to making a decision about what we value, and about those possessions we consider Important enough to keep them around, rather than tossing them, giving them away, or donating them to charity. You'll also find that your taste in Things will now turn towards Quality rather than Quantity.

On a deeper level, this transit also coincides with a time when we begin to examine those qualities in ourselves and in others that are important to us. Remember, the second-house reflects our self-worth, too, and Saturn only gives you what you've earned—no more, and no less. So it's also possible that we may now feel undeserving of what we've got, or inadequate in the Earnings Department. Eventually, either symptom can turn out positively, through our search for a better-paying job, or, again, concern about finances that leads to budgeting or saving. One thing's for sure: at the end of this two and a half year period, we all tighten up our belts—whether it's by choice or necessity. Remember, with Saturn, Preparation is everything. If you see him about to sidle into your second house soon—or even not so soon—your best bet is to balance the checkbook, regularly, be realistic about your finances, and Take Care Of Bizness now.

THIRD HOUSE

The third house has everything to do with your Small World—the world that you travel through on a daily basis—and all the folks that you know from within that small circle. It's also all about the way you conduct yourself when you're on Auto-Pilot, whether it's by driving around your neighborhood or performing tasks that are familiar enough for you to do them without consciously thinking about them, step by step. In other words, this is the side of you that comes out when you're operating on Home Turf, or learning those basic things you need to know to function on a daily basis on your corner of the planet.

When Saturn passes through this house, something about your automatic functions change. It's no longer easy to cruise through the neighborhood on a short trip, for example. The reason for that might be that your neighborhood is being restructured in some way, and construction around you is certainly one of those ways. It's also possible that your freedom of movement may be restricted. What all this boils down to is that you may have to learn to live without a vehicle for awhile, or you may simply find that life suddenly requires you to be spending a lot more time in your immediate environment—your Little World—than you were before.

Since the third house also relates to neighbors and siblings, you may find your relationships with those folks to be especially taxing for awhile. They may seem to be heaping responsibility on you for their lives, or unnecessarily interfering with your time. Ever heard the expression Just Say No? Well, now's when you'll probably have to learn how, if what you're being tugged into isn't a valid use of your time—but it might not win you any popularity contests. On the other hand, you may get more involved with a neighborhood project, or you might end up heading a committee of some kind that's designed to Clean Up the community. Your relationships with siblings may also begin to mean more to you than they have in the past.

Now, this house also relates to the Way You Learn, and the way you communicate. With strict old Saturn here, your best bet is to seriously begin studying something that directly pertains to your daily life—writing, communication skills, or navigating. He's here to get you to Think Seriously, and Pay Attention to the world you ordinarily fly through without a second thought. If you're feeling a bit depressed or heavy-minded for a while, then, get yourself involved with a project that requires a lot of concentration.

Remember, Saturn loves it when we Apply Ourselves. And when Saturn is happy, we're, um....well, we're not unhappy.

FOURTH HOUSE

Your fourth house is the spot in your chart that relates to your family, the way that you were raised, and the way you were nurtured. Since it has so much to do with your early life, then, and your childhood, it's also a symbolic storehouse for your Emotional Experiences, all those memories of How This Felt the last time you tried it. Whenever you react from the gut, it's this house that dictates what those reactions will be based on. When Saturn comes through this house, then, with his ultra-cautious attitude and need to see everything On Paper, you may find yourself a lot less willing to take chances—especially in regard to situations you've tried before that haven't panned out very well.

Saturn in the fourth house reminds you of The Past, so it's also possible that you'll be dealing with childhood fears now—in particular, those that were never really resolved. You may also become interested in Your Heredity, and begin researching the family tree. In a nutshell, Saturn is testing your Emotional Foundation when he visits this house. So if there are any weak or wobbly spots, now's when you'll need to see them honestly, face them realistically, and work towards putting them to bed, once and for all.

You're also looking for stability and groundedness in your present home-life. Now, that can mean many things on the physical plane. You may decide that stability means it's time to build a home, (because Saturn just loves to build foundations), or buy a home. Problems with the structure of your existing home may also surface now, demanding that you reinforce or re-build. If your physical home is in good shape, you may opt to co-habitate with someone. Or, if you're already living with someone, you may decide that now's the time to make that Commitment (a famously Saturnian issue) more solid, and begin to urge your Other towards marriage. This transit can coincide with the birth of a child, too, or the arrival of a relative who needs long-term care, or some other long-term life situation that makes your home-life more filled with Responsibility than it was before.

With Saturn's famous fondness for Hard Work, you may also find yourself staying in your home a lot more than before. In fact, since Saturn is the planet that inspires career aspirations, working from your home is possible at this time, as is starting a business that deals with homes, families, or children—like real estate, architecture, or child-care. Saturn also rules the elderly— folks who've been on the planet long enough to have paid their dues. So you may also begin working with the elderly, in Home-Care situations.

In all, this is the time that The Universe has set aside for you to Take Responsibility for your nest on the planet and demonstrate your emotional stability, as well. Batten down the hatches, then, and make The Cosmic School-Teacher proud.

FIFTH HOUSE

Well, here's Leo's house, the place that's built for All Play and No Work. At least, that's how it is until Saturn arrives and tells you to get off the bicycle and put your toys away. Sound like a drag? Well, not necessarily. Although this transit doesn't ordinarily coincide with a period when you've got much time for playing, which is just hell for the Geminis out there, it might just mean that your idea of What's Fun changes. You may begin to actually enjoy working—not quite so far-fetched if you do it by turning your hobby into a business. If you do somehow make time for rec- reation, you'll enjoy structured games or entertainment much more—where someone's In Charge of the activity. And don't be surprised if that someone is you.

Love affairs are also under the jurisdiction of the fifth-house side of you, so with Saturn here, who isn't known for being the most romantic guy out there, don't expect much in the way of flowers, candles, or trips to Tahiti. Saturn doesn't like frivolities— they're a waste. He is rather good, however, at Getting Serious, so if you've been casually involved with someone, you may decide to make a commitment to your Other at this time. You may also become involved with someone considerably younger—or older— than yourself. In that case, the flowers and candles won't be quite so absent.

This house also relates to children, so it's possible to find that they're taking up a lot more of your time and energy than they have in the past. This might mean that your relationships with your own children take on a more serious note—maybe you've got to 'draw the line' with them, or set down new rules due to behav- ioral problems. Maybe you find yourself dealing with Authority figures with regard to your kids. Or maybe you decide it's time to have one of your own, a most sobering—and yet rewarding—experience. And it doesn't even have to be only your own children that are somehow looking to you for guidance. You may be put in charge of a child-care center, or made Principal, or head up a committee concerned with kid's problems.

Since this house also refers to gambling and speculations, and since Saturn shakes his long, bony, finger at Those Who Waste Their Resources or Take Unnecessary Chances, now might not be the best time to head to Vegas or invest in a risky financial deal. Now is the time to take a look at what amuses you, and see how you can put it to work for you.

SIXTH HOUSE

Here's the house that's concerned with Your Daily Schedule, and with the things you must necessarily do to continue functioning in your life. Basically, that adds up to your health (what you do to keep your body functioning), and your work (what you do to keep your checkbook functioning). Add a dose of Saturnian seriousness, and you may simply find yourself more concerned with Doing What's Necessary to keep both of those aspects of your life operating more efficiently. Sure, that can mean added responsibilities at work—and maybe even feeling burdened or overwhelmed by them. Saturn doesn't come over to play, and he expects full value—and more—for his dollar. So you're definitely going to work hard now. But don't worry. Although the old Nay-Sayer may not be generous, he's also not blind to what you've accomplished, although he's so darned quiet, it may seem like he hasn't noticed that you've worked overtime every day for the past eight weeks. He has. And when the time is right, you'll receive your justly earned reward—a raise, a promotion, or a chance to become a partner in the firm—and maybe even a bigger expense-account.

Of course, Saturn also notices if you haven't done your share, and then there'll be hell to pay. At worst, you might find yourself at odds with the Authority Figures in charge of your paycheck, or at odds with your co-workers over issues of Who's Done What. At best, however—if you cooperate, that is—you'll be amazed at the new level of efficiency you'll develop, and the new respect for your own abilities that you'll emerge from this transit toting around.

By the way, if you are having problems with your boss, and you're honestly sure it's not your fault, it might just mean that Saturn is trying to give you the nudge to Take Charge of this area of your life, and get away from an Authority Figure who's not qualified to order you around. (Remember, he doesn't always side with the Powers That Be—only the ones that are justifiably in that position). In that case, you might now consider opening your own business, and becoming the Authority Figure yourself. Now, making that decision is a tough one—it's entering into an ultra-responsible situation, through having to deal with the Saturn-like details of owning, operating, and being responsible for the success of not only your own paycheck, but that of the others you hire. So don't do it lightly, especially not now. But if you know you're qualified, and the time is right, Go For It. Especially if you're interested in a field that's also Saturnian in nature, like business, accounting, or management.

Now, as I said a paragraph or two ago, health concerns might come up now, too. But, again, relax. Being concerned about your health can mean that you decide to diet, quit a bad habit, or join an exercise class—so finish the paragraph before you run off terrified that you're going to come down with a chronic illness. Although Saturn's visit here certainly can coincide with the emergence of a problem that's going to require a lot of steady tending to work out, most commonly, you'll just find yourself much more serious about the condition of your body.

Your Daily Routine also gets a bit less flexible than you're used to when Saturn comes through this house—unless you've got Saturn or Capricorn here natally. In that case, you'll enjoy this transit, and the added self-discipline it will afford you. On the other hand, this transit is hell on folks with Uranus in this house, who are used to having their day go more or less as they feel it should, who don't like to deal with time-frames, schedules, or appointments. In a nutshell, you're about to Get It Together, on a daily basis, so whatever you do, every day, regularly, will need to be much more regulated and stabilized. Get yourself a Daily Planner, learn how to make lists, and be on time for all your appointments.

SEVENTH HOUSE
Here's another Get Married transit—and a Get Divorced transit, too. If that sounds a bit odd, remember that Saturn rules the concept of Quality—so when he marches through the seventh house, he just won't settle for anything less than The Best in all your relationships. If your current One-to-One relationship has

been less than rewarding, then, or if you've been feeling starved or overburdened in some way, now's when you'll come to terms with The Reality Of The Situation. You may decide that if you're going to have to take care of everything on your own, without any material or emotional support from your partner, that you might as well be on your own. You might also take a good, long look at your current partner and decide that they really are The One For You—so why wait? Or, with Saturn's love of Older Folks, you may become involved in a relationship with an older or younger person—especially if the natal chart provides for this. Regardless of what happens, know that all your One-to-Ones are going to reflect your newfound Search for Nothing But The Best.

Now, since this is the house that also shows how we relate with anyone on a One-to-One basis, keep in mind that all your relationships are going to be much more serious than they have been in quite a while. That goes for best buds, professional relationships, and open enemies, another traditional group o' folks you'll find here. You may be put in a position of handling someone else's business affairs, or just feel as if someone you're very close to is heaping responsibility on you. All this may mean that you're not much in the mood for One-to-One encounters that aren't worth your time. This is another transit that weeds out the folks you want to keep in your life from the ones you won't mind losing. Remember, Saturn wants you to get a return for your investment, no matter where he's passing through at the moment. Anyone who's not going to earn their keep in your life, then, will probably exit now.

EIGHTH HOUSE

The eighth house is all about the way we share—both of ourselves and our resources. Since there are many ways to do just that, Saturn's trek through this house can mean a lot of things. First of all, since this is the house that shows our sexuality, this may be a time of celibacy, when we're not interested in getting physically close to anyone. Or we might pull inward and become less trusting of the outside world—less willing to Become Intimate on a mental or intellectual level. That might mean that we spend more time alone, preferring our own company to that of folks we're not quite sure about.

On the other hand, as per Saturn's fondness for trial and effort, now may be when we decide to become intimate with someone who's been tried and true—a Quality Partner that's worthy of our secrets, intellectually, physically, and emotionally. And, like the seventh house, this transit can also point to the start of a relationship with someone quite a bit older, or younger, than ourselves. If a relationship does start during this time, by the way, it's certainly not going to be a One-Night-Stand—on any level. You're out to sink your trust into someone right now, but they're going to have to prove themselves to you before you give it out.

Now, since this is Pluto's place, it deals with inheritances, taxes, and joint resources, too, so you may receive a financial settlement, a tax refund, or a loan from a large institution. You might also find yourself dealing with the IRS or other government agencies. Just stay away from Underworld Groups— and remember, this isn't the time to make a deal with the devil, whether the devil is a loan-shark, a finance company, or a partner you're not quite sure you trust.

This is also the house that deals with Death. That doesn't necessarily mean you're going to die, of course, or that anyone close to you will, either. Although it's quite possible to lose someone when Saturn treks through Pluto's house, most of the deaths you encounter will be symbolic ones. You may need to make very difficult decisions now, to separate yourself from people or situations that have gone past the point of no return—and making those tough decisions can make you feel as if a part of you has died in the process.

Remember, this house is where we keep the Crisis Manager in us—so if life does require us to deal with crises when serious Saturn passes through, the lesson we're about to learn is about just how strong we really are.

NINTH HOUSE

Well, here's Jupiter's house, the place where we deal with Growth—whether it's through travel, education, or new experiences, where we're always sure that the grass is much greener just over that hill. This is also the house where the side of us lives who's got very set opinions on The Big Issues— philosophy, religion, and politics, for starters. Now, Saturn isn't a big fan of growth, because growing means you're pushing past the neatly-laid-out boundaries he's worked so hard to establish.

So if there's going to be any growth right now, it's going to have to be for a very good reason, and it won't come without his signature on the paper. This can play out in several ways.

First of all, since Saturn just loves to see proof of credentials laid out on paper—and especially on Official Documents—if we're due to receive a diploma or certificate of some kind, and we've honestly earned it, now's when the Higher-Ups will Sign Here. This can mean that we finish our education, finally get The Book published, or that our lack of education or credentials becomes clear, and we take ourselves back to school to learn what we need to further our career. (This is an excellent time to write, by the way, especially if you're working on a technical journal or a textbook, and it's also a great time to do advertising for institutions or political parties.)

Since this house also relates to The Higher Courts, we may also find ourselves dealing with laws, lawyers, and judges for awhile. Of course, since Saturn only metes out What You Honestly Deserve, it's best not to expect more in legal situations. If you've been waging a legal battle for some time, however, and if your cause is upright, reputable, and deserving, now's when the situation may draw to a close—but not without the usual Saturnian delays, roadblocks, and stalls. Remember, you've got to jump through hoops to prove yourself to this guy.

Again, this house relates to politics and religion, and how we believe the world should be run. So now may be when we choose a party, return to church, or change our political or religious affiliation to better reflect the person we are at the moment. And even the fire and air signs may find themselves surprisingly conservative in those choices during Saturn's passage.

Now, if you're going to do any traveling, chances are good that it's going to be for work or business. That doesn't mean you won't be able to play while you're there, however, especially if Jupiter is also adding his two cents to your current planetary clime—only that you're going to need a justifiable reason to hop on a plane. The high side of any Jupiter/Saturn combination is Controlled Growth. If you take careful steps during this two and a half year period, the old Nay-Sayer will allow you to expand—but just a little hard-earned bit at a time.

TENTH HOUSE

Well, now, here's a match made in heaven—if you've been an Upstanding Citizen, that is. Saturn just loves it here. He's home for two and a half years, ready to work hard and Be Recognized by the world for what he's accomplished, ready to be seen as a serious player in the game of life. This transit of Saturn across the very top of the chart is much like the Saturn return—and it just about always pertains to how you've done with your choice of life's work. All of a sudden, career matters are primary. It's a time when you either answer The Calling or decide you're fed up with your career and call in sick—permanently—then switch occupations.

Folks also seem to get married when Saturn visits the Midheaven (10th house cusp). Marriage, after all, is a change in our public status, to a more serious, more legitimate reputation. Think of all the Saturnian professionals you know—politicians, especially. Any of them single? Nope. In fact, it's a well-known fact that pols often get married just before a big election—because it helps their chances of winning if the world sees them as stable. Well, marriage will do that for you. (At least, that's the rumor).

Now, if we haven't been good, Saturn is only too happy to point that out to us. When he travels through this house, he's going to do it publicly. So anything you've done that's not a credit to your reputation—especially your business reputation—will probably out now. On the other hand, if you've been working very, very hard to master your chosen field, or climb the professional ladder, now's when The Authorities will take note of your skills and reward you accordingly.

This is the transit that makes or breaks us in the eyes of the world. We're being watched very carefully, and our contributions to the planet are being recorded. The best we can do is to work hard and touch all the bases.

ELEVENTH HOUSE

Your eleventh house is the spot in your chart where you keep the side of you who's the Team Player. It's the You who emerges under group situations only, the slice of your personality who decides who and what you consider Your Peer Group. When Mr. Authority Figure enters this house, then, his first order of business is going to be to get you to take a long look at your group associations, to make sure they deserve you. This can show up in your life as a time when you disappear from group events, perhaps because you see the truth about the folks you've been with, and you don't like it. You're going to be very concerned about how your affiliations make you look in the eyes of the world, and if you're no longer proud of those affiliations, now's when you'll make your excuses.

If you are still quite pleased with those you've chosen as Kindred Spirits, you may Do Saturn by coming to the forefront of your group, by becoming a leader or by publicly representing the group's interests. You may also be surprised at the amount of Responsibility your group of friends heap on you now. Even if it's time-consuming, all that will simply point to the fact that you've become respected by the Others you've chosen, and that your knowledge and expertise is now sought-after and applauded.

On the other hand, your group may also seem to be pushing you away now—as if they no longer want you with them. If that's the case, consider that Saturn is the planet that rules age and maturity, so you may well have outgrown them—and although that can be a painful experience, it's a wonderful statement about You. When we Choose Sides, we're making a strong statement about how we see ourselves, and what our goals for the future are all about. If our group involvements change, our goals have changed, too. Now's the time to be sure the folks you spend your time with are deserving of your time and energy.

TWELFTH HOUSE

"I vant to be alone." Betcha anything Garbo was having a 12th-house Saturn transit when she didn't make that statement. This is the house that describes the side of us who comes out when we're totally alone, in safe places, or on retreat. When self-sufficient Saturn passes through this house, then, even the Libras out there may suddenly find themselves enjoying time alone, and actually even preferring it to the company of others.

This can mean that we take up a Very Serious Discipline, that we begin to meditate daily, or that we begin work on a project that requires us to Go Away for awhile. So chances are good that we're going to become very monk-like—especially since the twelfth house is the place where we're at our most spiritual, most understanding, and most reclusive. If we think of Saturn in that spiritual sense, then, as a wise Native-American grandmother who doesn't waste words, this transit can be a time when we develop a quiet wisdom, and a realistic understanding of The Mysteries of our wonderful Universe. All that said, it's quite possible that we'll spend much more time in places of sanctuary or retreat—and that all our newfound knowledge makes us into a guru in the eyes of others.

But that's not what's important to us now. Truth be told, when Saturn visits this house, Others aren't important to us at all. We're looking for Quiet Time—Quality Time alone with ourselves, to research who we really are, and what we've accomplished. We're completing a cycle of sorts, taking a realistic look at our strengths, fears, and inadequacies. Basically, we're symbolically cleaning up our subconscious. Now, if there are things we've done over our lives that we're less than proud of—and who hasn't—this transit may not feel especially wonderful for the whole two and half years Saturn spends here. His specialty, remember, is Pointing Out What's Wrong—so this transit may mean that we spend time brooding over past mistakes, or regretting things we've done. If that's what you're experiencing, remember that nobody's perfect, resolve to do better next time, make amends, if you can, then let it go.

This is the house that's traditionally been associated with Our Greatest Undoings, Our Secret Enemies, and places like hospitals, jails, and asylums. Saturn's transit through here has usually been described as a lonely, unhappy time, when we're confined in some way, possibly against our wishes. All those things were written Way Back When, however, when humans were a lot more group-oriented, and being alone meant you were pushed away by society. Nowadays, it's not a bad thing to be alone—so this transit doesn't have to be bad, either. Of course, if there's something we've done that's really awful, now is certainly when we stand a chance of being ostracized by others—and confinement is one of the ways society ostracizes.

Remember, however, that Saturn is the planet that grounds us, that brings us an awareness of who and what we are. Teaching us to accept ourselves, complete with flaws, is what Saturn's mission through this house is all about. If we take the time to understand ourselves, and to accept everything we find as simply part of The Whole Package, this transit doesn't have to be terrible. It can show up, simply, as a time when we restructure our Inner Self. So don't panic—and do ponder.

SATURN/SUN

The Sun is the Executive Director in our chart, the planet that describes our urge, literally, to shine through doing what we love and being recognized and applauded for it. It's who we really are, at our core. When Saturn visits our Sun, with his briefcase full of boundaries, structures and guidelines, our entire lives become much more focused on Achievement. We're out to prove ourselves to the Authority Figures around us, and we're not unwilling to work to do it. What this boils down to is that for the time period that Saturn is within orb of our Sun, we're much more Serious about our lives than we have been in quite a while, which may seem to temporarily put a damper on our personality. If that's the case, don't sweat it. These times aren't about having fun—that's what Jupiter's for. Now is when we're dealing with The Reality Of Our Lives—and that's serious, necessary business. And what's wrong with being a bit more reserved, polite, and humble for awhile?

Although much of this will apply to our career aspirations, there's a lot more to Saturn's visit than just Making It in the eyes of the world. We also become very concerned with our bodies, the vehicles that get our Sun around. So this is another Saturn transit that's tailor-made for dieting, quitting smoking or drinking, and concentrating on the structure of our physical forms. Remember, in the physical body, Saturn correlates with the bones and the skin, and all the other physical structures that keep our bodies together—internally and externally. We begin to realize now that we truly are what we eat, and perhaps that some of the habits we've allowed ourselves to fall into aren't good for us. In other words, we begin to feel Responsible for ourselves, in many ways, and responsibility for our health is just one of those ways.

When the Sun is conjoined by any planet, we become that planet—so now's when we're about to become just like old Mr. No himself, when our self-discipline and willpower will be at a peak, when our ambitions for the future will be all-important, and when waste of any kind will disgust us. Our eyes are open now to just what we've accomplished in the past, and what we want to accomplish in the future. If we know there's more we're capable of, we'll feel both guilty about not having done it sooner, and resolve about taking care of it now. If we have been responsible in the past, now's when we'll feel respected by others, and proud of ourselves. Remember, the Sun is the Be All That You Can Be planet—and Saturn isn't about to stop pushing us until we're honestly doing all that we can to achieve our goals.

When Saturn aspects the Sun by square or opposition, we may find that The Powers That Be seem to be blocking our paths, or putting difficult challenges in our way. We may literally come up against The Authority Figures in our lives, and they may seem to be completely unpleasable. All that can make us feel quite inept and incompetent for a while, but only if we know we haven't been performing up to our personal standards. Then again, if we know in our hearts that we've followed all the rules and touched all the bases, it's not uncommon for us to end a job or a relationship under these transits—especially if the restrictions we're trying to live with don't seem logical, rational, or necessary. In that case, we'll end up leaving a situation so that we can set up our own rules—guidelines that pertain more closely to who we really are and what we want. Although the more difficult transits can certainly play out through more taxing, difficult times, the end result is the same: we're more in charge of our lives than we were before, living by more realistic Standards.

The trines and sextiles are usually quite wonderful times, when Saturn lets you know he approves of what you've done. Doors open, your accomplishments are duly noted, and your rewards arrive. The best part of the perks we receive under Saturn/Sun transits aren't the kind that show up on paper or in a paycheck, however. The knowledge that you're being given recognition and rewards because you've earned them is a much deeper, more personally satisfying feeling, and that's what Saturn/Sun is really all about. Under the trines and sextiles, we also have the ability to conjure much more self-discipline and willpower than we've had for awhile. These transits are also great for trimming down or stopping a bad habit, since they allow you to deprive yourself without feeling deprived. Remember, this planet is an expert at Doing Without. When he's visiting your Sun, you'll need remarkably little from your environment, and be amazed at just how much comes from within.

SATURN/MOON

Our Moon is the place where we're at our most emotional, where we toss facts and figures aside to react strictly from our hearts. She's the side of us that nurtures ourselves and others, that deals with our children, our mothers, our families, and our homes. She's the urge we've all got to express our feelings about what the world is throwing at us, whether that means crying, or laughing, or giving someone we love a hug. Now think of how she's going to feel when Saturn comes along. He's the guy that's totally devoid of emotions, the guy that operates strictly on Rules, Regulations, and What's Supposed To Be Done Under This Situation. And he has no patience with cry-babies.

Now, on an emotional level, your experience with Saturn is going to depend on the condition of your Moon in your natal chart, as well as the type of aspect Saturn makes to your Moon. Remember, aspects are like conversations the transiting planet initiates with your natal planet. When Saturn conjoins your Moon, he's speaking the same language. So now may be when you feel quite justified about your feelings, no matter what you're emotionally involved with. After all, a great deal of the problems we encounter with our Moon arise from feeling that we just have to express an emotion that no one wants to hear. In that case, you'll be amazed at just how confidently you're expressing your feelings when Saturn's around.

Then, too, Saturn is the planet with the rings—built-in boundaries. And boundaries can be a blessing. For example, if there's a crisis that comes up now, you'll be quite able to Keep It Together and handle it. This is especially handy when we're dealing with life situations that require us to separate our feelings from Doing The Right Thing.

This emotional self-sufficiency can also point to a time when we can't find our emotions, however, when we feel hardened or shut-down in some way. If you're experiencing that side of Saturn right now, remember that he's the planet that's in search of Quality. So if your emotions aren't going to be appreciated by whoever or whatever is Out There, he's going to protect you from being wounded by turning down the volume, and making you much more cautious and self-restrained about emoting to an unfriendly audience.

Under the difficult aspects, Saturn may seem to be arguing with your Moon. That means you may find that your relationships with your Mom, your kids, or the folks you live with are also a bit difficult, possibly due to the addition of more responsibility for their lives. You may also find that your commitment to take care of these folks is taking up a great deal of your time, and feel guilty about resenting that. This can also end up making you feel quite heavy or serious emotionally, as if life is forcing you to be On Duty at all times, and your only defense is to bury your own feelings and keep on performing your duties.

If you're trying to buy or build a home now, you may also have to deal with roadblocks, problems, or delays. You may have a child of your own, too—and be astounded at the responsibility of raising a tiny person. Or you may be put in the position of having to act against your feelings—which is never a comfortable experience. These transits are not classically good times, so I won't tell you that they are. But after they've passed, your Moon will be much stronger—which means you'll be a bit tougher emotionally, and bit more equipped to handle whatever life tosses at you in the future.

Saturn's trines and sextiles to the Moon, on the other hand, are easy conversations, and can be wonderfully stabilizing times. We find just the right home, finally get through to the kids, and develop a deeper relationship with our Moms or our families. A healthy child arrives, and we're ready, willing, and able to set about the business of caring for this new person. At any rate, under easy Saturn transits, situations come up that put us in charge, we handle them successfully, and we're proud of ourselves. As a result, we feel grounded, settled, and secure. Regardless of which conversation Saturn initiates with the Moon, the idea is to firm us up emotionally—to build our resolve. So even if the circumstances that arise now are harsh or depressing, know that Saturn's structure and discipline is what will enable you to keep on going. On the physical plane, any Saturn transit can be fed by simply tidying up your physical home, repairing the structure, or reorganizing the closets.

SATURN/MERCURY

Mercury is ordinarily a rather happy-go-lucky kind of planet, a place where we enjoy New Information, word games, tooling around in the car throughout the neighborhood, and conversation with others. He's the spokesperson for our Sun, our own personal Mr. Microphone. Whenever your Mercury receives a visit from another planet, then, if we listen, we can hear that planet 'speaking'—in our voices. So let's imagine what might happen when Professor Saturn arrives at your Mercury's door with his briefcase, textbooks, and clipboard.

First of all, you're not going to be up for any Light Social Chit-chat—and your conversations with others are going to reflect that. No, now's when you'll be communicating strictly to Gain Information and Set The Record Straight. You'll be looking for data—facts, figures, and proven methods of problem-solving. Never mind what the neighbors are doing—what are the latest statistics like about crime in the area? This is a transit that prompts even the most optimistic among us to become pessimists, too. It's hard to think light, happy thoughts when Saturn's standing behind you, warning you that what you say and what they say carries a great deal of weight, so you'd better check every word before it emerges.

As with Saturn's trek through the third house, since Mercury rules our ability to get ourselves from Point A to Point B, it's also possible that we may have to deal with delays in our travel-plans, or postponements. If that's what you find yourself dealing with, remember that Saturn's job is to hold us back until the time is right—so it could be that we're being held back from progressing because we're going too fast for our own good.

With the conjunction, all these symptoms are possible, along with an urge to take up a very serious study of a subject we've always wanted to know more about. In that case, Saturn's ability to discipline our thoughts and keep even the fire and air signs among us in their chairs long enough to study, will be a Godsend. We may also begin teaching under the conjunction, as our Mercury responds to the urge to Instruct. Since our Mercury is also in charge of the paperwork we encounter, there may be an Official Document to read over, or a situation may arise that brings Registered or Certified Letters our way more often than usual. We can be quite rational and objective when Saturn touches Mercury—and not as liable to Venture A Guess without doing our homework first.

Under the squares and oppositions, our thoughts and our general mind-sets can be very heavy—as if we're unable to see a light at the end of the tunnel, or the positive side of any issue. We may also tend towards sarcasm, a famous Saturnian technique to keep a wall up between Us and Whoever Is Out There. These are also times when The Universe gives us the chance to make a difficult decision, acting on what we know is right, rather than on what would be easier, but not necessarily more logical in the long-run.

When Saturn trines or sextiles our Mercury, our ability to apply ourselves to a serious mental project increases, and we may actually be able to concentrate better. Saturn can also help us to improve our memory. He's never been famous for letting anything out of his grasp until it's time to let it go. And if we need to take tests, make serious, long-term decisions, or be painfully realistic about a life situation, now's when we'll be quite able to handle it.

SATURN/VENUS

Saturn transits put us in the mood to Get Serious about something. We start thinking in terms of what might be a safer move, which prompts us to act more cautiously than we might ordinarily. Apply all this to our Venus, and you've got a transit that marriages are made of—literally, for better or worse. Yes, when Saturn touches Venus, we start feeling as if it would be nice to have Someone there when we get home from work, so it might be time to take a deep breath and say "I Do." This even goes for Venus in Sag and Aquarius, who'll want to Get Serious, too, but with someone who's unusual or different in some way. Saturn's conjunction to our Venus may bring this urge to couple permanently into our lives, but only if something about our partner makes us believe they're reliable, steady, and worth the emotional investment.

He's also the kind of guy who inspires a concern for finances. We become more reluctant to spend our hard-earned paychecks on anything we don't see as Quality Goods, and able to live on a shoestring, if circumstances demand it. Then, too, now may be when we put ourselves on a budget, begin a savings program, or decide to take on a new job with regular paychecks—even if we always thought working for tips or commissions was the only way to go.

The squares and oppositions, as usual, can coincide with conflicts, or feeling pressured in some way. When we toss Saturn and Venus into the mix, it's money matters, relationship issues, or the burden of taking care of possessions that bring the tension into our lives—and maybe even a combination of all three. Then, too, when Saturn makes a difficult aspect to Venus, we may decide that our present relationship just isn't working—that we're investing more than we're taking out. In that case, we may opt to end a situation and resolve to choose a partner more carefully next time.

When Saturn trines or sextiles our Venus, our financial situation often stabilizes, and we've got a reliable, regular income. As with the conjunction, we begin to value Quality in our possessions, and what we buy at this time reflects that Taste For Nothing But The Best. Our more grounded finances may mean that our credit is good, and we're able to afford what we want. Most likely, if we're involved, we'll be content with our current Other, feeling the loveliness of a solid, stable, one to one relationship. If we're alone, or just dating, we'll have the wisdom and patience to keep from jumping into anything too soon. If we start up a relationship now, chances are also good that they may be someone quite a bit older—or younger—than ourselves, or that they may be someone we previously saw as an Authority Figure.

Regardless of the aspect it makes, we can learn to get along on very, very little under Saturn transits to our Venus. Saturn, in fact, teaches luxury-loving Venus the high side of admiring something and not needing to Own it. So Saturn/Venus transits can be times when we learn what, and whom, we really value—and what we're willing to do to keep them in our lives.

SATURN/MARS

Mars is our own personal sword, the part of us that we use to Defend Ourselves and protect our personal interests in the world. He's ordinarily a pretty rambunctious type of guy, not particularly concerned with what might happen after he attacks, with a built-in tunnel-vision that only allows him to see a straight path between Where You Are and What You Want. He's the side of us who sets out after and pursues our goals, the energy-pack that describes How We Take Action of any kind. Without him, we'd never do anything, much less assert ourselves, say No, or stand our ground when we need to.

Now, when we take that same Mars and add a thick dose of Saturn to him, we're adding Caution to all our actions. That can play out as self-restraint, or a crippling inability to act. Depends on us—on the way our Mars is aspected natally, and the type of aspect or conversation Saturn is initiating.

Under the conjunction, our Mars is wearing a uniform—a general's uniform. He's In Charge—no doubt about it—and he's ready for any challenge. He's strong, confident, and able to hold himself back until the time is right. In a word, we can be totally unbeatable now. When Saturn takes our Mars' side, he also lends a reputability and righteousness to the way we assert ourselves. In other words, under the conjunction, we may be able to count on the support of Higher-Ups, or we may be placed in the position of becoming an ally to someone who needs our back-up. Then, too, we may find ourselves doing battle with The Authorities, in order to gain our place among them. Again, it all depends on the condition of our natal Mars, and on how we deal with Saturn, in general.

The squares and oppositions are a bit more interesting, as the Chinese say. We can all tend to be really, really picky under any Saturn transit—crotchety, even. That's especially true of the more difficult transits Saturn makes to Mr. Mars. Here's where we're already quite competitive and combative, anyway. When that side of us is activated by a hard aspect—engaged in an argument or debate, that is—from Mr. Cranky, then, we may feel as if nothing is done well enough or fast enough to suit us. We can be critical, sarcastic, and impossible to please, never seeing anything positive in any situation. In other words, we can all become Mr. You-Didn't-Do-That-Right Himself when we're being adversely affected by Saturn.

Whatever we're showing to the outside world, however, is simply a reflection of the inner tension we're dealing with that's forcing its way out. It's time like these that try our souls, test our patience, and put us up against seemingly Immovable Objects— like authority figures who refuse to see our point of view, for example. Since Mars also rules the muscles, Saturn's tougher aspects can mean that we have I've fallen and I can't get up syndrome—that we're too drained to try again, or feeling too sure of impending failure to bother to answer a challenge.

Under the easier transits, we're strong, steady, and patient. Every move is well-planned, thoroughly thought-out, and carefully executed, with an eye towards What Could Go Wrong Here. We're expert trouble-shooters, and, in fact, life may put us in a position to do just that, for ourselves or for others. We can count on support from the Powers That Be, because we've earned it in the past, and proven ourselves in their eyes as worthy of an investment. We've also got the ability to mete out our energy—and our anger, if necessary—in an organized, rational manner now.

Saturn's visits to Mars are lessons in self-restraint. Regardless of the aspect Saturn makes to our Mars, we're being taught to Know When To Hold Up. We're learning the art of discretion, too. Most importantly, Saturn teaches Mars to aim carefully before he fires.

SATURN/JUPITER

Jupiter is the side of you that's ultra-positive, optimistic, and generous to a fault—the astrological equivalent of Santa Claus. He's where you keep your supply of laughter, enthusiasm, and high spirits. Whenever you try something new, take a risk, or hear yourself say, "Oh, what the heck"—that's Jupiter. This is the side of you that's always ready to Boldly Go Where You Have Never Gone Before, to get out there and explore, because whatever's on the other side of the mountain is an experience you just can't wait to have. He's also the side of you that tends to be a bit excessive, always choosing to have more than you need, rather than risk not having enough. Jupiter is the principle of expansion, where growth is the order of the day—and any type of growth will do just fine.

Now, as much as Jupiter represents that urge or need to expand, risk, and grow, Saturn is the side of you that withholds, contracts, refuses to take chances, and resists change. Saturn is the Head of the Department of Walls, Boundaries, and Rules— the Honorary Principal wherever he goes. Saturn builds walls to keep change out, talks us into segregating ourselves at times to get some work done without any distractions, and prompts us to Just Say No to just about anything.

Needless to say, we've got some conflicts going here. Jupiter and Saturn are, well,... not exactly the closest of kin. Saturn limits, delays, restricts, and makes you wait. Jupiter hates to wait. He encourages growth, acceleration, incorporation, and Just Doing It. When your Uncle Jupiter gets a visit from Saturn, he's got to do a lot of things that just aren't natural for him. He's got to go on a crash diet, for starters—because the source for whatever you're used to having plenty of is about to run dry. It's just as well, however, because Saturn won't let your Uncle Jupiter keep wearing that horrible, loud plaid sports-coat. He's going to bring along a neat pin-striped suit, which Jupiter will have to wear for the duration of Saturn's visit. Now, Jupiter won't like this. Pin-stripes absolutely ruin his easygoing image, and this one comes with a tie, of all things. (You can just imagine how Jupiter, ultimate fan of freedom, feels about ties, the ultimate in restriction.) To add insult to injury, he'll also have to promise Saturn not to rip it, stain it, or lose the jacket in a card game.

How's this going to pan out in real life? Well, if the aspect Saturn makes is a difficult conjunction, or a square or opposition, you're going to feel as if life is forcing you to Get Serious, like it or not. If your Jupiter is already in Capricorn, or in aspect to Saturn, it won't be quite so bad, but if you've got the type of Jupiter that tends toward being a bit too generous, excessive, and impractical, this transit is going to be a rude reality check. Your expense account may be cut in half, or taken away entirely—if you've abused it. Anything you've overdone in the past will now show up as a problem that absolutely must be resolved, and debts you've been promising to repay will now come due. It's a very sobering experience, but a necessary one. We can't run forever on our charge accounts, after all, and we've got to make good on our promises if we're going to be respected in the future.

Our relationships may be the setting for a tug-of-war of sorts, under these tougher transits, too. Saturn's demands can force even the most generous of Jupiters into feeling over pressured, stretched past the limits, and out of patience. If that's the case, make sure you've kept all your promises, but don't allow your good nature to be taken advantage of.

Under the easier transits of Saturn to Jupiter, the two of them are getting along just swell, and that means that your life is going along just swell, too. You're given the nod by Mr. Stern—which means you've used your Jupiter well in the past, and you're going to reap your just rewards. Promotions, raises, and career advancements come along at these times, along with lucky breaks, like meeting someone powerful who'll help you become successful, or getting noticed by the President of the company because you took a chance that paid off. In relationships, when Saturn makes easy aspects, or touches Jupiter in favorable ways, we're steadied or bolstered by someone else's help, guided along by an older person who acts as a mentor to us, or happy to do the same for someone younger who needs us. The best side of Jupiter/ Saturn shows up either through benevolent relationships with authority figures, or becoming a benevolent authority figure.

SATURN/SATURN—AND THE SATURN RETURN

When Saturn aspects himself, he's bringing a double-dose of seriousness your way. After all, your natal Saturn placement is a spot where you know The Rules you ought to be living by. This is the planet that prefers Just The Facts, Ma'am, that likes reality delivered with a capital "R."

How you handle this serious time has everything to do with how you deal with Saturn already. If you're in touch with your own Saturn, it's a place where you already know all about discipline, where you've learned the virtues of patience, endurance, and responsibility. This planet teaches you to respect your elders, follow the rules, and Do It Right The First Time, and if you're familiar with all those concepts, you'll be respectful, serious, and conservative when those attitudes are called for.

In this case, your Saturn will have already taught you to Do The Right Thing, listen to your conscience, be decent and civil to others, and neither borrow nor lend. He'll have taught you never to expect something for nothing, and to be keenly aware of the concept of earning what you get. So regardless of which aspect Saturn makes to himself, you'll rise to the challenge, take on any new responsibilities with confidence, and apply yourself just the way you know you should. Under any aspect Saturn makes to himself, in fact, professional rewards and public respect are quite possible.

If you've resisted Saturn's structure most of your life, however, refused to cooperate with The Authorities, and rarely taken responsibility for your own actions, then you'll see your Saturn as the critical parent inside you. In that case, transits of Saturn may emerge as times when you delay, inhibit, or stall yourself—mainly because your fear of failing in the eyes of this critical parent is so strong, you'd often rather not act at all than act inappropriately or incorrectly.

You may also meet up with heavy challenges from Authority Figures at this time, and feel as if they're blocking your every move. Saturn is unavoidable, however, so rather than try to avoid these challenges, your best bet, again, is to work hard, keep your nose clean, and Follow The Rules.

Oh, and just so you know—it doesn't always have to be that way with Saturn—sometimes he's a great guy, standing there with a big smile—okay, a grimace that might be a smile, under the right circumstances—on his face, and a certificate of Accomplishment in his hand. This holds true especially during The Mother of all Saturn Transits—the Saturn Return, that is. This transit comes along at age 29 1\2, when Saturn returns to its natal placement. At this time the foundation you've laid out for your life will be stressed—from within—by itself.

See, over the first 29 1\2 years of your stay here on the planet, you've learned what it takes to be a Grown-Up, how to run your own show by your own rules. At 29 1\2 that Young Adult inside you is called out to get to work on the project and show the world what you're made of. It's a serious time, more serious than you've seen in a while. Lots of folks change jobs, get married, get divorced, or get degrees—whatever they feel they need to accomplish to gain the respect of others, and themselves.

Remember, when a planet conjoins its natal position in your chart, you're receiving a double dose of that planet. Twice as much Saturn is twice as much seriousness—and although it's not a great deal of fun, now's when we stand to make our mark on the world, gain respect in the eyes of the Higher-Ups, and become known as a serious player in the game of life—all of which will make the next 29 1/2 years on the planet much easier to get through.

Again, no matter which transit Saturn is making to Saturn, you've got to work hard, be responsible, and show a proper respect for your elders. It's The Right Thing To Do. And don't ever try to get away with anything under Saturn transits—you get what you truly deserve at these times. Nothing more, nothing less.

SATURN /URANUS

Uranus in our natal charts is the place where we're at our most unpredictable. It's the place where we'd much rather fight City Hall than conform, where fighting for Our Cause and our own individuality is much more important than following any ridiculous societal rules. At least, that's how it is until Saturn comes along, with a list of Things You Can No Longer Get Away With.

These two planets aren't the easiest to blend, needless to say. It's like putting a thunderstorm in a pressure-cooker and keeping the lid on it for as long as you can—eventually, it's going to blow, and it's most likely going to blow when the aspect is exact, and the pressure is at its greatest.

Now, this pressurized feeling is most keen under the difficult conjunctions, the square, and the oppositions, but the circumstances will differ. Under the conjunction, our Uranian urge to break free of restrictions may mean that we decide to Declare Our Individuality, no matter what the consequences— in which case, we're truly on our own. Those around us are sure to see us as radical, rebellious, and erratic—and they won't want to be involved with someone so unstable.

Or we may end up taking on the Saturnian qualities of righteousness and resolve in this area of life where we're already pretty darned unrestrainable. In other words, no matter how rebellious we seem to be, our attitude will reflect a perfect certainty in what we're doing, and The Authorities will cooperate with us, seeing our genius and the necessity to act against rules that no longer pertain. This is the type of transit that action-heroes are made of, those rule-breakers we all love to cheer for at the movies. In real life, however, it's tough to rally support around us if we're not absolutely sure of both our motivations and our skills. Under the easier conjunctions, and the trine and sextile, this is easier to pull off, as Saturn lends us an air of reputability, no matter which rules we're breaking.

With the square, this battle plays out internally, as an unbelievable tension. The side of us who wants to Be Drastic is being held on a leash, and straining at it continuously. We may find ourselves being held back against doing what we know we've got to do, and it's Authority Figures, Society, and legalities that hold us back. This can wreak havoc on the average bear's nerves, and cause even the most stolid among us to take up nail-biting. We're definitely doing battle now—but the battle is on the inside. Under these transits, we need to find a daring adventure to keep us occupied, and to keep communications open with those Over Us so they know what we're doing.

The square is also the argument aspect, so it's also possible that we may find ourselves in the position of having what feels like No-Win battles with Others who stubbornly insist on adhering to the Rules, no matter how outdated and inapplicable those rules are in the present situation.

Under the opposition, our personal freedom is challenged by responsibilities Others place on us—possibly for their own actions—and we can react either of two ways. First, we can find new ways to accommodate both our own needs for freedom and

Others' needs to make drastic changes by becoming an example. We can help them see how to Get Themselves Free, reassuring them that no matter what the consequences, living with oppression isn't living. On the other hand, if those around us are asking too much of us, it's also possible for us to run away from them, or cut them out of our lives suddenly.

In all, this combination is the stuff that new rules are made of—and we need new rules all the time, because nothing ever stays the same. And not all rules—or laws—are good ones. After all, if no one ever had the courage to break a rule, slavery would still be legal. If you make sure the end you're after justifies the means, Saturn can be the most powerful friend Uranus ever had.

SATURN/NEPTUNE
Picture the Goddess with the pink smoke machine, snugly at home in whichever house she resides in the natal chart. She's got *Terms of Endearment* plugged into the VCR, a glass of wine or herb-tea on the coffee-table, and a box of tissues she knows she's going to need on her lap. Reality? Who needs it? Neptune's always in the mood to dream, be romantic, and ignore whatever she doesn't want to see. In our lives, this means that our Neptune position is the spot where we're expert escape-artists, where we prefer to see life the way we'd like it to be, rather than the way it really is. It's here that we keep our ability to enchant, hypnotize, and enthrall Others, with a whole range of techniques, from illusion to delusion to fraud. In a nutshell, here's where we're more than capable of fooling most of the people most of the time—including ourselves.

Now picture that same Goddess answering a knock at the door and finding Saturn there, ready for a nice, long visit. Needless to say, she's going to be depressed. He has no respect for sentimentality, isn't the slightest bit romantic, and doesn't want to talk about her dreams. She can't stand him, in other words.

She might, however, need him occasionally. We can't hide from reality forever, that is, and we all need to see the flaws in our idealized view of reality now and then. So although Saturn's visits to our Neptune aren't always times we enjoy, they're often quite necessary. Take the conjunction, for example, when Neptune is forced to deal with Saturn staying right next to her for just about a year. This is the ultimate in Reality Checks, gang, when our eyes are opened to the world as it truly is, when all our castles in the air disappear. If we've been lying to ourselves or to others, then, or even just living our lives a bit too unrealistically, now's when we'll experience the disappointment of seeing how our illusions have led us to waste valuable time. If we've been fairly well-rooted, however, and we've only used our Neptunes to help us imagine how perfect our lives might be some day, now's when Saturn will contribute his planning abilities and structures to those dreams, and help us build A More Perfect World for ourselves.

Under the more difficult transits, reality barges into our world, and we find ourselves dealing with a Prince that isn't really a Prince at all, or a castle that's built out of plywood, not stone. In other words, we're forced to see things as they really are. That might mean we suddenly realize that someone has been lying to us, that we've been working toward a goal that can never come true, or even that we haven't been seeing ourselves clearly. We can become disillusioned and depressed, and possibly a bit paranoid, as if everyone Out There is against us. In that case, we may try to pull back into our shells by whatever method of escape we ordinarily use, only to find that right now, there's nowhere to hide. It may be Authority Figures that corner us now, too, demanding facts and figures, rather than fiction.

When Saturn and Neptune meet up in more civil fashion, however, under the trines and sextiles and the easier conjunctions, we're open to seeing things more clearly now. We're ready to work at making all those wonderful dreams into reality, and willing to work in a concrete way to actually help others and ourselves to become better, rather than just deluding them— or us—any further. In that case, we can actually become a spiritual guru or mentor to others—or we may find a Saturnian representative to provide that for us. Mediation may come more easily for us, too, since Saturn gives Neptune a resolve and a stick-to-it-iveness she doesn't ordinarily possess.

In a nutshell, Saturn's visits to Neptune may not initially seem to do much more than force us to face facts, and that can be a crushing experience. But if, again, we see Saturn as the wise Native-American grandmother who guides us patiently and protects us when we need her, then our Neptune can look forward to her spirituality, compassion, and imagination being given real roots in the real world.

SATURN/PLUTO

Here's another interesting astrological combination. Start with Pluto, the place in all of us where we just love Total and Complete Change. Add a visit from serious, staid Saturn, the greatest fan ever of Just Hanging On. Needless to say, this pairing can give rise to amazing inner conflicts. Whenever your Pluto is triggered, your urge to trash everything and start over again is also triggered. When it's Saturn that's doing the triggering, however, the same restrictions that you're feeling the urge to cut unceremoniously out of your life may just be the ones that seem to refuse to let you go. The Old Nay-Sayer never did know when to quit—and Pluto is always up for a challenge. It only makes him stronger.

See, Saturn loves to build walls to Keep Change Out. Pluto erodes everything eventually, walls included. He's the purveyor of Change, the planet that understands that Nothing Lasts Forever. So imagine the type of circumstances you might come up against when Saturn tries to hold Pluto's evolutionary urges in check.

First off, especially in the case of a difficult conjunction, Pluto will only take this Holding On Thing for so long. Then he'll lose his patience. In other words, we'll make changes—and they'll be absolute, fueled by the determination we feel after fighting a war for too long. If the conjunction is a bit easier, as described by the condition of Pluto in our natal chart, and a past history of cooperating with Saturn, then this can be a time when inevitable changes come to us easily, when we're strengthened by the support of the Powers That Be. Under these circumstances, we often find that Authority Figures understand our situation, and see the necessity for us to stop fighting a losing battle.

Under the square or opposition, the issue is learning a difficult lesson through Trial and Effort, and, after many lost battles, winning the war. It's kind of like what happens at the end of a *Friday The 13th* horror movie, which, of course, takes place at a Summer Camp, a few days before it's due to open. The cast of teen-age counselors is inevitably reduced to One, and that One is obviously in charge of killing the killer. But no one said he'd go down easy. First, our hero strangles the maniac. He stops, gasping for breath after the struggle, and leans cautiously over the killer to make sure he's not breathing. Of course, the demon jumps up and grabs the hero by the throat, and the battle is on again.

After another amazing struggle, during which the killer is shot seventeen times, then thrown out of a canoe into the lake, the hero settles down on the front porch of one of the cabins for a good cry. But wait—here comes the killer again, dragging his bloody body across the lawn, this time armed with a pitchfork. The hero leaps into action, tackles the killer, and finally does kill him. Roll credits.

No, it's not a day at the beach for the hero, but what a great part to play. He's gotten himself noticed in the eyes of the camp directors, the parents of the kids who might've been killed if they'd been there, and the State Cops who arrive just seconds after the killer finally, finally dies. Our hero is exhausted from the struggle, but empowered by the battle. His life will never be the same, but his character has been bolstered by the odds he's overcome and the fact that he did overcome them.

Now, things are a bit less dramatic under the trines and sextiles from Saturn to Pluto. The cops show up at the beginning of the movie, and our hero has the potential killer tied up and properly incapacitated. Oh, and the teen-age cast gets to live. In other words, we see a problem coming early on, solve it easily, and still get the medal of honor. All Authority Figures are much more cooperative when Pluto gets an easy visit from Saturn— and all our battles end more quickly and easily.

This is another of those powerful transits, when we're capable of almost superhuman deeds. The circumstances may differ, but the result will be the same. We'll emerge In Charge of our lives, with a confidence that will get us through even the most difficult times in the future. Remember, both Saturn and Pluto are relentless. It's up to us to use that endless energy to overcome obstacles, end situations that have gone past the point of no return, and become our own hero/ine.

CHAPTER TEN

INTERMISSION

The Outer Planets and 'I Will Never' Syndrome...

Well, here we are at the Outer Planet Section. Now, I know we've already talked about the differences between Outer Planet Transits and Inner Planet Transits, but let's go over it again. Just for the heck of it. First off, and most importantly, all three Outers tend to stay put for a long, long time. Uranus, the quickest of the three, spends about 7 years in a sign, for example. If we give a transit a 5 degree applying and 5 degree separating orb of significance, that means for a third of that time—roughly 2 and a half years—Uranus will be in the neighborhood of your natal planet. He'll make three to five passes across the exact degree, shaking things up, rocking tradition, and daring that planet to try anything and everything—or stay in that rut. Neptune and Pluto hang around for at least three years—during which time your planet either Gets Religion (as with Neptune) or Gets 'Way Intense (as per Pluto). Regardless of which of the three Outers comes to visit, your natal planet forgets what life was like before they arrived—and begins acting out a lot of the qualities of the visitor, just as we often pick up expressions or habits when we live with someone, or new accents when we move across the country, or across the ocean.

Well, it's true that The Outers hang around far too long to be ignored. But there's another thing that happens under Outer Planet Transits that's rather specific to Uranus, Neptune, and Pluto. It's called the "I Will Never" Syndrome. It happens when the Universe provides opportunities for us to eat our words, and we take those opportunities—with gusto. You know exactly what I mean here, because we've all done it. Taken oaths we swore we'd never break, made resolutions we were sure would hold up, and promised ourselves never, ever to do certain things—and then done them. It's all part of being human. Well, in the spirit of adding a bit of humor and understanding to the process, let's take a look at this common affliction through a Fictional Reenactment. Let's have some fun with The Outers—since they often seem to be having so much fun with us. So sit tight and pretend you're watching *Cops*, or *911*, or *Baywatch*. (Okay, you ladies forget *Baywatch*. I hate it, too.) Anyway...

PICTURE THIS SCENE, IF YOU WILL:

Three rather striking figures sit casually around the edge of a circular cloud, staring into the center, sipping some wonderful potion and bemusedly watching the activities of The Mortals below. Occasionally, they elbow one another and point. You've heard of Surfing the Net? Well, it's similar. This version, however, is called Surfing the Populace—and you've got to be an Immortal to get on-line. Just in case you're not—an Immortal, that is—and just in case you're a fire-sign, and, as always, in a hurry to cut to the chase, allow me to introduce you to The Immortals I'm talking about, The Cast themselves, Uranus, Neptune, and Pluto.

Uranus is dressed in a long white robe—a cold, frozen, robe that crackles when he walks like a sheet that's been left out on the clothesline too long in February. He, of course, isn't really watching the show, and he isn't really sitting around casually. He's pacing, tapping, and staring off straight ahead into space, icy blue eyes fixed on The Future, automatically understanding exactly what the end result of all actions will be.

To his left is Neptune, dressed in her most beautiful pink gown, trusty pink smoke machine by her right side, bucket of pink dust on her left, ready to snap the machine on and toss a handful of dust down on whoever or whatever she sees as a little too harshly realistic for her tastes. Occasionally, she sniffles and dabs a tear away when one of The Mortals does something Dreadfully Romantic or Wonderfully Compassionate.

Pluto, dressed—you guessed it—all in black, is glaring over the edge of that same cloud, arms crossed, head cocked attentively forward.

Sound familiar? Well, if it does, here's why: Remember the scene from *Clash of the Titans* that showed the Gods and Goddesses seated around a circle of clouds, watching and discussing whatever it was Perseus was up to at the moment? Know what They always say about movies? That It's Only A Movie? Well, maybe They're wrong about that one—maybe the gods and goddesses really do that—check in on us, that is. Maybe they listen to us, too, and monitor our conversations pretty darned carefully, particularly when they catch any of us righteously making this proclamation:

"I will **never**...."

Doesn't matter what you finish that sentence up with—if you started it with those three words, somebody sitting around that cloud-circle is going to hear it. Then, whoever's On Duty at the moment, (whether it's Uranus on a swing-shift, Pluto on night-shift, or Neptune just snapped out of a daydream), whoever it is that hears you utter those fateful words leans over, taps Mercury on the arm, and says, "Jot that down."

Mercury, of course, looks a lot like Matthew Broderick in his role as Phillippe "The Mouse" in *Ladyhawke*. Although he understands exactly what's about to go down, he's still operating from a very keen memory of what happened to someone called Prometheus, (concerning the vulture and the cliff), the last time he tried to help The Mortals, so he snaps to attention and dutifully records the latter half of our sentence. Whatever we decided we'd just never do is now public record, up on Mt. Olympus. That done, The Outers return to sipping nectar, and the matter is ended.

That is, it's ended for the moment—but only until one of The Big Three happens to be in the neighborhood of that planet or point we were righteously proclaiming would never...Whatever. The Outer in the neighborhood of our planet stops, pulls out their galactic cell-phone, and dials up Mercury, who answers immediately, of course. They say something like "Hey, I'm in Seattle—pull Whatzername's 'Never' file and fax me the Moon section, wouldja?" Mercury sends the Never file along, and the Outer gets to work on the project.

Oh, sure, it sounds crazy. But what other explanation could there possibly be? How else could The Outers know just how to completely turn our lives upside down? How else could they know exactly which corners of our neat little existence to shake out and shake up?

Now, granted, that's a humorous way of looking at what sometimes are quite serious situations, but it's also true, isn't it? Don't we find ourselves doing everything we swore we'd never do, under Outer Planet transits? Everything from taking up golf to quitting—or starting—smoking, moving out of the house we lived in for twenty years—whatever. Isn't it true that no matter what we were absolutely adamant about never, ever doing, that's exactly what we do, at some point, via an Outer Planet Transit?

Sure it is. That's why you're sitting there shaking your head.

So why do you s'pose that is? Why do we find ourselves doing everything exactly as we swore we never would when one or more of The Big Three are in the neighborhood? You don't think it's because we want to, do you? What a thought! Maybe all that time we were spouting all that Never stuff, in reality, we were just trying to talk ourselves out of doing those things—and maybe those things were what we most wanted to do, but couldn't work up the Ooomph to do them yet.

Hoo, boy. That type of possibility really wreaks havoc on your head, hmm? Especially if you take a moment to consider all the Never's you've uttered recently.

Well. Needless to say, Outer Planet transits aren't boring. They are, however, disruptive. Just how disruptive they are depends on how true you've been to yourself thus far, and how stifled or repressed you've kept the parts of yourself that are about to be set off by Uranus, Neptune, or Pluto.

See, all of the Outers have a "Make Things Change" Clause built right into their contracts. They show up, symbolically speaking, when it's time to shake us up, to knock us out of those tight little ruts we've been comfortably stuck in. Sometimes we're conscious of how badly we want Out of wherever we've been, and sometimes we're not. If we are conscious of needing a break in our routine, well, then, even when situations come along that are less than ideal, we're more able to gracefully surrender what seems to be leaving our lives, and set to work re-creating New Stuff. If we're not conscious of how badly we want Out, on the other hand, we may view these Big Changes as bad. Either way, however, Change Happens, and our best bet is to cooperate. In a nutshell, then, the Outers represent times when we make Evolutionary Leaps. Deciding where to leap, and how fast, is what these next three chapters are all about.

CHAPTER ELEVEN

URANUS: A VISIT FROM THE LOON

Your Uranus Kit:

A Surprise Visit From Captain James T. Kirk
A Copy of all the *Star Wars* Films
A Lightning-rod
A Winning Lottery Ticket
A Fall-Out Shelter
A Computer, With World-Wide-Web Software Already Installed,
and Free Internet Access
A Copy of Your Astrology Chart
A Junior Scientist Kit
A Ride On The Space Shuttle
A Subscription to *Discover* Magazine
A Shock-Absorber

Uranus Transits:
Just Get Yourself Free...

There's a planet out there who believes that Independence is the order of the day, every day, that rules are made specifically to be broken, and that total and complete personal freedom is the only way to go—regardless of the consequences. He's always at his rebellious best, ready to surprise even you at the things he'll inspire you to say and do. Meet Uranus, the Head of the Department of One Never Knows, the planet of shocks, surprises, and sudden reversals. As much as Saturn is the technology we use when it's time to conform, go by the rules, and Act Appropriately, Uranus is the planet we look to for help when it's time to do the unpredictable, the erratic, and the unstable. Remember, this is the planet who just can't stand "shouldn't's," who considers "No" and "Don't" invitations to Do Just That.

Now, life on this planet provides plenty of situations where we're put in the position of not being able to act the way we really want to. When Uranus is in the neighborhood, however, holding back will only last for so long. He wakes you up to how confined you feel, breaks you out of your rut, and gets you free. These are times when even the most conservative among us suddenly (and I do mean suddenly) break tradition, in order to shock and amaze the masses.

See, Uranus loves suddenness—he's in charge of all kinds of sudden events—everything from lightning and tornadoes to winning the lottery or witnessing a plane crash in your front yard. He's also a computer wizard, the planet who's most involved in mass communication. Wherever he's traveling in your chart is a place where you'll have genius potential, where you'll be bold enough to ignore the old way to solve a problem, and, instead, find a whole new way. You might even invent something in the process. Major scientific and technological breakthroughs like the Space Program, the World Wide Web, and the Information Superhighway were all inspired by just that type of Uranian genius.

Under all Uranus transits, we do the unexpectable and unpredictable. The subject is freedom. And Uranus transits are not boring times. We act exactly as we shouldn't—according to society's standards, at least—to let everyone know how Different we are. We feel inspired, invigorated, and unrestrained—for the first time in Forever. Exciting, unusual circumstances happen along. These are times when The Universe seems absolutely bent on helping you to get yourself free. You're about to be liberated, Big Time. In a variety of ways. You'll be amazed, in fact, at just how many ways you'll find to display your newfound independence. And the more unable you've felt to Be Yourself, the more surprising the transit will be—both to you and to others. Sometimes we humans get so embedded in our routines that it takes a good jolt to get us out of it.

URANUS AND 'BUFFERS'

Quite often, temporary people arrive under Uranus transits to provide that jolt. I like to think of them as "Buffers." They walk into your office or your local hangout one day, say something that captures your attention and holds it, and within weeks, they're inspiring you to make radical changes in your life—changes you would have thought were totally Out Of The Question not too long ago.

Most often, they do their job by providing just exactly what you've just recently realized was sorely, sorely missing from your life. Might be freedom, might be romance, might even be financial independence. Depends on the house or planet Uranus visits with. Whatever. Somehow, they epitomize your heart's desire. They support you in your quest for it, tell you why you're right to want it, and stand by, nodding, with their arms folded while you A) quit the job you've had and hated for five years, B) end your marriage because you want to try true independence, C) move to Sri Lanka, or D) who the hell knows. Then they leave. Yes, just like that. They're Outta There. And don't doubt for a minute that they're permanently gone, too, because they are—no matter what they tell you, up to five minutes before they actually walk out the door.

Sure, you're crushed. And scared, too. You've just trashed something you thought you'd never be brave enough to even change a little bit. You did it because you had the support of your Buffer, and now they're gone. Poof. Just like they were never there at all—with the exception of the holes you'll say they punched in your life. What you'll discover later on is that these folks aren't meant to be permanent fixtures in your photo album—and much later on, you'll realize that you really wouldn't have wanted them to be, anyway. Buffers function as exciting, pretty "lures." They're messengers you choose because of their message. So no matter how crazy that message seems at the time, if it feels right to you, if it feels like you're breaking free of should's and ought to's, en route to doing what you truly want to do, you might want to listen up.

Keep in mind that you've allowed this person into your reality just long enough for them to wake you up to what's got to go, right now, if you're going to get on with your next step. Buffers usually bring about a serious tumult in your life—but they're also pretty darned exciting. When they arrive, recognize them, enjoy them, and think about what they're providing for you. Don't try to hold on when they get up to leave either. Just enjoy the ride.

Uranus Through The Houses

In general, with Uranus, it's best to remember that he doesn't have lot of patience, and he's got other stops to make. When he bangs on the door of one of your houses and invites you to go, just get in the car and buckle up. Forget packing anything—whatever it is, you won't need it. It belonged to who you were, not who you're going to be at the end of the ride. Besides, he'll be happy to leave without you—for the moment. Problem is, he'll come back, because he knows your itinerary much better than you do, and he's your ride to the next stop. The next time he happens by to pick you up, however, he may not bang on the door of your house— he may drive through your living room window.

What all this adds up to is a wonderful, frightening, liberating, frightening, invigorating, frightening time. As with all of the Outers, we notice his presence most when he first enters a house. It's as if someone powerful has just moved into your home, for a good, long stay, and you're suddenly put in the position of hosting them—and rebuilding your life around your guest. With Uranus, the guest is totally unpredictable. So, at first, the house he moves into is a place where the Status Quo is totally upset, and schedules are impossible to keep. You can no longer keep your life in order—especially if he's touching a planet that happens to live there.

On the downside, all this disruption means that the side of you who lives there is going to seem erratic, unstable, and inconsistent to others—and the Others you handle with that side of you will seem equally off to you. Remember, this is your transit, you're in charge, and sometimes you've got to completely disrupt things to set them straight.

On the upside, you won't care. You'll have a whole new attitude with regard to the matters that pertain to that house, and Being You will be your first priority. When The Great Liberator arrives, whatever you really want to do will be exactly what you'll do. If he enters your sixth house, for example, you may quit your job on the way to work. When he raps at the door of the seventh, you'll A) tell your spouse or Significant Other that you need much more personal freedom than you've had, so you're off to L.A., B) find your Other saying the same thing to you, C) look for a partner who allows you to truly be that side of your personality, no matter how radically you decide to act it out right now, or D), who the hell knows. Remember that D) is always an option under Uranus transits, and that no matter which Uranus transit you happen to be having, there's really only one stock line that works, only one thing to say that will cover it all. Stay loose, fasten your seat belts, put those tray tables in the Up position, and be ready for anything.

FIRST HOUSE

Who was that, just then? That's what folks will say when they see you walk by—even if they've known you for years. They won't be able to recognize you from one encounter to the next—much less understand why you're acting That Way. See, this is the Front Door of your house, the place folks see before they get in close enough for a visit. Any planet that enters changes the entire appearance of the house by its presence—and with Uranus, that can mean many things. You may decide you'd just love to have purple hair for awhile, or that it's time to pierce your nose, or that you're going on a crash diet. Maybe you're suddenly aware that you don't like the way you dress, and you trash your entire Donna Karan wardrobe to dress in Birkenstocks, purple Peruvian vests, and reflector sunglasses. Whatever the changes are that you make right now to your appearance, they're going to be striking. And your new "Look" will be set off marvelously by your new Attitude.

See, when Uranus enters the house, it's time to let go, stop worrying about What They'll Say, and Be Yourself—and you'll especially want to demonstrate all those sides of You you've been stifling for so long. So if you've always thought of yourself as a cowboy or cowgirl, you'll now become that cowboy or cowgirl. Remember, we make outer changes so that they'll act as a billboard of sorts, so that others will see The New Us, and have no choice but to accept us. We'll also be out to shock and amaze Others when this transit hits—and there's no telling what we'll do to make sure the message gets across. It's even possible that we'll surprise ourselves with what we'll do when this Wild And Crazy Guy crosses our Ascendants. One thing's for sure: we won't be boring.

SECOND HOUSE

Congratulations! You've just won the lottery! Um, I mean, Your company has been downsized and you've just lost your job. No, wait, you've just been called into the boss's office to ask if you'd like the position of Junior Partner—and, of course, that would involve doubling your current salary. Yes, any and all of those scenarios are possible when Uranus enters the second house— along with a thousand others neither of us could possibly imagine. See, your second house is where the side of your personality lives that selects and cares for possessions, and keeps track of the checkbook. When Mr. Unpredictable gets into town, one never knows what might happen to your financial situation. Might be great. This is the type of transit that Overnight Million- aires are made of. Might not be so great. This is also the type of transit that Overnight Paupers are made of. So in some cases, you might feel as if The Universe is rearranging your income without having a meeting with you about it.

Then again, this is the planet of Independence, and the second house reflects what we're willing to do for our daily bread. Which means we might just decide that it's time to take the show on the road all by ourselves and start our own business, or branch out on our own for the first time ever. Who knows? (This is one of those D) transits, in other words.)

Of course, if you're financially set, and you don't experience a major change in your money situation, keep in mind that your taste in possessions is about to undergo a change, too. You'll begin shopping for unique items—for the one thing that no one else has. You may also develop an interest in gadgets—electronic ones, maybe. Because Uranus rules computers and space-age technology in general, this transit can also mark the beginning of your career as the proud parent of a computer—which will wreak havoc on your checkbook, regardless of which model you choose. No matter which (and it may be all) of these scenarios you experience, remember to keep careful financial records with this guy rummaging around in your pocket. It may not make the changes any less drastic, but it will help you to keep tabs on where the money you do have is going.

THIRD HOUSE

Whoops, gotta go. Right now. When Uranus enters this house, better get used to that. This transit is all about moving quickly— both intellectually and physically. Now, this can mean that life suddenly requires you to make lots of quick trips throughout your Little World when you least expect it. Maybe your new fondness for Sudden Movement means that you join a Storm-Chasers group and set off driving through the panhandle of Oklahoma, pursuing tornadoes with a group of interesting strangers. Who knows? Even if you stay put in your neighborhood, the routes you automatically take to travel through it may suddenly change, forcing you to change directions at the last minute.

Your ability to move through your day may also change— due to a move or job change, for example. Or your method of transportation may become erratic, unstable, or unpredictable at times. This house reflects your habits, remember—and when Uranus arrives, habits and routine are hard to keep the same. Nobody loves to shake up routines like this guy, and nobody's better at coming up with a most unusual way to shake you up, Wake You Up out of your routine, and get you to see where you are and what you're spending your days doing.

Now, in addition to navigation (which is simply the way we communicate with our environment), this house also rules the style you've developed to learn basic tasks and have light conversation. So it might be your mind that gets the wake-up call, and you may be suddenly drawn to learning a very Uranian thing, like computers, astrology, science fiction, meteorology, or a science. Regardless of which level you're experiencing at the moment, learn to expect the unexpected from your thoughts and your environment. Fasten your seat belt, and pay attention.

FOURTH HOUSE

This house is where you stash the side of you who handles The Nest, and the emotional memories you built it from. Your childhood home, your family, and your present digs are all part of that. When Uranus hits town, all kinds of things are possible. The classic interpretation is that you may move suddenly, but someone may also move in (or out) of your home without much notice. A child goes through a divorce and moves back home suddenly, or your roommate may decide to leave for

Sri Lanka—tomorrow. Maybe you're stunned to learn that you're going to have a child yourself.

Then, too, if it's not a person who serves as the agent for change in your home under this transit, nature could step in. A tree falls on your house during a storm, and although it seems like a tragedy at first, the insurance money allows you to rebuild a whole new room or two. Maybe it's just the tone of your home that changes—it's suddenly much, much busier, with all kinds of unusual folks visiting. Uranus rules electricity and electronics, too. Apply that to your physical home, and you might experience anything from needing to re-wire the whole house to turning your den into a computer-room.

Now, this house is also where you keep your Memories, as I said. With Uranus here, then, don't be surprised if you find yourself suddenly remembering things from childhood you hadn't thought about in years. You may also find yourself feeling much braver and more independent than you have in the past— a signal that you're ready to break free of some type of emotional conditioning that's kept you suppressed or stuck for too long. At any rate, there's something about your physical abode, your emotional roots, and your view of The Past that's about to change. When Uranus roots around in our symbolic cellars, there's no telling what he's about to bring up the stairs with him. No matter what that is, it's designed to help you to see that all influences from the past aren't necessarily important to your emotional security forever. Enjoy this transit, whether you end up living in the south of France, or spending your time in front of a computer.

FIFTH HOUSE

Okay, so he (or she) is seven feet tall, of an entirely different race, religious or ethnic background, and maybe even the opposite gender than you ordinarily date. Who knows? Who cares? Well, you do—but you're not going to be at all concerned about What The Neighbors Think of your new Other. You're going to care about Expressing Yourself through your playmates and your lovers— and the more shocking they are, the better you'll like them. See, when Uranus sets up shop in this fifth house, the side of you who determines what Fun might be is ready for anything—the wilder the better. And if you're going to be radical in your choice of entertainment, you'd better have willing partners. So The Ideal Date might be quite radical too—at least to the outside world.

What's going to be fun? Well, if you're experiencing the radical, rebellious side of Uranus, fun might be skydiving, or driving a race-car, or bungee-jumping. Anything that's completely out of the ordinarily will do. If you're feeling more of the scientific side of this planet, however, you may find yourself spending every evening out in the driveway with a high-powered telescope, looking for the next Hale-Bopp comet with your new Other, who happens to be an astronomer. Whatever else happens, you're out for Brand-New Experiences, and exciting, unusual people to share them with. Just be careful, and remember—unless you've got some pretty radical tastes in relationships to start with—it's only a transit.

On the other hand, this house also refers to the side of you who hangs with The Kids. So you might suddenly find yourself spending lots more time in the company of young folks. If that's the case, they'll look at you as a shining example of Independence, Individuality, and Personal Freedom. They'll see you as unlike any other Adult they know. Of course, during this transit, you're going to be unlike any adult they know, Just make sure you don't cross any lines you'll regret crossing when Saturn comes to town.

SIXTH HOUSE

This is the house that rules health, and work, and The Rhythm of Your Day. Needless to say, then, just for starters, you can forget about keeping any kind of schedule when Uranus arrives. That's out of the question now. You won't know what to expect from one day to the next—and that's going to suit you just fine. You may find that your present job suddenly changes somehow, or that your co-workers change rapidly, or that they're much more interesting people. If you've been feeling as if your personal freedom or individuality is restricted at work, you may also quit your job, quite suddenly. On the way to work, for example. See, when Uranus gets here, you won't be able to stand spending all those Quality Hours of your life doing anything you don't absolutely feel is a genuine expression of Who You Are. So if you've been trying to fit yourself into a situation that's just not right for you, all it takes is one good Mars transit to inspire you, and you won't be able to bring yourself to go back to that place of imprisonment any more. And you may do that several times when Uranus is in this house— so don't expect your work-history to be stable for awhile.

On the other hand, if you're a conservative soul who never quit a job without notice in your life, maybe you'll simply change jobs, in orderly fashion—to take up work in a Uranian field, such as astrology or science. If you're already interested in Deep Space, you might get hired on at NASA. Whatever it is, it better be different enough on a daily basis to keep you interested, or you'll quit, start an entirely new job at an entirely new place, and do it all over again. Then again, this is one of the transits that indicates that it's time to strike out on your own and become self-employed.

Now, as I said, this house also relates to your health, since it's the side of you who Takes Care of Bizness and performs those tasks or duties you need to perform to keep yourself Functioning down here on Planet Number Three. So watch your health quite carefully now, too. This doesn't necessarily mean that a sudden health crisis will come up, only that you'll need to watch carefully for any signs of changes in the condition of your body. On a much less serious level, you may suddenly gain or lose weight, too.

In all, this transit is all about learning what types of conditions you enjoy on a daily basis, and what type of daily schedule you can set up that will best suit your natural, internal clock. Listen carefully, and don't try to keep yourself chained up to a job or a time-clock that just isn't right for you.

SEVENTH HOUSE

Well, now, here's the house where you keep the side of you who decides what A Partner should be. See, we tend to choose our One-to-One partners (both business and personal) because they allow this side of us to come out and play when they're around. When Uranus gets here, everything you've previously seen as qualifying factors in that choice will change. If you've always thought commitment was the way to go, you might now decide that's not right for you, that it's not rational to expect any of us to have only one person in our lives forever. In that case, you may decide you'd rather not be married after all—the day before the wedding, or after 32 years. Or you may hire the part out, and the person you really want may burst through the church doors just as you reach the altar and voice their objection to your marriage. You'll probably leave with them, too. Ever seen that in the movies? Well, it's entirely possible for it to really happen, right now, with Uranus in this house. On a less striking level, you may also find yourself simply longing for more personal freedom in your primary relationship. Regardless of what the circumstances are, you're looking for change now—and that's that.

Then, too, you may decide that you do want a partner, but find that your choice of partner has changed, and that you're now much more In The Mood for someone Uranian—a scientist, astrologer, or computer whiz would be ideal, but anyone who's unlike anyone you've ever known will do just fine. This is also the side of us who comes out when we're simply relating on a One-to-One basis—regardless of the intimacy of the connection. Which means that you may find yourself meeting the most unusual people you've ever met right now—under most unusual circumstances, too. There's something about the way you ordinarily relate to An Other that's got to change now, to allow you to truly Be You, no matter who you're facing—and you're ready to burn bridges, if need be, to do it.

EIGHTH HOUSE

Here's the house that's traditionally given to Pluto and Scorpio, the purveyors of Heavy Stuff, like Sex, Death, Loss, and Taxes. Sounds scary, huh? Well, relax—because basically, this is just the side of you who handles situations of power and control—and that conjures up a number of possible scenarios when you add the element of Unexpectability. First off, let's deal with The Death Thing—and please don't expect that everyone in your family will die suddenly when Uranus transits this house—I don't care what the olde books say. Although I'd be lying if I said you might not experience the sudden loss of someone or something when Mr. Unexpected visits this house, that's not all there is to it. In actuality, anything that abruptly changes your deepest emotional ties is read as a crisis—or a death— by your inner self. Marriage, (traditionally seen as a good thing, legend has it), is a great big crisis, for example. There goes your independence. All of a sudden, you're sharing everything. All it takes to trigger this Crisis Director in you is a change—for better or worse—that's inevitable, final, or profound. Think of how it feels to win the Presidency...talk about a crisis,

Needless to say, crises come in both good and bad packages, but regardless of what happens now, these sudden life occurrences will provide you with the opportunity to be objective, detached, and scientific in your handling of them—a la Uranus' gift for standing back from a situation to take a good look, rather than being too involved. So don't be afraid. Understand that it's time to learn all about how to handle Sudden Change without falling apart—and that you were due for a huge evolutionary leap, anyway.

Of course, this is also the side of you who's up for Intense Experiences, the side of you who craves Life-and-Death scenarios. After all, you never really know what life is until you're standing at death's door. And speaking of The D Word, remember that there are also many types of death. Moving. Career changes. Cosmetic Surgery. Anything that puts a rapid-fire end to who you were en route to making you someone new qualifies. Remember also that each type of death is immediately followed by the birth of something new, and that the rebirth process starts as soon as an end is finalized. Although Uranus will bring these changes about when (and how) you least expect them, it's because it's time to clear the boards for new life—it's time for a rebirth of some aspect of You. Besides, surprises are his job.

Now, this is the side of you who handles the issues of taxes and joint finances and inheritances, too. Or shared resources, as They say. So you may well be audited for the first time in your life, or decide to invest in a computer company with a partner, or receive a large sum of money from an Uncle you never met. Who knows?

Now, Intimacy, both physical and otherwise, is also handled by this side of you, and Uranus isn't the warmest, cuddliest guy out there—he's much more into experimentation. So this may also be a transit that brings out the more, shall we say, unusual side of your sexuality. You're looking for exciting, extreme ways to bond—or to cut those bonds. Just realize that this transit is all about waking you up to who and what you really are underneath the exterior trappings. Pay attention to how you react to life during this time, and you'll learn a great deal about the mystery of You. Quickly.

NINTH HOUSE
When Mr. Unpredictable enters any house, it's time to shake things up a bit. When he pops into your ninth house for a nice, long, seven-year stay, it's time to stretch your consciousness in ways you never thought you would. So since this house refers to long trips, among other things, better make sure your passport is current, because One Never Knows where you might end up.

Paris? Sounds great—after all, you've always wanted to go there. How's next week?

Will it happen that suddenly? You bet it will. You'll be quite open to changes of scenery now, and quite open to changing your mind about which scenery you'd like to see, too—suddenly. This is the transit that flying to Vegas for lunch was born from—if you don't decide that Cabo might be warmer, that is, minutes before you're about to board. See, when Uranus trips through this house, you're game for anything and everything, including last-minute turnarounds—as long as you end up being somewhere or doing something exciting. Remember, the ninth house is the side of us with perpetual Grass Is Greener Syndrome. It's where we're always looking for newness—for what's just over the next state line. Uranus inspires that side of us to Just Do It—all in the name of learning something new.

Now, speaking of learning, keep in mind that you don't absolutely have to become a Jet-Setter to get a bird's-eye view of the planet. You can educate yourself, too—a most mind-expanding hobby. So don't be surprised when you develop an interest in sci-fi, computers, astrology, or UFOs, and find yourself signing up for classes or out of town seminars on one or all of those topics. Uranus' love of the odd and unusual mixes well with the ninth house's quest to Learn Everything.

Since this house also has everything to do with politics, religion, and your own personal philosophies, you might also get ready to Rebel, Big Time, against whatever the current Conventional Wisdom happens to be. If you've always been conservative, now's when you'll be amazingly liberal—with a revolutionary streak, to boot. If you've always been liberal, now's when you'll start looking for Lyndon LaRouche's address, to start your own chapter. Likewise, your views on whatever religion you've been raised into also stand to change. Even if you were weaned on a very traditional belief-system, you may discover Animism, or Wicca, or decide that you've been a closet agnostic all these years. Whatever it is, your new religion is going to reflect a taste for the decidedly-not-mainstream.

In all, your wide-angle lens is about to get even wider—suddenly. Life will provide you with opportunities to let the conscious side of your mind come out to play. Remember, we're only wide-awake when we're in unfamiliar territory, or learning something brand-new. Again, make sure you've got a passport, and that your college transcripts are current. You're about to embark on a learning adventure.

TENTH HOUSE

After ten years in the business, you decide you don't want to be an interior decorator, after all. You'd much rather be a computer analyst, astrologer, or a self-employed Whatever. So you resign from your position at the office, impending promotion or no, and strike out on your own. That's what it's like when Uranus enters the tenth house. Self-employment is really big under this transit, as are drastic career changes. So if whatever you're doing isn't helping you to display your individuality to the world, if you're feeling as if you've been performing duties, rather than Being Who You Really Are For All The World To See, don't worry. All that's about to change. And by the way, it's also possible to become quite famous—or infamous—now. This is the transit that overnight successes are made of—especially if you happen to be taking up a career in one of the more Uranian fields of endeavor, like science, telecommunications, astrology or anything else that's futuristic or unusual. You may change your mind several times over this period, too.

This tenth house also refers to our attitude about Authority Figures, those folks who are in charge of our lives in some way. Now, you know how Uranus feels about Them—the Authorities, that is. He sees them as the Keepers of The Past, the folks who want to keep you stuck inside rules and regulations, rather than allowing you to grow as an individual. So when he's here, you may have a bit of a chip on your shoulder when you encounter one of Them—even if the individual happens to be the signer of your paycheck. Often, when Uranus is especially active in our tenth house, we send out very subtle messages to The Higher-Ups that we're not going to cooperate. They, of course, don't appreciate this much, so they tighten up on us even more. We, in turn, inspired by The Loon, pull away even further, say "No, I won't," a few more times, and cross our arms a lot.

Eventually, we end up getting fired, and much as we won't admit it, we're secretly delighted. We're free, out from under Their thumbs, ready to become Master or Mistress of all we survey. It's called Professional Liberation, and it's what we're really after—but we can't tell our Saturns, so we play through.

Now, career is just a part of our Public Image. This is also the side of you who determines what the public sees and knows about you—your reputation, that is. When Uranus gets here, your life opens wide—for all to see. Lots of folks get married suddenly, get divorced suddenly, or do something that forces the world's eyes to turn to them in shock and amazement. Basically, you're about to make a spectacle of yourself in the Publicity Department. So when you see that Mr. Amaze-The-Masses is about to pass through this house, make sure you don't do anything you won't want to see on the front page of the newspaper tomorrow morning. Because you might.

ELEVENTH HOUSE

Although this house has always been given over to Friendships, and Goals—which didn't make sense to me, for a long time—there's a lot more to it than that. This is the place where we discover what Strength In Numbers is all about. It's the side of us that comes out when we're in the company of Kindred Spirits—the side that's acutely aware when we're not with them. So when Uranus transits this house, you're due to discover a whole new peer group. Suddenly you realize that you have absolutely nothing in common with most of your friends. If you've always hung out at Tommy's Bar and Grill, drinking long-necks with bikers, you may find yourself suddenly wanting to sip a nice Chardonnay with the lawyers at the Sheraton—or versa vice. You'll be looking for your true Equals—and you may switch groups several times over this transit before you find the right ones.

Now, about the Friends and Goals thing. See, believe it or not, the folks we associate with have everything to do with who we become when we grow up. If we're hanging at the Sheraton, it's hard to make contacts for the Toy Run, and if we're hanging at Tommy's, it's tough to chat with the DA. So when you see yourself changing your group affiliations, pay attention to who and what you're leaving, and what you're heading toward. In general, when Uranus is here, we're drawn to more unusual types of folks— fringe-groups, you might say. The odder and more eclectic, the better. So don't be surprised to find yourself standing in line to get beamed aboard the Enterprise at a *Star-Trek* gathering, trading paperbacks at a Sci-Fi convention, and, yes, sitting in a classroom at an astrology conference. These times are tailor-made for discovering more about yourself through who you decide you've got a lot in common with.

Your behavior in group situations will also change abruptly now. Again, Uranus loves to make a spectacle of himself, and when he's in this house, he'll inspire you to do just that when you're in the middle of any gathering of three or more. So expect to see what friends you do keep standing around you in stunned silence as you suddenly stand on the kitchen table, wrestle the microphone from the speaker, or stomp from the room in righteous indignation. You're making a statement about the group ideals you're a part of—and you won't stop at anything to be sure everyone hears.

TWELFTH HOUSE

Classically known as the house of Greatest Undoing, and Secret Enemies, you've got to wonder why you'd want a twelfth house at all. I mean, this is the place Ptolemy called The House of the Evil Demon. Hoo-boy, huh? Well, it's not all that bad. This is really just the side of you who comes out in secret places, places of sanctuary, or when you're completely alone. See, it's the room where you hide the side of you who only peeks out when it's absolutely safe. Now, back in olden days, if you had something to hide, it was usually something you could be banished or imprisoned for. Society was much more group-oriented, too—so if you were alone, it wasn't usually for a great reason. Nowadays, however, it's okay to spend time alone. It's perfectly acceptable to be a private person, and undoing simply means not doing. Makes sense if you consider that Doing is under the job description of the side of you who lives in the opposite house, the sixth. In other words, it's all right to retreat from The Others, to pull back and recharge your batteries. It gives you strength for the next round.

Now, retreating is the specialty of your twelfth-house side. Here's where you're an expert at Doing without really Doing, Acting without really Acting, and Being without really Being. This is the side of you who just loves to hide, who feels comforted by silence. You've stashed all the tenderest parts of you here, the parts of you that your environment and your early upbringing (and possibly your past-life history) taught you aren't totally acceptable in public.

Needless to say, this is ordinarily a pretty quiet place. Well, when Uranus arrives, that changes. You find yourself in quite unusual places, telling secrets to very unusual people, doing quite unusual (secret) things. Maybe you decide it's time to unload, and you seek out a therapist. Maybe you head off to a New-Age retreat center to find yourself, or you decide it's time to join a re-enactment group, dress in funny costumes from another time period, and play pretend. Whatever. You're looking for solace and privacy, but whatever that used to be for you is different now. You may also find that those periods of withdrawal come in rather erratic doses now. On Thursday, you're fine, and ready to go out in the world and Do. On Friday, however, you tell everyone you'll be gone for the weekend, take the phone off the hook, and crawl into bed with a good book and the six videos you've rented.

This is also the house that's always been known for its connection to hospitals, asylums, and other wonderful places. So although you may not end up in a straight jacket or in quarantine, you may find yourself dealing with others in those places. Your job, in that case, is to observe what it's like when life steps in and relieves you of all duties. Above all else, remember that this twelfth-house side of you is very shy, and very bruisable. Whatever it is you decide you need to do to recharge, do it. Give yourself time to Be Alone when you need it, and you'll be fine.

URANUS/SUN

In general, during Uranus/Sun transits, you may feel like you're inside one of those Winter Snow-Scene bubble ornaments. You feel as if your life—your whole life, as per the fact that the Sun represents your very core being—has suddenly been picked up and shaken, by what seems like outside forces. What's really happening is much more profound, however—and a lot more exciting. Since the Sun is the real You, and the core You, any planet that transits it signifies a change in the way you see You. Since we're all in charge of just what we fill our lives with, that inner change will manifest through outer events. A job change. A change in your primary relationship. A huge, sudden move. Or maybe all three. Under Uranus transits to the Sun, you may even change your name—quite literally—since you're changing your identity. Other signature aspects of your personality are also up for suddenness now—like your appearance, for example.

Now, with the tough aspects, you're going to be positive that there are Powersomethings That Be out there, busily at work haphazardly and randomly rearranging your life for you—with absolutely no regard for your feelings on the subject. You may get fired "suddenly," for example, or your spouse may casually mention over dinner one night that they've decided to leave you and move to Zimbabwe with someone else—next weekend. Now, you're necessarily going to be shocked, appalled, and dismayed.

Understand, however, that when something like this happens, believe it or not, it's usually for the best. If you examine your feelings honestly, you may also discover that you've been feeling stifled by that job or that relationship. Rather than quit your job or leave your marriage and appear irresponsible, however, you may have been sending out rebel messages, in the form of tiny "resistance" behaviors, until finally, The Boss or your spouse decides enough is enough, and you're ousted, or deserted. Again, on the surface, you'll be quite surprised—but in reality, you're really going to be relieved. You're free. Under tough Uranus/Sun transits, as with any transit, it's really You that does the changing. You're just doing an awful lot more of it at these times, a lot more quickly, too.

The traditionally easy aspects Uranus makes when it touches your Sun bring along changes that are a bit less disquieting than ones that occur under the tough ones—but these changes are just as sweeping, in the long run. As with the harder aspects, once this transit kicks in, your image of You will not be anywhere near what it is before the transit starts. Now, the only way to complete the change, to truly see yourself in that whole new way is by becoming someone new, and that means changing your whole life.

If you're in any ruts when Uranus raps at your Sun's door, you'll have to be ready to get out of them now. The circumstances that jolt you out of your ruts under the easier transits do seem to be a bit smoother than they are under the squares or oppositions, however. Instead of being fired, you get a job offer that's different from any other position you've ever been offered. It's a radical change—in fact, taking the job requires that you move to Africa— or New York City. You're scared, but the company's offered to foot the bill, and they've sent you all kinds of literature on the area where you'll be working, and it looks just beautiful. You've been thinking it was time for a big change, anyway, so....

Go for it. It might be wonderful. Besides, if you don't go, you'll still have to change your whole life.

The real difference between the challenging transits of Uranus and the easy ones seems to be the clean-up period afterwards. With the tougher transits, you've got a lot more to reassemble, wash up, and replace—mainly because the changes happen so abruptly. Regardless of what type of aspect you're experiencing and what actually occurs, you're still going to see yourself in a whole new way. And that's scary, and exciting, and terrifying, and wonderfully invigorating. No matter what else you do now, do yourself a favor: look at Uranus/Sun transits as a chance to be totally You—a chance you won't have again for some time. Enjoy. These transits are only tough to deal with when we try to hang on to what we used to be.

URANUS/MOON

How about moving to Zimbabwe, or Sri Lanka? No? Well, how about moving into a tree house with seven people you're doing a science project with? No? Well, all that might sound like it's out of the question if you're not in the midst of a transit from Uranus to the Moon, but if he's anywhere near this lovely lady in silver in your chart, you're probably shrugging your shoulders, nodding your head, and wondering what the weather is like in Zimbabwe this time of year. See, your natal Moon is a place where you have the urge or need to Root Yourself to the physical world through a home—a home that gives you a safe place to retreat to, no matter what the world tosses your way. As much as our Moons want to stay put, then, we can't grow emotionally if we never go out of the house. So even the most grounded of Moons will now find themselves living with the most uncertain of circumstances, and considering the wildest of living situations, when The Loon stops by.

Under the conjunction, as with the conjunction of Uranus to all our planets, we often feel for some time that a change is coming, and plan for it, internally. We don't actually do anything that those around us can see, however, until the very last minute—which makes our behavior seem totally Out Of The Blue to them. But we know better. We know that we've been growing tired of this place, this town, and this living alone (or with someone), just waiting for the right time to change all that. When this lightning-bolt strikes, then, we're ready. Now's the time. Why wait? We fix dinner on Tuesday night, and pack everything up and move on Wednesday.

The tougher Uranus transits can make you feel as if you're living with an earthquake constantly shaking up the ground beneath you. You want to move—or do you? Or you want to have a child—but do you? You're never quite sure of what you're going to do until the transit happens, (and with Uranus, it seems that the actual event happens when Uranus is exactly at the degree of your natal planet). The jitters are what you'll feel before, as you're considering the action, and after, while you're realizing exactly what you've done. Oh, and speaking of the jitters, let's not forget that there's an Emotional Thing that happens when Uranus grabs our Moon by the collar and turns her around. We feel nervous, and excitable—and it may even be hard to sleep.

Under the easier transits to the Moon, (which, again, depends on our natal Moon's opinion of Uranus to start with), we're less nervous about what we're going to do, and more stimulated by how drastically our lives are going to change afterwards. We're looking forward to Zimbabwe—regardless of the weather, or happily making plans to move into a commune. Group living situations like communes and ashrams, by the way, are a distinct possibility when Uranus touches the Moon, by any aspect. She's out to change where she lives and who she lives with—and in the process, she's going to make sure she can emote more freely, from now on. A rather Uranian urge to adopt may also come along now— and the adoptee may be a stray critter, a computer, or a child from Bosnia. Any transit to the Moon brings out our nurturing instincts—Uranus means we want to nurture someone or something unusual in an unusual way.

Our relationships with our Moms (and the rest of our families, and with women in general, too), are also due for a quick turn-around under any Uranus visit. If we're very close, we might find, suddenly, that we feel distanced from her. If we're not ordinarily close, we may find ourselves spending more time with her, seeing a new side of her. Or she may do something—like announce that she's leaving Dad, or joining the Peace Corps— that knocks our socks off, and allows us to see her as a real individual, instead of Just Mom.

No matter where you move to, what you adopt, or what happens with your Mom, remember that this time is all about you uncovering a previously hidden side of your emotional nature, in order to get to know the You on the inside better.

Don't be afraid of the changes that happen now. Enjoy the scenery, and the newfound freedom of discovering who you are when you're no longer on familiar Home Turf.

URANUS/MERCURY

Think of Mercury as he's always been known—as The Messenger of the Gods. It's his job to shuttle information back and forth from Out There to In Here. Your Mercury is in charge of everything you're aware of, from sights, scents, and sounds to gestures, words, and symbols. Whenever you communicate with your environment in any way, it's your Mercury that's doing it. Now imagine what it feels like when Mercury become Uranus-ized. First of all, the tempo of your life definitely picks up. There's an electric quality to every moment of every day, along with a definite element of Unpredictability. So all your communications with Out There will be quite charged for quite some time, as will your responses to them.

I remember when Uranus last made a major aspect to my Mercury. It was back when he was in Sagittarius, and I loved it. There was always something unexpected waiting for me in the mailbox or on the e-mail, and all kinds of phone messages on the machine. See, this transit links the King of Mass Communications with our own Communication Central. It's like having your personal switchboard on High. Someone from High School contacts you after 20 years of silence, or you bump into someone you knew from Hawaii at a Farmer's Market in Maine. Maybe you find yourself wanting to learn new and unusual ways of communicating, like sign-language or Morse Code. Whatever.

Your mind is having a party right now, enjoying all kinds of New Thoughts and New Ideas. It's fun, it's stimulating, and you probably won't be able to sleep very well. You'll also find yourself just as amazed as Others are at the words that leap from your mouth, unfiltered. Uranus doesn't care much about what others think of him, and when he passes that rebellious quality along to Mercury, whatever you think will quite promptly be what you'll say.

With the conjunction, all this is especially true. You'll be amazed at the thoughts that leap into your mind—and please be sure to jot them down. Uranus' inspirations are often strokes of genius, but they won't stay long, so keep a pencil handy. You're about to be awakened to a new type of understanding of the world. Lots of times, that involves finding astrology, or taking a science class, or becoming fascinated with severe weather. In truth, this transit has the effect of a tornado on your consciousness.

In the case of the tougher transits, breakdowns involving electronic or electrical devices are quite expectable. Your daily trips through the neighborhood may suddenly turn into exciting adventures, too. Sure, that might mean that your car breaks down once or twice, but that's okay. You're supposed to be breaking routine right now, and think of all the interesting people you might meet and have stimulating conversations with if you have to resort to mass transit for a while. And if the copy-machine breaks down just as you approach it, or you end up dealing with electrical problems in your home, don't fight it. Just use that Uranian Genius quality you've been temporarily endowed with to invent a new way to get the job done. Expect to hear all kinds of news that breaks up your daily routine, too. Although all this uncertainty can be pretty darned unsettling when it hits, try to stay loose, be flexible, and enjoy the variety life will insert into every day. And stay away from the coffee-machine—if it works. You won't need any added stimulation—trust me.

Under the easier times, you may be a bit less jangled by unusual life situations, but you'll still learn a valuable lesson on living in unpredictable times. The same messages will arrive on the machine and in the mail-box, but they'll most likely be news of your Liberation in some way. A long-standing obligation will end suddenly, and you'll be free to think of new ways to spend your time. You'll most likely discover what it's like to be owned by a computer, and you may find yourself resenting anything that takes you away from the World Wide Web. Regardless of the transit, you're about to have your eyes opened to the wonders of the technological world. Enjoy your trip on the Information Super-Highway, and be sure to take notes.

URANUS/VENUS

Venus in our natal charts represents who and what we love, and how we love it. So in addition to having your finances do the Feast and/or Famine at least once, via various types of lightning-bolt circumstances that neither you nor I could possibly predict or describe, you should also prepare to be courted by the most amazing assortment of suitors you've ever met. Under these transits, we're attracted to—and we attract—quite an unusual array of prospective Others, some of whom we'll consciously choose because we'll enjoy their rebelliousness, others who'll choose us because we're sending out shock me now vibes, whether we're conscious of doing it or not.

Now, I like to call these folks Buffers, (see the first page in this chapter) and it's only fair to warn you that it's quite possible that these folks may not hang around for too long. Remember, their purpose is to jolt us out of our present circumstances by appearing to provide us with just exactly what we were sorely missing. That done, they may just disappear, leaving us with our lives in a shambles. If that happens, enjoy your Buffer while they're around, and allow them to inspire you to break out of your rut. Just don't get too comfortable, and don't allow yourself to lean on them. Enjoy this new relationship for what it is. Use it to see what it is in yourself that's struggling to break free—the side of your personality that this Other allows you to do. Oh, and one last thing: don't let them drive. (Kidding. Just kidding.)

Now, on the other hand, not everyone who enters your life now is destined to abandon you suddenly. There are Uranian types out there everywhere, not the least of whom are astrologers, computer whizzes, and scientists. So you may also begin a relationship with someone who falls into one of those categories now.

Under the conjunction or the tougher aspects, expect your finances, relationships, and personal values to hit both ends of the bell curve, swinging drastically up and down, probably due to outside circumstances you'll have no way to see coming at you. Expect, too, that your choices in partners may not be welcomed with open arms by Others, and that you may find yourself involved with someone who's making you feel a bit stressed by directly or indirectly showing you how confined you are, in some way, by some aspect of your lifestyle.

When Uranus makes an easier aspect to Venus, you'll be invigorated, excited, and quite ready to make sudden changes to allow who and what you love to more accurately reflect the New You. Your taste in clothing and decorations may change drastically, too. If it does, chances are good you'll be wearing most unusual garb and shopping for One-Of-A-Kind items—anything to let the world know that you're Different now, and not about to conform to society's standards of what you should wear or own. If you've always had a station wagon, you may opt for a red sports-car now, or a motorcycle. If you've always had a motorcycle, you may decide it's time for a motor home. Remember, D) is always an option under Uranus transits—Who The Hell Knows?

URANUS/MARS

What's the last thing in the world you'd ever expect yourself to do right now? Well, that's exactly what you can expect under a Uranus transit to your Mars. Uranus is the planet that revels in suddenness, remember, the planet that delights in last-minute plan changes, complete reversals, and shock effect. Mars is The Way You Take Action—so all your actions will reflect that sudden urge for freedom—100% freedom—to do exactly what you want, exactly when you want to. Mars is also your personal Rambo, remember, so don't be surprised if you seem to have no control over your temper. You're not supposed to be controlling it now—you're supposed to be letting loose. Now, that doesn't mean you should take the neighbor out because they're playing their stereo too loud, too late—but it does mean that you'll be quite ready to knock at their door and mention that you've got to get up early, even if you'd ordinarily just stick a pillow over your head and put up with the noise.

Under the tougher conjunctions, and the more difficult aspects, you'll need to wear a muzzle and have an advisor on hand. See, these are times tailor-made for Being Mad As All Get-Out And Not Taking It Any More—and expressing that anger rather quickly. Picture your Mars, in a combat uniform, being visited by Uranus, The Loon, with a cattle prod in his hand. No matter what you're angry about, then, no matter what you feel you really need to do to defend yourself, you'll do it, regardless of the consequences. Just try to get your Saturn involved before you behead someone.

If you channel all this quick-acting energy into an appropriate project, like taking on an adversary who's been unfairly stifling Your Cause, you can work wonders and become known as a force to contend with. If you attack someone who walks across your lawn, you can bring down the sudden opposition of the police, the military, or other Enforcement Agencies. It's not a bad idea to operate machinery rather carefully now, too. The tougher Uranus/Mars combinations are the stuff that accidents and injuries are made of. Be sure to fasten your seat belt, no matter who's driving, and don't get behind the wheel when you're angry.

When Uranus makes an easier aspect to your Mars, you've still got all the energy you'll need to solve a problem suddenly, but chances are good that life won't present you with quite as many conflicts along the way. Whenever Mars is triggered, life is interesting, as the Chinese say. Add a bit of Uranus, and it becomes interesting even more rapidly. Remember, these are times when you're learning to act quickly, on your own behalf, and to use ingenious methods to Assert Yourself. Just take it easy on the innocent bystanders while you're asserting.

URANUS/JUPITER
Well, now, this is quite the combo. Jupiter is where you're at your most generous, ebullient, and lucky, where you're always ready to take a chance, because you just know in your heart that everything will work out fine. Uranus is a mad professor, a genius/madman who pushes us to rebel, break tradition, and Be An Individual—no matter what the cost. When your Uncle Jupiter gets a visit from Uranus, then, the subject is Risk-Taking, Big Time.

See, neither Uranus nor Jupiter have ever been known for discretion. Both are perpetually In The Mood to jump a little higher, push a little harder, and see just how far they can go in their mission to torture Saturn. So don't be surprised at anything you do when your Jupiter is transited by Mr. Erratic—especially when it's by conjunction. Your optimism reaches new heights now, with an added twist. Maybe it's time to learn parachuting—or maybe you're not risking yourself physically, but you're game to invest in some rather risky stocks. Doesn't matter. Either way, you'll get the great big rush of excitement you're after, and that's what counts, when these two get together.

With the more difficult transits, you may feel as if you're on a roller-coaster—that no one in your life is reliable or responsible. Of course, you may be subtly pushing them away—but you won't see that at the time, most especially if the aspect is an opposition, and you're projecting your restlessness onto An Other, anyway. With the square, you might still feel as if you're on that roller-coaster, but all the ups and downs will be internal, and not quite as noticeable to the outside world—until you snap, and do something everyone Out There will see as crazy.

When the two get together in one of the traditionally easier aspects, the situation is much more mellow, but still far from boring. This transit is the technology behind long-distance conversations, foreign e-mail, winning the lottery, and sudden trips overseas—or all of the above. You may find it very hard to settle down at all, in fact. You're craving New Stuff, Right Now, and with the inspiration of these two egging you on, you'll undoubtedly get it.

URANUS/SATURN

I have a theory. I think Uranus really, really enjoys his transits to Saturn. Saturn's job is to Build Stuff: walls, rules, boundaries, you name it. Now, Uranus, as you know, is the planet who loves to Tear Stuff Down—Suddenly. I mean, one of his official titles includes being the Head of the Department of You'll-Never-Guess-What-Just-Happened. He's the kind of planet who's in charge of gleefully producing The Absolute Last Thing You'd Ever Expect. His job is to snap you into attention and out of that rut you've been in, (see Saturn), to get you to wake up, see the future, and Get what your part in it will be. So when he touches your Saturn, regardless of the aspect, it's time to trash all those carefully-laid plans you've been keeping neatly in place. Needless to say, this makes Uranus one happy planet.

See, Uranus knows that sometimes folks get stuck in ruts they just won't leave—either because they're afraid of what might be up ahead, or afraid of What The Neighbors Might Think. (See 'Saturn,' again.) Neither of those fears, however, are relevant, valid, or worthy of consideration to The Loon, so when he touches Saturn, especially by conjunction, chances are good that he's going to aim his lightning-rod of change directly at whatever you feel are the most stable, solid, unchangeable aspects of your life. Since handling Your Career is one of Saturn's primary job duties, this is often where Uranus begins wreaking havoc—especially if you've been responsibly hanging on to a lifestyle that doesn't suit The Real You. This is another of the unsettling transits, but it's also the most liberating.

Under the tougher transits, the plot thickens up a bit more. The square from Uranus to Saturn marks a time of tremendous inner tension. It's as if you're struggling to Stay Put, (as per your Saturn's demand that you never, ever Change, much less suddenly and drastically), but no matter what you pile in front of the door, someone or something still seems to be able to push it open, a little at a time. You're curious to see What's Out There, but you're still hanging on to Should's. With the opposition, it's your Others who seem to be pushing you to change your life—

for them. In reality, you've simply sent them signals about who and what you're really longing to be, and they're just following orders. This is one of those transits under which marriages are made and broken, careers are trashed and restarted, and life directions are turned directly around.

Whatever the aspect, keep in mind that Uranus isn't out to topple your life and ruin your reputation—even if it seems that way at first. He's here to jump-start you on the path to Who You Really Want To Be. Although cooperating can be tough, especially if you feel as if your life is falling apart, remember that if you listen to the beat of that Inner Drummer, you can't go wrong.

URANUS/URANUS

Any time Uranus touches his own position in your chart, he's home for a visit, and ready to have a chat with you about Freedom and Individuality and the unfiltered expression of those qualities in your life. First off, he has a quite regular orbit of 84 years (which I'm sure makes him crazy—he hates to be predictable). That means we all experience the first sextile visit around puberty—14 or so— the first square at around age 21-ish, and the first trine at about 28, (right around the same time as the Saturn Return). The opposition shows up at around age 42, the second trine at 56-ish, the second square at 63 or so, the second sextile at 70-ish, and the conjunction at age 84.

Now, if you think about those ages, and the periods in human development they represent, you'll understand a lot more about The Loon. At age 14, we've discovered The Opposite Sex, and all the wonderful things they do to our brand-new hormones. Talk about Individuality—we argue with our parents about staying out too late, staying on the phone too long, and Going Too Fast when we tell them we're in love. We're absolutely sure they just don't understand us—and we're right. This is the first real call to Freedom we all experience—and since we're all unique individuals, no one but us could possibly understand what true freedom is, to us.

This transit would be a lot easier if it weren't accompanied by Saturn's first opposition to itself, also around age 14, which brings in the power-struggles with Them—The Authority Figures who won't give us the absolute freedom we think we need at that time. Fortunately, this first major aspect is a sextile, one of the traditionally easier transits, and more often than not, we can expect some understanding and support from our environment as we discover just how unique and separate we are from the family unit we were raised into.

The first square is a bit more dramatic. We're 21, and we're legal. Full-fledged adults. We can vote, drink, and move out if we want to—and some of us are just finishing up with college, too. Our whole adult lives lay stretched out in front of us—a road map just waiting for us to Start Our Engines and proceed. The friction of the square often coincides with our changing directions several times before we get it right, and since this transit also occurs with the second Saturn square, we may, again, meet up with obstacles or roadblocks in our quest to Be Free.

At age 28, (again, just in time for a Saturn transit—the Saturn return), we're having our first trine from Uranus to Uranus. We find that it's easier to be ourselves, since we've got a bit more experience under our belt about who and what we are. Changes definitely occur around this time period—marriages, divorces, career changes, etc.—but we're less likely to rebel for the sake of rebelling, and more likely to see the need for keeping some elements of the past.

The opposition is traditionally associated with The Mid-Life Crisis, because it arrives at about age 41 or 42, when most of us are taking a look around ourselves and thinking about what we haven't done yet. Most folks I've talked with during this time period say the same thing. They're ready to trash at least a major part of lifestyle and start over, because it's suddenly dawned on them that their A) Job, B) Marriage, C) Home, or D) Whatever, is not what they want, and they don't want to waste any more valuable hours on any activity that's not 100% What They Want To Do.

I've got one client who quit his day job with an accounting firm to pursue a career in music, another who left her marriage to live on a horse-farm in a teeny little room, and another who (seriously) joined the Peace Corps. Remember, the second Saturn opposition occurs around age 43 or 44. Since Saturn is how we draw boundaries and set direction in our lives, these transits inspired each of them, over a two to three year period, to re-draw the boundaries suddenly, to make new rules, and to set off in an entirely new life-direction.

The second trine arrives at age 56-ish, a year or two before the second Saturn return. That is when folks often retire, which combines the urge to be free with reaping the benefits of what you've invested in life, a la Saturn. Of course, this is also a time when marriages dissolve, second marriages occur, or folks start their own businesses—the ultimate in Uranian freedom and Saturnian responsibility.

The second square comes along at about 63, right around the time of another Saturn square. This is often a reawakening of some kind, a time when we all realize we're not as young as we used to be, and we need to hurry up and do all the things we really want to do—while there's time and energy left to do them.

The second sextile from Uranus to Uranus arrives at age 70, with the third Saturn opposition. Now's when folks seem to really revel in their uniqueness, and in the person they've become. There's a peacefulness that most folks I've known at this age possess, and it strikes me that it comes from being able to look back and see how you've managed to remain Yourself while still living by society's rules.

Now, I'm personally of the opinion that if we live long enough to reach the age of 84, we've earned the right to do anything we damned well want to do. And you will, too, when and if you have the transit of Uranus to Uranus. This sense of freedom to do— and say— exactly what you want to is something only completing an entire Uranus cycle can bring. Traditionally, this transit was seen as a final chapter of sorts, a time to review what we've accomplished in our lives, and to get ready for our next life— if you're a fan of reincarnation. Nowadays, this transit can mean a lot of things. With life-spans growing longer all the time, and folks staying younger longer, rather than looking at this transit as the end of our lives, we might be better off to look at it as a new beginning.

URANUS/NEPTUNE

Ever have the experience of being rudely awakened from a deep sleep, only to find yourself on another planet? No, huh? Well, think of how Dorothy felt when she woke up in Oz, and you'll understand the types of feelings you'll experience when Uranus touches Neptune. Think of it this way: Neptune spends her time massaging your temples and telling you everything is just fine as it already is, all the while handing you magic spells to alter your current reality as you see fit. She's in charge of smoothing the rough edges of your life, of silently creating a smoke-screen for you to hide behind when reality gets a bit too harsh.

Uranus, however, is The Great Awakener. First off, remember it's this planet's job to Free You Up—by whatever means are necessary. If you cooperate, he doesn't have to resort to Drastic Measures. If you don't, he gets a bit cranky. That might mean you start to experience the damnedest things at the damnedest times—and it might mean a shock or sudden surprise, to boot. When Uranus passes through the pink haze your Neptune has created, then, it's time for Sudden Insights.

Under the conjunction, the gift for Understanding that's built into every Neptune is made a bit more radical by Uranus. This could mean that you suddenly decide it's time to Get Active in whatever charitable cause you're drawn to, and that you become absolutely fanatical about it.

When Uranus makes a difficult aspect to Neptune, it's easy to see how much we wouldn't want to see whatever he's shining his bright light onto. It's as if someone has barged into your bedroom with a spotlight and a boom-box. You're up, but you didn't expect to wake up this quickly. You're confused about where you are and what's going on—and the light hurts your eyes. Symbolically, this can correlate to a time when you wince away from reality. Under the easier aspects from Uranus, we often find ourselves being tremendously enlightened—and glad for the new insight. The light is still quite bright, but we're more willing to rouse ourselves.

Any of the transits from Uranus to Neptune seem to work best when we involve ourselves in a spiritual quest of some kind. Again, working with charities, or with organizations that are dedicated to improving life on the planet for all of us, is a great way to combine these two Heavy Hitters well.

URANUS/PLUTO

Picture Pluto, Lord of the Underworld, Master of Secrets, the Ultimate Detective in Black, opening his thick, dark chamber door and finding The Madman there. Sure, he'll let him in—Pluto has nothing to be afraid of, and this visitor is just nuts enough, and just change-oriented enough, to be an ally. See, like no others, these two planets are big fans of The Future. They love change, too—ongoing change. No matter how sweeping the changes they engineer when they get together, then, keep in mind that it's only the beginning of The New You. The best—and I do seriously mean

The Best—is yet to come. In all, there's really just one rule in this book, kids, one phrase that pays, one catchall kind of Perot-like line, no matter which aspect Uranus makes to Pluto. No matter what happens, Don't Get Comfortable. Don't. Stay loose, flexible, and open to whatever The Universe, in its infinite wisdom, tosses at you—and at the rest of your generation, all of whom will be going through the major changes you're experiencing.

Individually, remember that Pluto in our charts is where we're gifted with an X-Ray Vision of sorts. Uranus loves to illuminate and expose—suddenly. So whatever you see now, whatever new understanding he presents your Pluto with, take advantage of this opportunity to investigate the mysteries with a genius at your side.

Whatever the aspect, don't forget to be excited about all this. After all, when was the last time you went for a ride through a dangerous part of town with a madman—and lived to tell the tale?

CHAPTER TWELVE

NEPTUNE

Your Neptune Kit:

Rose-colored glasses

An autographed picture of your favorite movie-star

A nice, long nap—with your favorite pillow and blankie

A Dream Interpretation Book

An All-Expense Paid Weekend For Two In Vegas

A Magic Wand

A Crystal Ball

A Bottle Of Your Favorite Wine

A Cup Of Herb-Tea

Lawrence Welk's Bubble-Machine

All of Enya's CDs

A Packet of Calgon, and A Dozen Candles

A Disguise

A Harlequin Romance or Two

A Two-Week Cruise On The Love Boat

Your Very Own Merlin

A Vial of Love-Potion #9

A Book of Susan Seddon-Boulet's Artwork

Neptune Transits:
Dream A Little Dream Of Me...

Neptune's gift is her ability to dissolve boundaries—to make us see that we are all part of The One. In the process of any Neptune transit, then, we feel softer, and much more aware—in a very psychic way. That can be good, and that can be bad. When we're ultra-sensitized to Others, we can be at our most compassionate—and that's good. But being that sensitive can also make us uncertain about what to do next. In other words, our spiritual circuits can get overloaded with all those messages coming in, leaving us a bit cloudy on the subject of Personal Borders. Now, living like that—not being quite sure of where we begin and Out There leaves off—is exhausting. It's as if walking through a normal day is now like walking through a field of psychic land mines. Needless to say, after awhile of this, we may end up wanting to hide or escape from reality—until the smoke clears. That's not so good—especially if we choose to escape in an unhealthy fashion, through substance abuse, depression or mental illness.

See, Neptune's job description covers everything from compassion, romance and idealism to illusion, delusion and fraud. It's not up to her which end of the scale we choose—it's up to us. Either way, the harsher edges of reality will be buffed away. So if you're in the middle of a visit from The Lady Neptune, then, and you're feeling quite soft, as if reality is subtly changing its shape right in front of your eyes, there are a couple of things you can do. First of all, enjoy it. Put yourself in surroundings where you'll be able to enjoy your antenna being turned up to High. You'll begin to sense what your spiritual purpose is, and what will make you most fulfilled. You'll sense these things because you'll feel vaguely dissatisfied with your life as it is—but possibly not quite sure why. Neptune transits are times of Divine Discontent, when there's typically a whole lot of sighin' goin' on—but not a lot of action. And that's all right. You're not supposed to be acting now—just floating.

Secondly, if you're feeling a bit fuzzy about something, relax. Take a deep breath. You're definitely not the first. Give your brain a break and don't try too hard to figure it out—on that mental level—because you're not in the mood for reality, anyway. When Neptune is visiting, you won't want to hear the hard, cold facts about what's confusing you. So allow yourself to feel wistful, nostalgic, and even melancholy at times. This doesn't mean you should ignore what's going on around you—and by all means, do read on. But don't think for a minute that you're going to Get This— the meaning of the transit, that is—until it's over. At which point, you'll undoubtedly look back over everything that's happened, scratch your head, and say "It was wonderful—I was so in tune" or "Where the hell was I when all this was going on? Was I sleeping, or drugged, or just incredibly naive?" Both results are possible— simultaneously, even. See, reality is temporarily tabled when The Pink Goddess is in the neighborhood. And that's okay.

The periods that follow Neptune transits, however, are when we can experience both the best and the worst of reality. If we use this time of ultra-sensitivity to connect on a deep, spiritual level to Others and to the world around us, we emerge from a Neptune transit with a new understanding of how good life can be when we function as if we're a part of the planet—not separate from it. If, on the other hand, we've overdosed on Neptune's pink dust, if we've built someone or something way, way up, we can be a bit disappointed. If we've put our new love on a pedestal and refused to see any flaws in their character, or totally idealized a situation and refused to see the pitfalls, when the Reality Light goes on, it can be crushing.

In all, the best thing to do with Neptune is not to do anything at all. The subject is escape, romance, and alternate states. Play your cards right, and your Neptune transits will be among the best, most magical times in your life. Pay attention to your dreams, enjoy your new ability to just know things, and imagine how your life could be perfect—but don't fall into the trap of believing it's already that way.

Neptune Through The Houses

When Neptune enters a house, she's there for a good, long time, depending on the size of it. So if you've got an interception in your chart (that is, if a pair of signs are enclosed inside a house axis, rather than appearing on the cusps of the houses), and those houses are 35 or 40 degrees wide, well, then, you can expect her to cast her magic spell on that area of your life for up to 20 years. Even in the case of the smallest of houses, she'll be staying on for 8 years or so—long enough to scatter some of her famous pink dust around, and make that side of your personality a lot softer.

While she's there, then, all the matters that deal with that house become a bit more romanticized, and a lot fuzzier. The problem with Neptune is that you may not be aware of her presence at all, since her specialty is Operating Invisibly. But if you pay close attention, you'll find yourself much more sensitive, much more prone to daydreaming, and a lot more easily confused. Taking all that into consideration, you'll need to be a lot more understanding of yourself—and of the Others who are handled by that side of your personality—during her visit. Pretend you're playing host or hostess to someone who's sensitive, understanding, and nostalgic. Pretend that same someone is extremely vulnerable to outside influences, with such a great faith in the good side of Others that he or she sometimes misses their faults. Now recognize that it's you that's going to be acting and feeling in these ways.

As we've said before, every house in your chart is a side of you that only comes out in particular life circumstances. Each life circumstance has a cast of characters to call its own. Your sixth house shows your co-workers; your fourth and tenth house your parents; your fifth house your children, lovers and playmates, and so forth. As Neptune passes through each of the houses, then, recognize that your dealings with each of these folks is also going to carry a rather dreamy, idealistic, or romanticized tone. Regardless of the house Neptune is transiting, resolve not to make decisions of major importance until you get a nice, solid, Saturn transit to help you See The Light. Now let's take a look at what to expect as she travels around the circular lens of your chart.

FIRST HOUSE

The First House (and the Ascendant degree in particular) is the Front Door of your chart, the entrance to You from the outside world. Neptune, of course, doesn't like doors. She much prefers veils, and smoke screens. It's very easy to get lost, then, when she waves her magic wand across this entrance to You, to be unable to separate what's Out There from What You Are. And speaking of smoke screens, you'll be amazed at your new ability to infiltrate social situations easily, almost as if you're able to become invisible when you want to be. Remember, too, that Neptune rules Illusion—so when this pink goddess is in the neighborhood, you'll also be able to disguise yourself quite well, both physically and otherwise, and able to mingle where you will. In a nutshell, this transit is much like being endowed with the ability to shape-shift.

On the other hand, you may also feel like a walking mirror—like Other People are using you as an image, projecting What They Want You To Be onto what you really are. I can't tell you how many actors and actresses were born with Neptune in their first house, by the way, with a lifelong gift to change colors, chameleon-style, and take on the qualities of the environment. Remember that transits remind us of how someone with this natal placement feels all the time. With Neptune here, then, you may just decide to take up acting, singing, or magic—to add a more mystical quality to your personality. One way or the other, now is definitely the time to play with your appearance. This house has everything to do with the way you dress yourself, the condition of your body, and with your physical self in general, so don't be surprised if you have the urge to change or alter your Look so that your outer image reflects your new inner attitude. You may disguise yourself in some way, using Neptune's affiliation with the concept of glamour to change your hairstyle or color. Or your taste in clothing may begin to lean toward more ethereal, flowing styles. In all, remember that your presentation of You is about to undergo a tremendous softening. On a deeper level, it's best to be picky about the environments you enter when Neptune is here. With no Front Door to separate you from Out There, you'll be absorbing everything around you, for better or worse.

SECOND HOUSE

Neptune has never been famous for her ability to keep a checkbook balanced. She loses the deposit slips, spills something on the checks, or simply gives all her money away to an animal shelter. See, money doesn't mean anything to Neptune. It's a product of the physical world, and Neptune doesn't live in the physical world. You, however, do. So if you find yourself losing track of how much you have in your account, or even literally losing what you've got in your pocket, take a few precautionary steps. Get duplicate checks, or hire an accountant you trust. Underline the part about trust, too, because under this transit, your eyes can become quite misted over when it comes to numbers, making it possible to be deceived or taken in financially by someone with A Great Deal. Remember, if it sounds too good to be true, it just might be too good to be true. Keep a watch on just how much you're donating to nonprofit charities at this time, too—lest you become one yourself. Do allow yourself to donate what you can to an animal organization, (okay, so it's my favorite Cause), drop off clothing to a homeless shelter, or sign up to be a foster-parent to a child in a third-world country. Remember, this is also the house where our self-esteem is handled. When Neptune is here, any positive way you can share the wealth with less fortunate creatures will make you feel good about you by the help you're able to give them.

Of course, possessions are also handled by the second house side of you, since the objects we choose to surround ourselves with are nothing more than outer representations of those qualities we value in ourselves. So you may develop a fondness for All Things Spiritual when Neptune passes through here—like crystal balls, amethyst clusters, and magic wands. Or you may lose your possessions, or give them away. Since this house also represents How We Make Our Money, now may be when you turn a metaphysical or spiritual leaning into an income, by becoming a professional tarot-card reader, astrologer, or spiritual counselor.

THIRD HOUSE

Communication in general is handled by the third-house side of us, as is the whole idea of habitual navigation throughout our Small World, the places we visit on a regular basis. So when Neptune passes through, with her magical pink smoke-machine in tow, it's not unusual for this side of our personality to become a bit disoriented. This can show up in our lives in a number of ways. First off, our communications with others may take on a romantic, poetic, or confusing tone. That can translate into a newfound ability to write poetry or music, an interest in spiritual or romantic literature, or an inability to dash through our daily routines like we did before. Second, we may find ourselves daydreaming a lot more—just sitting and thinking. The high side of all this is that our imagination will be stimulated. But with all those daydreams in the air, our sense of direction may become a bit fuzzy for awhile, too—until we learn to operate on intuition, rather than directions. In short, this transit sensitizes the Auto Pilot aspect of ourselves to what's going on around us. With Neptune acting as co-pilot, it's best to allow ourselves to be guided through the ordinarily routine aspects of our life by symbols, inspirations, and notions. And do jot down those inspirations. Neptune has been known to deliver an amazing array of revelations to whatever house or planet she visits.

Now, Neptune's famous ability to create an illusion means that this combination is also the technology behind counterfeiting— behind fraudulent signatures, forged documents, phony contracts or staged conversations. So during this transit, make sure you have all important papers checked over carefully by a reputable agent before you sign on the dotted line. Remember, just because Neptune's subtle doesn't mean she's not potent.

Since this house also describes the side of us who deals with siblings and neighbors, we may also find these folks to be acting in Neptunian fashion. A neighbor may send us mixed signals, or appear to be involved in some secret activity. A brother or sister may take up a spiritual path, or begin using alcohol or drugs. If this is the case, use the third house's gift for communication to listen, add Neptune's compassion, and listen with an open mind, and an open heart.

FOURTH HOUSE

Pretend that a wonderfully romantic figure has just moved into a room in your home, for a nice, long visit. It's wonderful to have her there, of course—your whole family is softer and more sensitive, and you may find that you're much more in tune with each other than you have been in awhile. You'll reminisce about your childhood, and want to make your home as warm and snuggly and comforting a nest as you possibly can. You'll be terribly tempted to just stay home with your visitor, watching love stories with her and showing her your old photo albums. But after the pink smoke clears, and you realize you've got bills to pay, and promises to keep—in The Outer World, that is—what are you going to do with her? You've got your life to carry on, and you know that—but you just don't feel like participating right now—especially in the harsher aspects of reality.

Well, fond as Neptune is of water, you may opt to move to a home by the water, or put a pond in your backyard—so you'll at least have a soft, safe nest and the soothing sound of running water to return to after you've fulfilled your obligations Out There. Or you may decide that life Out There is entirely too hard—in which case you might pack up and head off to live on a religious or spiritual commune, and go permanently on retreat. You may decide to get yourself a cabin in the woods where there's no phone, no electricity, and no mail delivery—all of which suits you just fine right now, because you're in the mood to live alone and

Commune With Nature, anyway. If you don't do any of these things, you'll definitely find yourself hiding for at least some of the time that Neptune passes through this house—whether that's by taking the phone off the hook and pulling down all the shades, or actually going away. Since this house describes the cellar of the chart, on a much more mundane level, you may find yourself literally dealing with water in the basement—which is really a symbolic indication that there's some type of dissolution occurring at your roots. Your dealings with family members may also become confusing or unclear. You may begin to hold back or hide something from them, or you may feel as if they're withdrawing from you in some way. If that's the case, let them go. Whatever Neptune erases from our lives is meant to go, to free us up so that we can get to know the spiritual side of ourselves.

Then, too, because this house represents your emotional warehouse, you may simply find that you're much more sensitive in all your dealings with others, and that most of your automatic responses are suddenly influenced by old memories. You may become extremely nostalgic, or discover a much more intuitive side of you. In a nutshell, when Neptune passes through here, your gut responses will become a lot more prominent in your life. Your decisions will be based on emotion and intuition, rather than facts. Allow yourself to retreat, then, to use your home as a sanctuary.

FIFTH HOUSE

Adding a dose of Neptune to the fifth house can mean several things. First of all, since this house is where we keep the side of us who deals with children, we may find that our dealings with youngsters become much more profound—as if they're suddenly serving as tiny spiritual gurus. Without years of conditioning on How We Should Act, children do their charts in the purest ways possible—and manage to learn, play, and grow at the same time. With Neptune here, turning our sensitivity meter up on High, we see that innocence as evidence of how good life could be, if we'd just keep it simple and follow our inner voice. On the other hand, the children in our life may also go through a confusing or vulnerable stage, and need us to provide simple insights on how to deal with fears and insecurities they may be experiencing.

Then, too, in this fifth-house room lives the side of us who becomes involved in Love Affairs. As Neptune tiptoes through, then, tossing handfuls of pink dust on everyone we encounter, we can become involved in very romantic relationships, or secret affairs. We may also begin an association with someone who we feel we need to save, or someone who we imagine will save us in some way. Often, someone who seems to be just perfect comes along, but after the dust shakes off, we realize that in reality, our new love is not at all the way he or she seems to be. With Neptune here, we're not willing, ready or able to see the reality of our relationships with lovers. We're in the mood to fall in love. We ignore all the obvious warning signs, and let our imaginations fill in the blanks. Needless to say, it's quite possible to be deceived, disappointed, or taken in by someone. Of course, it's also quite possible to finally find the love of our lives with Neptune transiting this house. In practice, I've found that during the course of this transit, we kiss a lot of frogs—but if we're patient, the Prince does eventually show up.

On a personal level, don't forget that this house is also the Creativity Headquarters, and Neptune is the ultimate creative tool. She punches holes in our walls, and lets intuition and Divine Inspiration flow right in. So while she's here, with no creative holds barred, our artistic abilities are amazingly increased, as if we're in constant contact with a Muse who never sleeps. In all, when Neptune visits the fifth house, our love of life and the playmates it provides is heightened. Enjoy the magic— but realize that you're the magician.

SIXTH HOUSE

This is one of those transits with a terrible reputation. First of all, this is the house traditionally associated with the health of our body, and specifically with our immune system, which is basically the ability to keep our barriers intact, to resist illness and infection. When any planet enters this house, they're intruding in some way. Neptune leaves the door open to any room she visits—she dissolves it, in fact. So when it comes to the condition of our health, leaving the sixth house open means that it becomes vulnerable to whatever is passing by. It's as if we have no defense system in place to stop illness from infiltrating our physical borders. Add to all that the fact that Neptune has always been connected with poisons and viruses, (that invisibly infiltrate our bodies), and you can see where this tough reputation came from. While it's true, then, that Neptune passing through here can be a time when our immune systems and our ability to resist these intrusions may be lower than usual, it's not a guarantee of illness. To stay healthy during a visit from any planet, our bodies must only accommodate the visitor, and make them feel welcome. If we can incorporate the qualities of the planet that's visiting—one way or the other—we don't have an awful lot to worry about.

In Neptune's case, that's not as difficult as it sounds. She's a very spiritual lady who's only real goal is to point out our connection with the rest of life. So rather than fearing Neptune's time here, think of it as an opportunity to heighten your awareness and sensitivity to your physical self. In a nutshell, it's time to pay attention to our body, to key into what it really needs— and there are lots of ways to make our body's acquaintance. Meditation begins with listening to our breathing our heart beat. Yoga is a way of connecting with our muscles—and increasing our flexibility and strength by stretching those muscles. If you've been on a rigorous weight-lifting program, however, or if you're used to an hour's worth of intense aerobics, don't be surprised if your body begins to prefer more gentle movements—and don't force it. The softer ways of exercising are the best ways to use Neptune's transit through this house.

Now, this is also the side of us we take to work each day. With Neptune along for the ride, we may opt to pursue a more spiritual type of work, such as counseling, or service to The Other. Our preference for a work environment may change, too, so we may take up work in a shelter or retreat center. Metaphysical surroundings will also appeal to us now, as will work with an environmental or spiritual organization. Our relationships with our co-workers will take on a more Neptunian flavor, as well. We'll want to be around others who are working for a similar cause. If our actual job doesn't change, then our approach to it might simply become much less ego-driven.

Remember that both the work we do and the way we take care of our health are reflections of the rhythm of our day— the most important meaning of this house. Bringing in Neptune means operating at a more sensitive level—all day, every day.

SEVENTH HOUSE

Your seventh house is the place where you keep the side of you who comes out when you're in the presence of just one other person. Just the one. Doesn't matter whether it's your spouse of sixty years, or the person who just took the seat next to you on the bus.

Whenever you interact on a one-to-one level, your seventh house door is open. With Neptune tiptoeing around in here, not wanting to wake you up and disturb you with anything as petty as Reality, then, you're not likely to see Others clearly. This can mean you idealize the heck out of your Other, and turn Joe Shmoe into Robert Redford. Or you might find yourself being idealized by someone. Others may see you now as a guru of sorts, able to fix their problems simply by listening to them. One way or the other, however, it's time to incorporate a more spiritual quality into all your individual encounters.

This house reflects the type of partner we settle in with, long-term, too, since when we choose a mate, we spend a great deal of time alone with them, being our seventh-house person. So now is when your tastes in An Other will tend toward the Neptunian. On the high side, then, you may find yourself involved in a committed relationship with a musician, a spiritual guide of some kind, a poet or a metaphysician. Now may also be when you find a guru to work with on an individual basis, a spiritual teacher who'll subtly show you what Relationship is really all about. The tougher side of this transit involves Neptune's urge to rescue or save An Other—so be careful of a tendency to fulfill that urge by adopting someone who needs you. Plenty of co-dependent relationships like this are started with Neptune's passage into this house, but it doesn't have to be that way. Just be careful not to over-idealize anyone. It's only when we see others clearly that we exercise the highest side of Neptune in relationships: the ability to unconditionally accept someone as they really are.

EIGHTH HOUSE

This is the house that has everything to do with Intimacy, with the way we tear down our separateness to merge or bond with An Other. Now, merging intimately is most often connected in our minds with sex—but that's only the physical side of it. There are lots of ways to Become Intimate with another—through deep, penetrating, soulful conversation, finding someone we trust, and sharing our secrets. All of these are simply indications that we're confident enough in our personal strength to let another get close to us without being afraid we'll lose some of it—and these are the types of intimate interactions we'll prefer when Neptune arrives into the eighth house.

See, although it's natural to connect Neptune and the eighth house with romantic physical interludes, and to paint mental pictures—starring Us—that look like Harlequin covers, it's not always like that. Sure, an hour with Fabio—or someone we've turned into Fabio, via Neptune's magic pink dust—wouldn't be hard to take, and we certainly are in line for our share of at least one lovely, intense, romantic connection. But Neptune may also inspire us to want more. So instead of picking out a low-necked peasant blouse and deciding on an accent, envision a few year's worth of encounters that are far too spiritual to only point to sex. Picture yourself truly knowing An Other—and being known by them. Imagine, even, a connection with someone that's so precious to you, you don't want to know them physically—because that might spoil it. That's what Neptune here is really all about. Truth be told, this ethereal, mystical goddess is much fonder of tantric sex than of The Real Thing—because she's afraid to break the perfection of her fantasy by inserting an uncertain reality into the picture.

Now, this is also the side of us who handles The Other Heavy Issues—like death, and other losses or crises, and dealings with agencies in power over us. With Neptune here, we may feel as if people or situations are being spirited away from us— like it or not—or that a very subtle infiltration of our most closely-guarded Self is occurring. Again, regardless of the circumstances, remember that whatever leaves our life under an outer planet transit was meant to go, to make way for a new side of ourselves to be born. That's really the function of this slice of our personality, after all—to assist us in rejuvenating ourselves by eliminating conditions or situations that are outworn or no longer useful. Although it's the hardest thing to do, it's best to accept these losses and try to see what the future now holds that wouldn't have been possible without an ending of some kind first.

On a much more mundane level, this house also has to do with joint finances, inheritances, and taxes. Neptune's fondness for secret activities can mean that a behind-the-scenes investigation into our finances is carried on at some point by one of the Powers That Be, such as the IRS. We may also stand to inherit a spiritual bequest of some kind, or become the recipient of a gift from an anonymous source.

In all, remember that Neptune here heightens our perceptive side. She turns our already keen eighth-house antenna into super-receptors. Investigate the mysteries during the years Neptune spends here—life after death, and reincarnation, for example. Listen to the whispers of your subconscious, and pay attention to what your perceptive side picks up. And don't take candy from strangers.

NINTH HOUSE

Here's the side of you who gets bored, who decides when it's time to break out of your daily routine and Do Something Different. So whenever you go on vacation, take a class, or get to know someone from another country, it's this ninth-house piece of you who buys the tickets, signs up, or extends a friendly aloha. Now, add a bit of Neptune's magic pink powder to the ninth house and its perpetual quest for new knowledge and uncharted experiences, and what do you get? Well, first of all, a strong urge to travel—to exotic, romantic, secluded, or unreal places. In short, anywhere that's magical. You'll also be drawn toward meeting people from other, more spiritual cultures, who have a more open, humanistic view of the world. And as for the new knowledge this side of you craves? Well, now's when that quest for New Stuff will extend into the metaphysical, so classes on astral travel, altered states, and massage will hold quite the appeal for you.

Of course, this is also the part of you who needs to ponder The Big Questions—religion, politics, and philosophy, for example. So you may find yourself interested in Eastern religions, such as Buddhism or Hinduism. Your political views will probably soften, too—to encompass the party or platform you feel is most concerned with your particular Cause or Underdog, whether it be animal rights, amnesty for political prisoners, or preserving the rain forests. In all, the upcoming years will be a time of gradual, invisible, but profound change in your view of How The World Should Be Run.

TENTH HOUSE

This is the house of Reputation and Accomplishments, the place in our charts that's rather like our own personal bulletin board. It's a very public place, where everything we've ever done is put on display for all the world to see. It describes our future career aspirations, too. So when Neptune arrives, we can become famous for a number of things. Perhaps we become known for the reputation we've earned, working as a counselor or psychic, or as a spiritual advisor. Or our current career slips away, leaving us to ponder what's next for us—what our purpose on the planet really is. Then, too, since this is the side of us that decides what's best for our future, in a social sense, we may find that life is pointing us towards a path into the metaphysical fields, or towards holistic vocations, such as herbs or massage.

Now, this is also where we keep the side of us who handles the concept of Authority Figures—whether we are the authority, or we're simply in the presence of an authority. When Neptune visits this house, then, we may become the head of a Neptunian organization, such as a nonprofit group or environmental organization. Or our attitude towards Higher Ups may change, due to a new presence in our life—a superior or boss who is spiritual or metaphysical.

Of course, Neptune doesn't always illuminate and inspire. Sometimes she confuses. In that case, it's possible that we may still be put in charge of a major project, but not quite sure where to begin. If things aren't going well in our lives, we could also now become known for our escapist behaviors, especially if we turn to alcohol or drugs to avoid reality. Or we may feel that a superior is sending us mixed signals, and be uncertain of how to deal with them.

Regardless of what happens in the outer world, you should know that what's really changing is You—and what you'd like to do with the rest of your life. Listen to the soft whisperings from your soul.

ELEVENTH HOUSE

Ever been to a meditation group, or a twelve step meeting? Ever been part of a theatrical troupe? Well, now's the time when you may find yourself joining one—or many—of these organizations. Neptune's trek through the eleventh house inspires us to search out Kindred Spirits, much as Uranus does. The difference is that the common denominator you'll be looking for with Neptune transits is either Spirituality, Religion, Metaphysics, Music, or Self-Help. In short, you'll be on the lookout for folks who are unconditional in their acceptance of others, people who inspire by their words, their music, or the sharing of their experiences. Hook up with the right group now and you'll experience the wonderful feeling of being One with a group of liked-minded Others. You'll grow on a spiritual level. And you just might discover an innate talent for the theater, or for music.

Now, that's the high side of the transit. But there are other types of Neptunian groups out there, with members who express the lower sides of Neptune's energy. Lots of them hang out at Wally's Bar and Grill, chugging down one long-neck after another. These are folks who try to get lost in groups—to forget who they are and where they are. Needless to say, if you don't want to end up like Them, don't get involved with them—especially not now. With Neptune in the neighborhood, it's easy to be drawn in by group affiliations that are unsavory, secretive, or detrimental to your health. It's easy to have the wool pulled over your eyes by a religious or spiritual group that's really expressing more of the downside of Neptune's range—fraud, delusion, or artificiality—because you want to believe.

Then, too, Neptune also rules the concept of glamour and fantasy. So it's perfectly possible for you to also end up with group affiliations of the glamorous kind—with folks in the cosmetic industry, maybe, or in a medieval recreation group. Remember that Neptune is famous for her love of Playing Pretend. Groups that allow you to slip into a disguise and become someone else for awhile are just what the doctor ordered.

TWELFTH HOUSE

Ssh. Be very quiet. When Neptune returns home, to the twelfth house, it's Quiet Time. Time for naps, and baths, and meditating. In short, since this house holds the side of you who only comes out when you're completely alone, it's time for Quality Time alone with yourself. You'll find yourself feeling like it's time to go on retreat, to Be Peaceful, and just think. Everybody needs time alone, but you're really going to need it when Neptune passes through this house. Now, this is a transit that lasts for several years, and although you could, indeed, become a full-time hermit, you may simply find that you're now needing a period of rest and withdrawal after periods of intense social activity. If you can't get away for an extended period to live in seclusion, then, make sure you have a Safe Place to return to after a hectic day out there in The Real World.

Now's also when you'll be drawn to activities you can pursue in private, too. Secret activities will also hold a great deal of interest for you. Why, you may even have a secret affair when Neptune tiptoes through here. It's time to rest and regroup, to find out who you are when there's no one around, expecting anything from you. Take this time to rest, to undo from life's stresses and tensions by finding a way to Get Away From It All. Listen to soft music, light candles, take bubble baths. Or find a natural hot-spring, and soak reality away. Whatever else you do, remember that since Neptune is relaxed here, and feeling so safe in her natural home, she'll be far more likely to whisper her secrets in your ear and teach you how to do her magic. This can be a wonderful, peaceful period in your life, when you'll find solace in time spent alone.

NEPTUNE/SUN
Prepare to become a psychic sponge, to feel everything, to become so sensitive to the world around you that it feels as if everything Out There is really a part of you. The Sun is the very core of us—the center of our chart. It's the side of us who wants to be Someone. When Neptune visits, then, we begin to dream of who we could be—if Things were only perfect. That's wonderful, and inspirational—imagining something is the first step towards getting it on the road. But it's also possible to become so wrapped up in The Dream that we start to think we've already got it. We don't. Saturn transits are when you make things "real"—Neptune transits are when you decide what you want Real to be. So if you decide you'd like to be a star, or the CEO of a corporation, or just part of a team of folks sent to Zimbabwe to work with the natives, realize that there are changes you'll have to make in your life to make any of those dreams a reality.

Regardless of the aspect Neptune makes to your Sun, you may not see yourself clearly. Of course, with the conjunction of any planet to the Sun, we actually become that planet for awhile. So first off, you might as well give up drinking, smoking, and whatever else you do to escape reality, because you won't need it now—and it won't help the situation. If you want to escape for awhile, try classical music, hot tubs, or steam rooms. You can smooth the edges of reality in more ways than one.

When Neptune makes a tougher transit to your Sun, you may go through something of an Identity Crisis, as if whoever it was you believed you were is now eroding away, leaving you to wonder who you are. If this happens, don't panic—and don't get paranoid. You're still the same person you really were. But really is the important word there. Who are you—really? Well, now's when you'll discover that—because everything that's not you will dissolve away, leaving you feeling quite naked, vulnerable, and unprotected. Now, the high side of even the tough transits is that once all your artificial coverings are gone, you'll know who you really are. And that new You isn't really new—it's just more sensitive. Under the easier transits, you'll still feel as if your identity is slipping away—but you won't miss it much. You'll be glad to see it go, and maybe even relieved to find yourself again. Under either transit, your work, relationships, and appearance may also change or soften in some way—to reflect the real you that's been hiding under the facades you've built.

Now, you're also going to feel quite nostalgic, with Neptune transiting your Sun—regardless of the aspect. When this happens, do one thing for yourself: Go For It. Really. Wallow in it. Read old love letters from The One Who Got Away. Play Barry Manilow records. Watch *E.T.* if you really want to get down. Regardless of what it takes, don't ever run away from this new personal softness you'll experience under Neptune transits. The sensitivity you'll feel at these times is a part of Neptune's magic—her ability to make the ordinary into the extraordinary, to make the unobtainable into the Most Wanted, to turn everything and everyone into the very best it can be. Imagine yourself the best you can be—and go for it.

NEPTUNE/MOON

Our Moon is our soft underbelly, the planet that we use when it's time to react to What's Out There, rather than act, as our Sun and Mars do. When Neptune visits the Moon's place, she's punching holes in an already delicate shell. Needless to say, this is a time of extreme sensitivity to the environment—for better or worse—when our susceptibility to the outside world heightens to the point that harsh sounds can actually make us wince. In fact, I've often found that many folks just can't listen to music any more rad than Mozart during this period—especially under the conjunction of Neptune to the Moon.

Now, since the Moon is the instinctive side of our nature, and Neptune is the Queen of Intuition, under the easier transits, we often have truly psychic moments. We just know things—without knowing why. We think of someone we haven't seen in awhile, and then bump into them a day later. Sometimes our dreams are quite prophetic, too.

This combination in a tougher aspect can also conjure a Divine Discontent that we can't quite explain. We sigh, wish, and feel nostalgic—and we don't see things clearly at all. See, Neptune is a lot like Glinda, the Good Witch in *The Wizard of Oz*. Remember how she told Dorothy to just close her eyes and say "There's no place like home"? Well, that's what we all want to do when Neptune touches our Moon. It's also the best prescription anybody can offer you when your Moon is under the wistful spell of this Pink Goddess. So instead of wondering what to do, understand that you're not supposed to see or understand anything intellectually under Neptune, much less do anything. You're supposed to feel—everything—romantically, vaguely, and dreamily.

So expect to sigh a lot, and to wish for The Way Things Were—or The Way They Could Be. Expect, also, to forget about the arguments that drove you apart from your recently estranged Significant Other, the parts of the late job you truly hated, and the way the roof in the old house used to leak when it rained. Under Neptune, you'll remember how cute They looked when they smiled, how nice it was to walk down that sunny hallway at work in the morning, and how great the view was from the old front porch. In short, our memories become extreeeemly selective, and very, very tender when Neptune waves her magic wand over us. Since the Moon is the compassionate side in all of us, our sympathy towards other creatures deepens, too. In fact, we often feel with someone or something, rather than for them.

So what's the point? Well, at the end of this transit, we often wake up to realize that everything about us is different—that we've been changed and sensitized from the inside out. The reality we were living at the beginning of the transit has been gradually eroded or erased, right from under our feet—while we stood there on it. Often this pertains to our homes, and to the loved ones in our lives. Of course, after the smoke clears, which isn't until well after Neptune's moved on, we're able to see things a lot more clearly, and we begin to understand what the meaning of All That was. In the meantime, enjoy the new (or improved) psychic abilities you'll have—and be tender to critters, kids, and your elders.

NEPTUNE/MERCURY

Ever hear that expression The porch-light's on, but nobody's home? Well, that's how you're going to feel when Neptune touches your Mercury. At least, that's how you'll feel on an intellectual level. You'll be really good at sensing things during this mystical lady's visit, but not so great at figuring them out—even if you ordinarily consider yourself a very mental type. She's here to teach you all about mind-reading, dream interpretation, and the symbolic language of the Universe—and she's quite good at what she does. So if you pay attention to those symbols, keep track of your dreams, and try to understand the meaning behind a pattern of similar events, you'll learn far more than if you try to deal with facts and figures. This is all true in particular in the case of Neptune's conjunction to your Mercury.

See, this is another of the truly psychic transits, inspired by Neptune's special talent for dissolving boundaries. Again, this won't do wonders for your concentration abilities—but you won't have to concentrate to get by. Out of the blue, you'll reach for the phone, knowing that it's about to ring—and you'll know who's on the other end, too. Under the easier transits, that knowing will come to you quite easily. You'll sense the outcome of a situation long before Stage Two is in effect, much to the amazement of all parties involved. You may even be able to quite literally read other's minds.

Now, the danger with the more challenging transits of Neptune to Mercury (the squares, oppositions, and some of the conjunctions, for example) is that you may be so in tune with the psychic airwaves that you feel a bit confused—as if you're not sure where Their thoughts leave off and Yours begin. It's as if a pink filter is covering your eyes and ears, so that everything you see and hear is a bit muffled, and your ability to discern individual voices is gone. Needless to say, then, you can be very easily influenced by others now—so don't make any major decisions or sign anything important without the input of a trusted advisor. (Someone who isn't in the middle of a Neptune/ Mercury transit). You're also going to be inspired to write music and/or poetry, and as with transits of Neptune to the Moon, you may not be able to stand harsh sounds. So turn down the stereo, and lend an ear to the voice of the wind, instead. Let your conscious mind take a back seat for awhile. Take a deep breath, close your eyes, and listen. The Universe is speaking to you.

NEPTUNE/VENUS

Prepare to fall in love. Several times. In fact, prepare to fall desperately in love at least 22 times over the next 3 years—and to be equally sure that This Is It each time. Neptune's visits to Venus, (especially by conjunction), inspire us to set off an a quest—to Find The Perfect Mate. And we may just do that—eventually. In the meantime, however, each and every possible candidate for the position will look, for all intents and purposes, like The Right One—for a little while, at least.

See, Neptune inspires us to see only the good in all our prospective Others, to see the spiritual, tender side of them. Now, that's quite a lovely gift to give someone, and it can even inspire them to Be The Best They Can Be. But once reality arrives, and we're forced to take a good look at the mortal we've turned into a God or Goddess, it can be disappointing, too. For example, we may choose to ignore the fact that this new Other is taken or unavailable in some way. Maybe that's because we're so darned happy during the time we do have with them, it doesn't seem to matter that we can only have them on Thursday nights. But maybe it's because we're harboring a secret hope that if we continue conjuring Magic Moments via champagne, candles, and Hallmark cards they can't take home, they'll soon realize that no matter what the cost, they've just got to be with us.

Under both the easier and the tougher transits of Neptune to Venus, that might just happen. A note arrives at the office one afternoon, tucked between the petals of a dozen roses. It says that our Other has left Whoever, and they'll pick us up at five. We're elated. Life is wonderful, love is amazingly wonderful, and reality is tabled. We pass the note around the office, and don't get anything done for the rest of the day. We can't. We're in love, you see.

But here's where the difference between the easy transits and the tough ones comes in.

When Neptune is making an easy aspect to Venus, things may just work out. They pick us up, and their suitcases are in the back seat. We embrace tenderly, and head off together into the sunset. A peek in at the happy couple two months later reveals that they're picking out names for their children. Roll the credits. Fade to black. Under the tougher aspects, the suitcases are still in the back seat, and the embrace is every bit as warm and tender—but after just a week or so, we discover that spending time with The Beloved isn't quite so magical when it's spent grocery shopping—

especially if we're the ones writing the check at the register. They snore; they don't clean up after themselves, and they still don't have a job. Even if we're reluctant to let the dream go after we've stopped lighting candles, we may return home one day to find the television off, for a change, with a note from The Beloved taped to it—a farewell note. We feel used, abused, and misled. How could we not have seen this coming?

Well, regardless of the ending we actually experience—or how many times we experience either of them—the one thing all Neptune/Venus transits bring along is "Buffers." Now, these folks are different from Uranian Buffers. They're sent along with a similar mission—to get us out of our current situation—but Neptune's representatives do it by casting a spell to lure us away from where we were gradually. There are no sudden, drastic moves, like there are under Uranus transits, so we probably won't quit our job on Tuesday and join the Peace Corps on Wednesday. Instead, on the high side, we may find that this new person guides us, subtly, toward becoming more of what we really are, on the inside, and that this new person we've discovered inside us doesn't want to work in a real estate office. They want to be the manager of the local metaphysical bookstore.

On the low side, we may find that all our money is gone, and that the stress of worrying about Where They Are while we're at work eventually ends up in our getting let go because we're not performing. Either way, this person has subtly pulled us away from the life we were living when they arrived. They heightened our sensitivity to others, made us softer in our One-To-One relationships, and helped us to catch a glimpse of Divine Love— and that was the point.

But there's more. In addition to playing out in dreamy relationships, these transits can also point to times when we're either inspired or misled financially. Check the nature of the transit and the condition of your Venus to see which end to expect. Above all else, realize that each and every dance we do with another human is part of our path—so however great or terrible the experience, it's a learning experience. We may not get the point of the lesson until after the pink goddess has moved along, but the end result will be the same: we'll see how fine the line between perfection and deception really is. And that will certainly come in handy along the road.

NEPTUNE/MARS

He's totally spontaneous, the side of you that initiates all activity. He's in charge of how you assert yourself—so whenever you say No, it's him who'll be doing the refusing. He's Mars, he's red, and he's not at all shy about defending your best interests—even if he's got to get mad to do it. In fact, one of the best ways to get to know Mr. Mars is by thinking of all the phrases we use to describe anger. "Hot under the collar." "Seeing red." "All fired up." Needless to say, he's not shy, and he doesn't know what hesitation is. At least, that's how he is before Neptune enters the building.

Yes, these transits are interesting times, to say the least. When Neptune visits Mars, she befuddles him. It's like tying a pink ribbon on a handgun. She softens the red, fiery, action-oriented urge inside of you, and turns it into slowly burning embers, steaming from her watery touch. This can all be quite romantic, but it's not ordinarily a condition Mars enjoys. Remember, he's the ancient God of War, and he's not much into love stories. Neptune also traditionally withdraws strength from the planet she touches—and Mars prides himself on his strength.

What does this combination add up to, then? Well, first off, you may just feel tired—as if someone or something has pulled the plug on your energy. So even if you're used to leading a rather strenuous type of lifestyle, you'd better make arrangements to tone that down a bit. Mars rules the muscles in the physical body, so when Neptune arrives, you'll be much more in the mood for a massage, a slow dance or a Tai-Chi class than a triathalon. When this happens, no matter how hard your Mars tries to threaten, prod, or force you to keep at your usual pace, know that it's time for a break in the action. It's not a permanent situation, you understand, and you may just return to professional weight-lifting after Neptune's gone. But even after the transit has passed, you'll probably find your choice of exercise to be a lot more in tune with your body's needs, rather than your urge to compete.

Your competitive edge, in general, may soften now. Winning probably won't be quite as important, whether it's an argument or a foot race. On the other hand, since Neptune dissolves boundaries, you may also find that you're unable to control your anger—that it spills out, despite your best efforts to keep it in check. It all depends on you, and on how your natal Mars is aspected.

Under the conjunction, you may combine the best of both worlds, and become a Holy Warrior of sorts, fighting fiercely for what you believe in. Or you may suddenly not want to do battle at all, no matter what the Cause. You may also become a bit of a lightning-rod, and begin to feel that you're attracting others' anger. Under the harsher aspects of Neptune to Mars, you may also feel as if your efforts to Take Action are being met with subtle but impenetrable resistance—like you're punching a water-balloon. With the easy aspects, however, you may feel that all your actions are led by an intuitive force—as if you instinctively know just where and when to invest your energies for best results.

Regardless of which end of the spectrum you experience, remember that it's okay to slow down—and it's not a bad idea to soften up a little, either. And if you're in a situation where you feel defenseless and vulnerable, don't be afraid to ask for help. Even Mars deserves a vacation—and a helping hand—every now and then.

NEPTUNE/JUPITER

Again, as with transits of Jupiter to our Neptune, remember that this is the combination that Las Vegas relies on to stay in business. You know how Vegas is often called a Grown-Up's Disney Land? Well, that's what your life may seem to become when transiting Neptune touches your Jupiter.

Sounds great, huh? Well, it can be—if you don't get carried away in a casino. See, Jupiter's the kind of guy who's always game to take a shot at the brass ring. He's ultra optimistic, with unswerving faith in The Abundance Of the Universe. Only problem is, he doesn't know when to quit. His urge to grow and expand was never tempered by anything as restrictive as logic. Or caution. Or discretion. This is the place where we keep our supply of Everything Will Work Out Just Fine attitude, where we're ready to try anything—at least once—confident that only the best will happen. Add a dose of Neptune's pink dust, and you've got a team that truly believes in miracles. This is especially true when we're experiencing the conjunction of Neptune to Jupiter.

Needless to say, the boundless enthusiasm of this combination can be just wonderful. Imagining a miracle is the first step towards seeing it happen. And in fact, under Neptune's touch, this side of you that's already so positive and generous can be a powerful instrument toward making your own dreams—or someone else's—

come true. When Neptune visits Jupiter, especially by conjunction, we feel divinely inspired, as if we're magically gifted with the power to make the world a better place.

That type of thinking applies to both ourselves and others, so we may set our sights high, choose a lofty personal goal, and believe we can reach it. But with Neptune visiting, chances are also good that we'll be more concerned with playing Santa Claus to whoever we see as the Underdogs than making a fortune for ourselves. Remember, our Jupiter is also the place where we're the most concerned with Social Issues. So it's natural that adding Neptune's compassion will put us in the mood to take on a social ill and put all our good-hearted energies into Helping. That's the best side of what happens when these two conspire, and what we may experience under the easier transits.

But miracles don't always come true. They take more than just dreams to realize them. So sometimes, no matter how fervently we believe in our dreams, reality doesn't cooperate. That's what the harder transits are about. They can be times when we experience a Crisis of Faith—where all our hopes are dashed, and we feel as if we have nothing left to believe in. On the other hand, the push of the hard aspects can be just what it takes to make a risky venture into a lucky break. Who knows what will happen? It's like turning Jupiter loose at a blackjack table with your life's savings and a girl he wants to impress. Anything is possible. You may end up a millionaire—or a pauper.

The point behind this combination, no matter which aspect they hook together through, is to allow yourself to dream Big Dreams. It's where the best things in life come from. But realize that if you risk everything, no matter what the life scenario, you can also lose everything. Choose your ventures wisely, and see if you can't retain a Saturnian advisor to help with your decisions.

NEPTUNE/SATURN

Neptune's gift is her ability to dissolve boundaries, to turn us all into psychic receptors. When she visits with Saturn, the planet we use to erect boundaries and build foundations, there's a bit of a battle going on. Your Saturn—that is, your natural ability to separate—is no longer functioning up to par. So the boundaries between You and What's Out There are at their thinnest. Instead of seeing yourself as a separate individual, you're now open to all kinds of outside influences, good and bad. This means that you'll quite literally let your guard down in one way or another—and that can produce both positive and negative results.

First off, you may notice that the structures you've built your life upon seem to be dissolving, right out from under your feet. This is especially true in the case of the conjunction. It might be due to an outside influence you've subconsciously allowed access to, and it might be due to an attitude change. Either way, you're going to have to do some rearranging to get used to the uncertainty of it all. This is where the expression shifting sands probably came from. It's time to re-evaluate your life and your path, to learn to let rigid or over structured aspects of your life go.

Most often, since Saturn handles your career, regardless of the aspect Neptune makes, you may start to wonder if the one you've chosen is really right for you, and if something a bit more spiritual might not be in order. This doesn't have to mean that you start reading tea leaves or tarot cards for a living—although it could. But no matter what your vocation, if you're going to keep at it under this transit, you'll need to truly believe in it. Any work you do, in fact, will have to enable you to carry your beliefs along in your briefcase—or you won't be satisfied with it on a deeper level, and you'll want Out.

But the long-term effects of this transit on your life are far more profound than just changing careers. Remember the last scene in that great old cowboy movie, *Shane*? The part where the kid is yanking on Shane's arm, trying to get him to stay? It was the same lecture cowboys have been giving forever to little fatherless boys at the end of all the cowboy movies, the same one lots of heroes still give at the end of the movie, the speech that explains why they're going away. It's something along the lines of "Some day you'll understand, boy...but a man's gotta do what a man's gotta do."

Remember that lecture? Well, you may, but I'll bet you didn't understand it any more than the kid did—or he wouldn't have been hollerin' after ol' Shane as he rode off into the you-know-what. Know why both you and the kid didn't get the point ? Well, it's because those great-sounding lectures that inspire those noble, wistful, downright religious Big Finishes at the movies are brought to you courtesy of Neptune's visits to Saturn. In short, this is a mighty powerful combination, son, but not a pairing that's prone to inspiring razor-sharp, accurate, realistic memories of Just What Was Said. No, this is the technology that ordinarily produces one of three things: A) the ability to fool many of the people most of the time by portraying yourself as some type of noble guru on a mission few are deep enough to understand, B) the ability to actually become that guru, to yourself and others, by sensing what your true purpose on the planet really is, or C) Paranoia.

Now, A and C are what you'll probably feel with the harder aspects. You'll be dissatisfied on a personal level with anything as shallow as an illusion of success—and others will suddenly see through the illusion, anyway. In other words, under the tougher transits of Neptune to Saturn, if there's a nice picture on the box, but when you shake it, nothing rattles, neither you nor the outside world will be willing to perpetuate the myth. C) comes in when you begin to notice that They've noticed, and you wonder how long you'll be able to continue the facade. Under the easier transits, you'll choose B), and change your life around so that who you are and what you do—your life's foundation, that is—more honestly reflects your real self. It's up to you. Use this transit to examine just how sturdy your life's structure really is. Let what's not waterproof go—or repair it. This is your opportunity to become a whole person.

NEPTUNE/URANUS

Uranus in our charts is where we're radical, rebellious, and ready to fight City Hall—with or without a cause. It's the place where we're quite happy to shock and amaze everyone around us by proving to them just how independent and unique we really are. It's also a spot where we welcome sudden changes at the very last minute with open arms. Because here is where not knowing what to expect from life is just fine.

Needless to say, you can't be emotionally attached to situations and people if you're going to change your mind and take off for Europe on a whim. And if you're going to be a rebel, you've got to be charged up with a wired kind of energy—enough to get you through the picket line.

Enter Neptune, with her portable massage table. She throws a bit of pink dust into your eyes, and suddenly you're not feeling quite so radical. She rubs Uranus' temples, gets those nasty knots out of his shoulders, and hums a lullaby in his ear. She whispers to him to just calm down and relax. There's really nothing to get riled up about any more... and suddenly we're not quite so concerned with staying on strike until the Powers That Be meet our demands. Yes, this is a time when we may find that all our urges to break the rules are considerably softened. We may even begin to See It Their Way, and with Uranus' fondness for doing 180's, we may even end up on the other side of the battle. Under the conjunction, then, when Uranus becomes Neptune, that's certainly one of the ways we may end up.

On the other hand, depending on just how stubborn a Uranus we have, we may refuse to be led away from our Cause, and instead, become almost religious about it. Under the harder transits of Neptune to Uranus, we may even be riled up, striking out, and still fighting Them—but not sure of who They are, or why we're standing there with a sign in our hands. Under the easier transits, when Neptune cooperates with Uranus, we can also become even more convinced that we're right, so radically sure that Our Way Is The Right Way that we can't see any other way.

Now, with all that magic pink dust around Uranus, our lives can also turn a bit topsy-turvy. Reality seems to be suddenly transformed into a theme park—but all the rides are roller coasters. Remember that this is the pairing that inspires scandals—because scandals are really just secrets that get exposed suddenly. No matter what the aspect Neptune makes to Uranus, the best thing to do is to adopt a worthwhile, spiritual Cause—and set off inspiring Others to join us.

NEPTUNE/NEPTUNE

Next time you hear yourself sigh, or feel yourself slip into a day dream, think of Neptune. This is the planet that's in charge of romance, nostalgia, and magic. She's the side of you who delights in glamour and illusion, the side of you who's wistful, who wishes on a star and believes they'll come true. Neptune's place in your chart is a fuzzy, vague spot where you keep your pink smoke machine, where you're equally capable of fooling all of the people all of the time, and of being fooled yourself. Wherever she is in your chart is where you have that amazing ability we've talked about, to infiltrate your environment—but it's where you can be infiltrated, as well.

When Neptune touches your Neptune, then, you'll be capable of the very best and very worst this fuzzy planet has to offer. Remember, any planet aspecting itself is producing a double dose of that planet's symbolism in your life. So this can be a time of extreme compassion and sensitivity for creatures who are less fortunate than yourself—or a time of extreme self-delusion.

At these times, then, regardless of the aspect Neptune makes to herself, allow yourself to be drawn into charity or volunteer work. You're going to be keenly aware that We Are All Part Of The One, that there are no boundaries between you and What's Out There—so if someone or something around you is hurting now, you will be, too.

Since this type of sensitivity doesn't always mix too well with Reality, and since Reality can be downright unavoidable at times, despite our best efforts, this may also be a time where you'll try to escape, in a number of ways. Anything that gets you out of The Real World will do it, anything that makes you feel as if someone wonderful is rubbing your temples and telling you not to worry, that everything is just fine. Sleep, meditation, and prayer are the highest uses of this double Neptunian dose, but alcohol and drugs are also under her jurisdiction. So be careful not to overdo any kind of Altered State right now.

Now, although her official title is Head of the Department of Reality Avoidance, Neptune is also the Queen of Imagination and Fantasy. She's one of the most creative energies you own. Use this well of receptive energy to create, then, whether it's music, art, or poetry. This is a time when you can use your personal magic wand to cast Special Moments into other folk's lives. Keep your feet on the planet, and your ear cocked towards the whispers of inspiration.

NEPTUNE/PLUTO

The Pink Goddess Meets Darth Vader. Sounds like a great title for an awful movie, huh? Well, that's what your Neptune/Pluto transits will be like. You'll be secretive and magical, sensing all kinds of things. Remember, Pluto is the ultimate Detective, and Neptune is the Mistress of Illusion. So any and all mysteries will appeal to you now—and you may even want to create one or two around yourself.

Now, because these two planets are so far away and their orbits are so wide, we only get to entertain Neptune at our Pluto's place a few times over the course of our lifetime. And Most of us born over the past 50 years or so were born with a sextile between the two planets to start with—so we're collectively quite familiar with the meshing of these two energies. Religion and Politics, for example, on a large scale, or the concept of Being Empowered by Being Spiritual, on a personal level. When Neptune sets that sextile off by visiting Pluto, then, she's also going to aspect herself. So it's our collective beliefs that will be stimulated, either in positive or negative fashion.

But let's talk a bit about Pluto. This a spot in our chart where we're going to prefer trashing a situation to fixing it. Remember, this guy's a big fan of Starting Over From Scratch. Add a bit of Neptune's illusory, romantic touch and your Pluto may end up even more potent. She aids him in his efforts to Change Everything by adding the touch of a magic wand. All that means that when she touches Pluto by transit, you're going to be quite good at manipulating by creating illusions—or being manipulated by an illusion. Needless to say, under the harsher transits, it's best to avoid taking drugs or overindulging in alcohol.

Now, it's true that the square happens at a very young age right now—usually around 14 or so—so that word of warning might seem a bit out of place. But kids are experimenting with drugs at younger ages now, and 14-ish seems to be about the time they need to make a decision about how to handle the topic. So even if you've already had the transit, be aware of it for your children. The trine happens a bit later in life—usually within a year or so of the first Saturn Return. It's at this time of becoming an adult in the eyes of the Universe that Neptune's gift for inspiration added to Pluto's natal position can help us to envision what we really came here to give the planet. This is also typically when we begin to discover our personal power—and to see the results of our decisions. The opposition happens at about age 60 or so, and although drugs can still be an issue, (prescription drugs in particular), the hardest side of these two coming together at that age can be more along the lines of feeling as if our personal power is slipping away, perhaps because we're not capable of quite as much as we used to be. The highest side of the opposition is that it can also bring awareness—in this case, awareness of how wonderful a gift Life on this planet really is.

Regardless of the age or situation, when these two come together, we can all benefit from a bit of therapy. Neptune can soften Pluto's intense way of guarding secrets long enough to make great psychological breakthroughs. She can erase his suspicions, jealousies, and power issues by convincing him that it's quite all right to open up a little. So use your intuition to help you dig down deep when these two get together, and you'll discover a brand new inner world.

CHAPTER THIRTEEN

PLUTO

Your Pluto Kit:

Pomegranates

Dark Glasses

A Black Trench Coat

A Flashlight

A Surgical Kit

Fertilizer

A Book on Death and Dying

Scary Movies (*Arachniphobia*, for one...)

An Atom Bomb

An Illustrated Book on Spiders and Snakes

One Year's Worth of Free Therapy

Pluto Transits: Just Let Go

You remember Pluto, right? The Head of the Department of Extremes and Inevitables? The guy who looks a bit like Darth Vader—who's in charge of such delectable topics as Death, Destruction, and Endings? Well, although all that may make you want to forget about him, you can't. That's what the inevitable part is all about. And you shouldn't, either—because even if you could just ignore Pluto, what you'd really be ignoring is all the opportunities to evolve that life will present you with. And that's what Pluto's visits are really all about: evolution and enlightenment.

Now, enlightenment can't happen if you don't shed some weight—and Pluto wants you as light as possible when he arrives. See, he's trying to help you climb up the evolutionary staircase. Over the course of a transit, he'll come by to visit several times—to check your progress and weigh you up. He wants you to rise up easily. And if he has to, he'll lighten you up himself.

It's like this: Pluto doesn't like it when nothing happens. That's stagnation, and that's not going to help you on your quest to Change. He's a very big fan of changing everything, matter of fact. You might even call him ravenous. He doesn't want just a little bite of anything. He wants it all, and he wants it all at once. When he comes a-callin', then, forget telling him you'll quit cauliflower for Lent because you just love it and it'll be a big sacrifice for you, really. Forget that. Pluto's heard those stories, and he ain't buyin' them. He wants you to give up Everything— everything that's superfluous, that is. Everything that's excess baggage on your soul.

Needless to say, when you feel his breath on your neck, it's time to evaluate What's Really Necessary in your life—and to ditch what isn't. Remember, the harder you try to hold on, the more ungently he'll shake you off.

That's what Pluto transits are all about: they're a three-stage process of Life, Death, and Rebirth. Now, don't let that Everything stuff scare you. You'll get to keep The Real Things— everything that's really You. It's the useless things that pass away under Pluto transits—so an existing condition in your life is going to die, and that's for sure, but it's going to be one that's outworn it's usefulness to you. Yes, it sounds harsh, but you know what? Somewhere deep down inside, you always know what's got to go, under a Pluto transit. It's just tough to come to grips with the fact that now is the time. You also know that even if you try to hold on to someone or something, it will probably still leave your life—or you'll learn down the road why it would have been better to let go then. So tap into that inner knowing, and let Change happen. It's always best to cooperate with the tide you'll see about to peak in your life. Make plans for Stage Three—Rejuvenation Time—and release what's got to go gracefully.

Pluto Through The Houses

The subject is obsession, regeneration, and inevitable change. These are times of Transformation and Rejuvenation, when we shed our skin in a particular area of life in order to start over— but not without some expense. It's like watching a part of your personality go up in flames. The scary part is that you may have been comfortable with Things just the way they were. The great part is that they'll be better—and you'll feel like you've been reborn—after it's over.

It's like this: about two years after the huge fire in Yellowstone Park, I spent three days there. We stayed, of course, in the part of the park untouched by the fire, but drove through the pieces that were. The charred trees were coal-black to about waist-level, then orange, then white. The effect was eerie—like a perpetual sunset. Just at the feet of the blackened trees, though, a carpet of fuzzy green babies covered the ground, tiny pine trees and white birch that never would have been able to seed were it not for the heat of the fire which releases them. These lovely little green guys marched right through the burned forest, literally covering the ground. Once I spotted them, I wasn't sad any more— I understood The Process.

This is what all Pluto transits are like. They're times of death and regeneration. But this process is especially obvious with Pluto's passes through the houses in our charts. When he first arrives, we feel terrified. Things are changing, Big Time, in a particular corner of our lives. The side of our personality we keep in the house he's transiting begins to change. We see those changes first through what happens in our outer world—as the forest fire begins. As time goes on, we sense that the fire is out of control, that the part of our life ruled by that particular house is changing, completely—and that there's nothing we can do to stop it. On some level, we don't even want to. But since humans are notoriously bad at Change, there may also be a part of us who resists—or tries to. Pluto, however, is not a planet of Maybes. He's in charge of The Inevitables. So resistance is futile, as they say. Holding back from these changes is like telling ourselves to put the evolution of a particular side of ourselves on hold— and that's out of the question.

If we can understand that the changes are inevitable, we stand the chance of re-seeding our lives after the fire—and that's the most important thing to do when Pluto enters a house. See that the changes, both in the Outer World, and in our personality— are inevitable. Try to understand them. One of Pluto's gifts is the ability to see what's going on beneath the surface of things. Then cooperate. Re-seed. Get to know the Side of You that's left after the fire. It's the only real side that was ever there, anyway. Whatever is gone was unnecessary, or outworn. Now it's time for The Good Stuff to emerge—the brand-new life that was smothered or stifled by the old. When Pluto transits a house, the best thing to keep in mind is that new beginnings can never happen without endings. If there wasn't any fire, there wouldn't be little green armies inching their way up towards the sun in Yellowstone. That's the rebirth part of a Pluto transit.

FIRST HOUSE

Pluto's transits to the Ascendant initially feel like the biggest, darkest, most powerful person you've even known has shown up at your Front Door with a search warrant and told you to wait in the yard until they're done. It's your house, the place you feel safest, and now that's being shaken. You start to question who you really are, and what you're made of—if it's so easy for someone to just show up at the door and force you out of there. You'll feel quite violated for awhile, but then you decide that you're not going to take it any more. You charge into the house, ready to tell this Dark Intruder to get out. To your surprise, he hasn't touched a thing. He's just sitting there at your kitchen table, smiling. When you enter, he applauds you—and says "Sorry about the scare tactics—but I had to see what you were made of." Despite yourself, you're smiling. You sit down, pour some coffee for the both of you—and Stage Two of Pluto's transit to your Ascendant begins. You find you have an ally, not an enemy. A powerful ally.

Well, then. Let's talk about how you're going to act after all this happens. You've overpowered the intruder. You've faced your fear—your greatest fear—and discovered that it was nothing more than you being afraid of your own personal power. There's no longer an intruder—never really was. Only a New, Improved, You. Needless to say, as a result of the experience, you're feeling rather powerful. As if nobody and nothing can touch you. And that's quite true. In fact, Pluto's transit over the Ascendant and through the first house can be one of the most empowering times of your life. You have a New Attitude. So, of course, since the

Ascendant is our Front Door, you'll want to make sure the whole world knows just how In Charge of your life you really are by decorating that door appropriately. You'll probably redo your entire physical appearance, starting at the core. Physical stuff first. Then incidentals, like wardrobe—black, please.

Now, all that applies to what will happen if you respond to this transit by grabbing Pluto by the neck and shaking him. If, on the other hand, you buckle—if you do stand out in the yard, waiting for that figure in black to leave your home—well, it's going to be a long wait, first of all. And you're going to get mighty cold out there. In the process, you'll become angry (with yourself), resentful (also at yourself), and bitter (yep—you guessed it). All those bad feelings will turn into a Front Door that's sullen, sarcastic, and guarded—and no one will want to come near you. So if you're looking to spend an awful lot of time alone, (and, hey, maybe you've got a book to write...), then by all means, don't take charge of your life when Pluto enters your first house. Who needs it, right? Riiiiiiiight.....

Seriously, though—try. Even if you're scared. When you feel this big blast of power start working its way into your personality, use it—but use it appropriately. And when you're patting yourself on the back, reveling in your newfound power, remember that you're only in charge of You and your own surroundings—not the people who happen to stumble across those boundaries. Go easy on others. It's the truest expression of power and confidence you'll ever find.

SECOND HOUSE

The second house is the side of you who decides What You Hold Dear. It's the piece of your personality you take out when it's time to go shopping, balance the checkbook, and decide what qualities in yourself—and others—you find valuable. Pluto is equal parts Detective, Analyst, and Assassin. He's the guy with the x-ray vision, too—who always knows exactly what you've been up to. And he has an uncanny knack for being in the building when there's a power-struggle taking place. Needless to say, then, when Pluto enters this house, your financial picture is going to become quite interesting.

First off, since you'll be in the mood to start a secret stash of some kind, by all means, do—just in case. Put something aside in a safe deposit box, and swallow the key. Okay, don't really swallow the key, but do make sure you're the only one who knows where it is. You might also want to be prepared for the possibility of a verrry detailed investigation of your finances—yes, that means an audit. Yes, it sure could be the IRS. They're an organization that's long been associated with Pluto. And if you are audited, prepare to be asked for detailed accounts of every last dime you've earned and deducted. Pluto is nothing if not thorough, you know, (the Analyst), and nothing if not able to unearth even those minute details you thought you'd buried (the Detective). He's also not above attaching your pay, or making sure your monthly payments are high enough to cancel taking that trip to Europe you've planned (the Assassin—of your plans). Your best bet, when you see that Pluto will enter your second house in a few years, is to be very, very honest and aboveboard in all your accounting matters. Resist the temptation to be less than honest on paper, and don't make deals with loan-sharks—of any kind.

Now, you may also find yourself deeply enmeshed in power struggles over money at this time, whether that's because there just isn't much to go around, and you're having to fire-walk your way to paying the monthly bills, or because someone's trying to coerce or manipulate you out of what's yours. In that case, remember this is your Pluto transit. Stand up for yourself, and come out with both guns blasting. You may also feel as if nothing comes your way without strings attached.

That's the scary stuff, and I felt obligated to mention it first. However, remember that Pluto also empowers us—so this transit can also coincide with a time when you decide it's time to take control of the steering wheel in the financial department. In that case, it will simply mean that you begin to Take Charge Of Your Finances, to stop being dependent on whoever or whatever. Since Pluto also rules power, you may also be the recipient of a great deal of money—enough to make you quite powerful. No matter what else, remember that now is your chance to tear things down and start over. So it's a great time to close out an account that's been mismanaged for too long, and start over.

THIRD HOUSE

Here's your third-house Pluto lesson: words can be a very powerful weapon. Now, before you decide that's really nothing to concern yourself about, and that this lesson is going to be a piece of cake, consider this: ordinary words combined with Pluto's famous manipulative abilities are the technology behind Mind Control, Brainwashing, and Blackmail. Doesn't sound so harmless anymore, huh?

See, your third-house is the side of you who communicates with others and your environment. Pluto is the guy who's perfected the art of persuasion through his perceptive abilities. He's already got a gift for x-ray vision, for being able to see the real meaning of words and actions through paying attention to subtle body-signals and tone inflections. In short, he knows What You Meant By That, and he knows what you want to hear. So his transit through this house will bring you into contact with very manipulative and possibly coercive words—and the purveyors of those words.

As a result, you can expect folks with a gift for Sales to come into your life, for starters. Or you may become a salesperson of some kind yourself. That doesn't mean you'll necessarily take this on as a profession, but you'll definitely learn a bit about intellectual digging under this transit. You'll learn to use Pluto like a shovel, to tunnel beneath words and find the Meaning that's buried there. You'll learn a lot about doing verbal warfare in the process, too, as you see how delicately a twist or two in a sentence can affect the outcome of an entire situation.

Now, the power of words certainly isn't limited to their use in coercion. There are lots of positive ways to use powerful words to benefit yourself and others. You could learn to communicate with folks in crisis who need to hear the naked, bare-bones truth to be convinced that they need to make changes in their lives—right now. You can be taught to regenerate yourself, physically, spiritually, and emotionally, through The Power Of Positive Thinking. And hypnosis is an invaluable tool—whether it's to help you quit a bad habit, start a good one, or help you remember a trauma, long buried, that's sabotaging your psychological health. In short, words are very, very potent because they influence our thinking, and any time we change the way we think, we change the way we see the world.

Now, since this house also refers to your dealings with neighbors and siblings, you may also find that these folks become instruments of major Change in your life during these years. You may become Plutonian-ly involved in your neighborhood or community somehow, too—by starting a Neighborhood Watch program, or leading a citizen's action committee to fight a proposed toxic waste dump in your town. Remember, a Pluto temporarily gives you super-powers. Use yours for a good cause.

FOURTH HOUSE

The fourth house is our root-cellar. It's the side of us who handles New Stuff based on how Old Stuff felt. And lest you think that the past is simply the past, remember that everything that's ever happened to us has a direct influence on every future action or decision. When Pluto arrives, then, with his shovel and Analysis Kit, get ready to deal with issues of Power, Control, and Manipulation from the past—and to see just how powerful your memories can be.

Now, this can mean that you begin therapy to dig up, face, and purge yourself of an event from childhood that's affecting your current emotional condition. Or it can indicate a time when you do this on your own—when memories from the past seem to surface when you least expect them—and you're able to see their significance in your present life. Since this house also refers to the way we were nurtured, and the person who did the nurturing, now may be when you begin to see just how powerful and controlling one of your parents was—or is.

You may experience Pluto's transit through this house through crises that make you see the necessity for change in your present family situation, too. But before you start thinking of all the awful things a crisis can be, remember that anything that's radically different from what we're used to, whether it's traditionally thought of as bad or good, has a crisis effect on our lives. Matter of fact, there's a Top Ten list that's been published of the crises or major events we encounter through life that are the most emotionally stressful on us. That list includes marriage (or divorce), the birth of a child, and major moves. So any (or all) of those scenarios are possible when Pluto arrives. Even a family member striking out on their own or moving back home can have a gigantic effect on our home life—enough to qualify as a long-term crisis.

In some cases, you may find that you're doing some digging on a more literal level—by digging a hole in the earth and building a new home. You might end up Doing The Pluto by replacing a septic system or refurbishing the plumbing in your cellar. If that's the case, realize that outer events are all simply indications of inner change—and if your physical home is in need of regeneration, your emotional foundation is, too.

In all, this transit is about starting over from the roots up, which might mean tearing down everything—and I do mean everything—to start over. No matter what it is, then, that needs to be completely redone when Pluto enters this house, go for it. Purge yourself, your family, and your home of what's unnecessary. Then plant new emotional seeds for the future, and watch them grow.

FIFTH HOUSE

Here's a transit that often points to the beginning of a whole new attitude about Fun. I mean, imagine inviting Pluto over to play. First of all, what's he going to bring with him? It's a scary thought. He loves Ouija boards and monster costumes, of course—but he's also a big fan of anatomy, physiology, and forensics. So if you're about to experience a visit from Pluto, prepare for your appetite on The Mysteries to become quite insatiable. You may develop a taste for Steven King novels, or start listening to Anne Rice's vampire anthologies on your way to work. You might also take up an unusual hobby of some kind, that's quite Plutonian in nature— say, playing detective, or learning some psychology. Any type of digging will capture you—literally and otherwise.

Of course, Pluto also loves Life and Death experiences, so your taste in leisure-time activities may reflect his presence here by turning your interest toward death-defying sports— like sky-diving, mountain-climbing, or racing cars. Whatever you do for fun now, rest assured, it's going to get your adrenaline pumping. One client I have literally started fire-walking on weekends when this transit began.

Then, too, because Pluto is such an intense kind of guy, and this house relates to Love Affairs, you may start dating someone (at least one someone) who perfectly personifies any or all of Pluto's traits—and chances are, since this transit lasts a while, you'll experience both sides of the coin. They may be an agent for profound positive change in your life, or they may be very manipulative or possessive. You may take up with an investigator, an analyst, or a researcher. In extreme cases, this transit also points to relationships with quite obsessive folks—and, by the way, this is a good time to avoid getting involved with anyone who represents the negative side of Pluto's qualities. You could also become involved with someone in a very secret way when Mr. Behind-The-Scenes gets here. One way or the other, you won't be looking for a casual affair over this period. All your prospective Others will need to be intense and penetrating, or there won't be a second date.

Your relationships with your children, or with children in general, are also going to take on a much deeper, more penetrating tone. You may need to fire-walk your way through a difficult experience with one of your own children, or there may be power struggles between you and someone else about How To Raise The Children. Even if you don't have any kids of your own, you may find yourself involved in transforming children's lives through crisis counseling.

In all, remember that this transit is about intensifying and deepening the side of you who's in charge of enjoying life. Choose your leisure pursuits—and your playmates—carefully.

SIXTH HOUSE

This is another one of those transits with a very heavy reputation to live down. All the olde texts describe this as a major health crisis just waiting to happen—often with a very Plutonian ending, if you catch my drift. Well, I beg to differ. If this transit meant that we were all going to develop a fatal condition and die, then anybody born with Pluto in the 4th or 5th house would never live past the age of 40—and that's ridiculous. That doesn't mean that I'm downplaying the seriousness of Pluto's transit through this house, or failing to see its importance—only that I'm quite sure it's possible to live through it without a major health crisis.

See, it's like this: in this sixth house, we keep the side of us who chooses our work, tends to the health of our body, and decides what the rhythm of our day is going to be like. In short, it's the piece of our personality who's in charge of our daily schedule—and that's an area of life that turns habitual quite easily. (Unless, of course, you were born with Uranus here, in which case your only daily habit is not to have a habit at all.) When any planet steps into this house, then, it's arrived with a mission: to change those daily habits and rearrange our schedule in some way, either because we're stuck in an unhealthy rut, or not structured enough to keep our bodies going.

Now, the point of any transit is for us to incorporate those energies that the transiting planet symbolizes into the area of life they're visiting. So while it's true that we certainly do need to adjust our lives in a very major way to accommodate a visitor like Pluto, we don't have to become extremely ill to keep him happy. Pluto is the Clean-Up Man. His number one function by transit is to point out what's not working. Sometimes, then, Pluto's visit does coincides with a time when we discover something wrong, health-wise—something that we need to medically treat, surgically remove, or purge. (And since he has everything to do with the reproductive organs, it's often one of those parts that needs fixing—or removal). But the point of all those processes is to improve our health, not rob us of it—so if you do discover a problem when he's here, by all means, don't ignore it. Get thee to a physician and get it fixed.

On the other hand, this transit may point to an increased interest in our body. Lots of folks simply join a health club, go on a long-overdue diet, or quit a long-term bad habit—all of which are quite wonderful things to do for ourselves, all of which are quite positive ways to use Pluto. Then, too, as he's a rather focused kind of guy, some of us become rather obsessive with our health. We find symptoms where there really aren't any, and develop a good case of hypochondria. In all, Pluto only wants you to get rid of what's not doing you any good—and that includes excess weight, unhealthy habits, and/or an inactive lifestyle.

Now, this house has long been associated with pets (although I've also seen pets reflected more by the 4th or 5th house side of us—depending on how you see them). So—does this transit mean the death of a pet? Not necessarily—but possibly. It can mean that your critters simply take on a much more important part of your life, or that your attitude about pets changes drastically. Or it can mean that you lose one. Now, you know I hate to even mention this part of Pluto's visit, fond as I am of beasts with tails...but it does happen, unfortunately.

If you believe in reincarnation, however—which is another of Pluto's specialties—well, then, even if one of your fuzzy babes does pass over when Pluto gets here, do what I do. Tough as it sounds, try to keep in mind that their life-cycles aren't as long as ours. So do everything you can to help them pass over peacefully and painlessly. Then be sure to tell them to go get a new fur body, and get back immediately. And do allow yourself to mourn. A pet's death is every bit as traumatic as losing a person we care for— even more so for some of us. Then check for the right pair of eyes in every stray you see. (Hey, I think it works...)

Of course, this house also pertains to work, to what we do on a daily basis to earn our daily bread. With Pluto here, our position at work sometimes increases in importance—we become absolutely indispensable to our employer, or our power at work is intensified through added job responsibilities and/or a promotion. Sometimes we change our job around completely, and turn to investigation, analysis, research, crisis counseling, or a job that allows us to dig—literally. One way or the other, our health, our work, and the people and beasts that are part of our daily travels become more important to us.

SEVENTH HOUSE

Pluto is the guy who wants it all. He's Mr. Intense and Penetrating, the kind of guy who never could stand surface chit-chat, casual dates, or open relationships. Needless to say, when he sets up camp here in the seventh house and settles in for a nice, long visit, regardless of how long or short the encounter you have with An Other, there absolutely will not be anything casual about it. You'll be having deep, penetrating conversations with strangers you meet on the bus, asking them what they really think about whatever's on page one. They'll walk away a bit shaken, but you'll get them thinking about more than what's for dinner tonight, and that's good. And if that's what your quickie encounters are going to be like, you can imagine how much more profound your committed relationships will be.

Needless to say, if you start a relationship with Pluto in this house, it's going to be plenty intense—more like two souls pairing up than just two humans—and you're both going to have to fire-walk to keep it alive. With this newfound depth occurring in all your encounters, you'll notice that your tastes in prospective Others will change, too. You'll be far more interested in anyone who's Plutonian in nature or profession—a CIA agent, perhaps, or a researcher, analyst, or detective.

Now, this can also mean that your commitment to your current Other deepens to such a point that you truly feel connected to them on a soul level—and that you really couldn't possibly live without them. But Pluto also represents Letting Go of what's unnecessary. So if a relationship ends now, it's because it was bogging you down in some way, and stunting or stagnating your personal growth. In other words, if your current relationship doesn't support this new, deeper, more passionate side of you that's just now arriving, you'll want out. And you'll get out. The beauty of it all is that with Pluto here, on some level, you'll understand that—and the goodbye, although painful, will be easier because of that knowledge.

Now, this is also the type of transit that may coincide with the entry of unsavory individuals into your life. So don't allow your new craving for depth to draw you into relationships with violent or obsessive types, or those who are involved with the underworld in any way—whether it's organized crime or gangs. While it's certainly not the case all of the time, this is the technology behind fatal attractions and stalking—so be careful, and choose partners who reflect the highest side of Pluto's character. One thing's for sure: when Pluto enters this house of One-to-One relationships: nobody gets out the same as when they came in. This goes for both You and Them.

EIGHTH HOUSE

Listen closely... because that hissing sound you hear isn't really a snake—it's a soft, potent, "Yesssssss...," the first word I'm sure Pluto utters as he finally crosses the threshold of the eighth house. Ah yessss—Home again. This is where Pluto is at his most potent, where he's finally in surroundings that suit him. He's settled in for a nice, long return to his very own house in your chart—and that means that there's Changes to be made, Evolution to get underway, and psychological battles to be fought. All perfectly wonderful activities to engage in—if you happen to be Pluto, or if you're currently experiencing his visit to your eighth house.

This is also the house that holds the side of you who's interested in what goes on behind the scenes. So at this time, you may develop an interest in some of those things. Life after Death. Exorcism. Grief therapy. Or maybe just recycling. Don't be afraid, and don't think for a moment that you're being morbid. With Pluto here, it's all part of the package.

Now, Pluto always did love turmoil, and life and death situations—and he will be operating unchecked when he's home. So you might expect Things to become a bit turbulent for awhile. It's nothing you won't be able to handle, however. You've been temporarily endowed with super-powers, able to leap tall buildings, do battle with arch-enemies, and save the world from Bad Stuff. In the process of tuning up your super-powers, you may become involved in a power struggle or two over joint finances, taxes, or other people's money. This is the eighth house, after all, where the issue of Ours is handled. That may mean there's an ugly battle over a divorce settlement, a family feud over an inheritance, or the threat of ending up responsible for a loan you co-signed for a relative or friend that they've reneged upon. On the high side, you may marry someone who's quite wealthy, or find yourself involved in a very successful financial partnership. Or your super-powers may be called into play to help you decide how to invest that sizable inheritance you've just received. Any way you shake it, you'll be up for it.

Of course, this is also the side of you who handles the issue of Intimacy—and with Pluto here, you're going to learn all about it, in all its forms. That means you may stand to become involved in a very intense physical entanglement that teaches you just how close sex can bring you to An Other. You may also find that all your relationships now carry an intense, penetrating quality, sexual or not. Then, too, there's the issue of Death, not just of the physical kind, but endings of all kinds. You can expect an awful lot to leave your life when Pluto is here, but relax. Although this isn't ordinarily an easy period in our lives, it's an educational one. It prepares us for anything the world throws at us, after it has passed. It toughens us up, and makes us more insightful into why Others do the things they do—and why we do the things we do. Remember, Pluto is the detective, the analyst, and the assassin. When any of those characters show up in your life during this transit, they're teachers. If you pay attention now, you'll learn more about Human Nature than at any other time in your life.

NINTH HOUSE

Imagine Pluto as your new teacher. He stalks into the classroom, dressed in black, and within moments, he's got you asking Why—about everything. You're no longer interested in the surface details of any subject. All of a sudden, you want to know more—about the inner workings of politics, the psychology of religion, the reasons why certain philosophies so attracted the people who lived back then.

This will mean that you'll begin to feel as if your daily life just isn't providing the kind of stimulation you need. Routine will bore you. You'll develop an obsessive, insatiable urge to wander—to see how other folks live, how other cultures run their politics. Once you hit the road, you'll find that every trip is a life-changing one, and that your life and personal philosophies are drastically, radically transformed by what you see or learn. Even if you don't spend the next several years in foreign countries, you'll need education and encounters with others from Far Away to help you broaden and deepen your intellectual horizons.

Now, if there happens to be a national election going on while you're having this transit, God help anyone who dares to differ with you on your choice of candidate, or your opinion on a major issue. You won't want to let them go home until they're wearing your team's colors—and all that new knowledge and experience will make you quite persuasive. In short, if you were at all interested in politics before the transit started, you'll want to get much more involved in the process now. If you're already involved, now may be when you come to power politically, too. Pluto's x-ray vision allows us to see How Things Work, on an internal level, and understanding what's really going on inside a political process is invaluable to anyone who wants to play the game.

Now, with this new teacher in Jupiter's ninth-house classroom, you're also going to develop a strong interest in current events, and contemporary issues, especially the more Plutonian issues—The Right To Die, Abortion, and the moral battles over Genetic Engineering, for example. In all, your conscious mind will be ravenous, starving for The Answers—and you'll be happy to dig to find them. Pluto is the kind of teacher who inspires your soul's need for Understanding of the deepest, most penetrating kind. You'll want to know Everything during this time when his class is in session. Just go easy on others who don't see it your way—and try not to take any political prisoners.

TENTH HOUSE

This highest spot in your chart is your Career and Reputation Department. It's your office, the penthouse suite of your chart, the place where your own personal bulletin board hangs, covered with clippings that detail the accomplishments you've made throughout your journey down here on Planet Number Three. The view from this house is an aerial view—and no other perspective lends such a broad glimpse of your entire life.

The Authority Figure in you lives here, taking questions from The Press, and planning your next career move. When any planet makes an appointment to visit this house, it's there to make you a deal: either incorporate its symbolic energies into your professional life, or it will set up camp outside the office door and hand out leaflets to everyone who enters.

Now picture Pluto walking into that office, black leather briefcase in hand. Talk about an offer you can't refuse...This guy wants one thing from you—to Take Charge of your life or Change it and start over. If you've already done quite well for yourself, then, this transit represents a time when you'll gain an amazing amount of professional power, and rise to the pinnacle of success in your chosen field. Others will begin to see you as The Final Authority—no pun intended—and your name will become quite well known. On the other hand, if you've spent much of your life drifting in and out of jobs, not really ever focusing on one thing, or if you've invested years pursuing something that really doesn't pertain to who you are, well, then, Pluto's going to demand that you get out of your chair and let him sit back there. Until you make a decision. The right decision.

In other words, if you haven't done it yet, circumstances are now going to demand that you choose a life path that absolutely reflects what you know you should be. Sometimes that means changing careers—and with Pluto sitting back there, you may choose a career in one of his fields. Detective work, psychology, or research, for example. Or anything that allows you to use your new ability to dig—figuratively or literally.

Then, too, because so much of this house is about what you've become known for, and since Pluto just loves to dig things up, you may also become rather infamous at this time. In other words, secrets you may have thought were long buried may now emerge from the depths. You might even need to admit to something you've done, and take the consequences—which may mean that your life, as you see it, is a shambles.

Not to worry. No matter what Pluto finds when he reaches into your past professional life, no matter how good or bad the file he brings to the newspaper really is, you're ready to handle it. You're super-charged in this most public area of your chart. It's like being on an evolutionary mission.

The Authority Figure in you will also feel the symbolic impact of this visit from the planet who so loves power and control. On the high side, you'll be feeling quite confident in yourself and what you've done. On the downside, you may feel pretty darned useless. Either way, look at this transit as a new beginning. It's an opportunity to get started on your path—if you haven't found it yet, or if you've strayed from it. And if you have been on the right track, now is your chance to get behind the steering wheel and decide where you want to go, and at what speed.

ELEVENTH HOUSE

Here's the side of you who's the team-player, the slice of your personality who comes out in group situations. This is the You who chooses your affiliations, and decides which pack of other humans you most identify with, based on what you have in common with them. Now, let's add Pluto to that house—the guy who's searching for intense experiences for you—no matter where you are or who you're with.

When Pluto tags along to your weekly meetings, then, regardless of whether it's a sewing circle, an astrology class, or a Greenpeace gathering, you're no longer going to be satisfied with superficial friendships. You're going to be looking for a purpose to your affiliations now, and since this house also holds your goals for the future, that purpose will need to be meaningful, to contribute to how you see yourself in the future. This may mean that you change peer groups entirely, if you don't find what you're looking for now. Remember, our peers are those we feel we share a common denominator with. When that common denominator changes, the folks we see as Kindred Spirits often do, too.

So if you do find yourself bored with the usual group activities, and drawn towards more Plutonian circles, make sure these circles reflect the highest end of Pluto's symbolic energies. That is, make sure you're hanging around with fellow detectives and analysts, and with those who are also interested in The Mysteries. Although it's easy to fall in with the wrong types now, if you let your common sense guide you, you'll find your niche in associations and organizations that strive to accomplish positive change. And speaking of Change, remember that Pluto loves to rejuvenate, recycle, and reform. Any group or organization that's involved in those goals will suit you just fine.

Now, Pluto also wants you to take charge—no matter where you are or who you're with. So don't be surprised if whatever group you're a part of now asks you to take a much stronger role in their leadership. In all, this transit is about purging you of associations that won't serve the best interests of who you're becoming, and giving you a strong hand to guide the ones that will.

TWELFTH HOUSE

Well, now, here we are again at the door to the twelfth house, the place where traditional astrology says you keep the side of you who's your greatest undoing. Yes, this house has a very tough reputation. Ptolemy even called it The House Of The Evil Demon. Scary stuff, huh? Well, no, it's really not. As I've said before, this is really just the side of you who only comes out when it's Safe— the piece of your personality you ordinarily hide, the side you carefully unwrap and take out only when you're alone, or in the company of someone you trust completely. Why would that be seen as a bad thing? Well, because being alone back when Ptolemy was around was a bad thing. Society was much more group-oriented than it is now, so if you were alone, it usually meant you were sick, banished or imprisoned. Nowadays, however, it's perfectly all right to spend time alone, and the more planets you have in here natally, the more you're going to need time alone, matter of fact—to rest, recuperate, and recharge your batteries.

Now, when Pluto pushes aside that filmy veil that separates the eleventh house from the twelfth, he's here to lend a new depth to your Quality Time Alone With You. This is the planet that loves to dig, remember. So when he visits this house, chances are that first of all, your Alone Time is going to be much more meaningful. You may spend a lot of time in very intense concentration on Deep Stuff. Or you may end up wondering What It All Means—your life, especially. Lots of folks turn to therapy at this time, to help them find answers to those questions, or to do the Pluto purge— by getting rid of old hang-ups.

This house is where we stash the side of us we were taught was inappropriate or not fit for public consumption very early on. Now, anything in our chart that's stifled eventually finds a way out—but if we're afraid to use it out in the open, then the ways we've found to express that side of us may be less than positive. Therapy is a great way to get to know this piece of our personality who's hiding behind the veil. Again, anything we hold back for years is in need of reassurance, acceptance, and a positive outlet, so that we can use it in a healthy way. With Pluto here, rummaging around in our subconscious, it's That Time.

PLUTO/SUN

Prepare to change everything about yourself—everything. The subject under Pluto transits is regeneration and inevitable change.

When Pluto visits the Sun, the Executive Director of that Corporation you know as You, it's time to clean house. This is a big one, gang, an important time when whatever has gone past the point of no return or is broken beyond repair will pass from your life. Definitely. So get used to it, and let it go. Make plans for the future to keep yourself occupied while these huge changes happen. You're molting, shedding your skin in some way—and although you'll be very different when this transit is over, what you'll have left will be real.

Now, Pluto's conjunctions to the Sun, like Saturn's, are not known for being rollickin' good-times—that's Jupiter's job. These are times, however, when you'll learn just how strong you are— what you're made of, way down deep. See, part of Pluto's job is intensifying. Also, remember that your Sun's going to take on the qualities of any planet that touches it by conjunction—so in this case, you'll feel as if you're a phoenix, ready to crash and burn and start over. In some way, circumstances in your outer world will assist that process, and everything you think you are may peel away from you—your job, the place where you live, and maybe even your relationships. When it's over, you'll get to really see yourself—without all those other things attached. In the process, many of the old lies or half-truths you've been living will pass away, too. But don't fight it. Remember, you can't hide from this guy. Pluto wants you to get to know You—and you can't do that if you continue your life as is.

Now, under the tougher transits, you may experience power struggles, or battles with authority figures who seem to have a hold over you. You'll be up for the challenge, but it's going to be a fight to the figurative death. Keep in mind that becoming empowered is the end result of any Pluto transit. The secret is to let go, accept the losses or changes, and make plans for the future. Under the easier transits, the changes will still come, but you'll make them yourself—so it won't feel so much like you're being forced to change by outer conditions. You may rise to the very top of your profession, or become famous in some way, too.

Any of these transits will change the way you see You. So you may change your name or your identity in some way, too. It's going to be exciting. You're going to be born again when you're done with this huge purge. Look forward to it. Watch as your Real Self slowly emerges over this three-year process. But don't get comfortable 'till it's over. All of Pluto's transits involve ongoing change, and all processes take time

PLUTO/MOON

Your Moon represents your home, your family, your relationship with your Mom, your security, and your children. It's the urge or need we all have to emote, too. It's one of the most tender parts of us, a place where we prefer to react, rather than act. When Mr. Intensity arrives, then, it's a given that you're going to be feeling everything far more urgently—and probably expressing your feelings in far more urgent a fashion than you're used to, also. Pluto turns up the volume on your feelings when he touches the Moon, to the point where you might find yourself feeling 'obsessed' with someone or something—and emotionally tied up in knots, too. Most often, the focus will be on family issues, again, having to do with your Mom, your kids, or your home. But Pluto also empowers, remember. So if your usual reaction to what the world tosses at you is to sit back and take it, you won't be doing that anymore. No, with Pluto here, you'll be changing from the inside out—much the way a caterpillar transforms into a butterfly after its 'evolution' inside the cocoon is over.

When Pluto conjoins the Moon, you're going to be super-charged, emotionally—and everything about your outer life will reflect this inner change. You'll take a new, stronger stance within your family, put your foot down and make final decisions at home, and be amazingly in charge of your feelings. You may become a mother (or a father) now, too—and whether or not you've ever had children before, this one will powerfully change your life. You may move, or make drastic changes to your home's foundation, or tear one down and build a new one in its place. You may also begin to realize the profound emotional connection you share with your mother. After all, this is the person whose body you actually lived inside for nine months. She was your original shelter from every storm, your life-source. You felt everything she felt while you lived inside her womb. So with Pluto here, you'll begin feeling with her again, although quite subconsciously.

Under the tougher transits, (and this includes the tougher conjunctions) you may find your relationship with your Mom undergoing drastic change—or a complete turnaround. You may separate from her in some way, too. At times, you may also feel as if you're a prisoner in your own home—but you won't take that for very long. There's nothing like a tough Pluto/Moon transit to open your eyes to any kind of emotional manipulation and inspire you to Just Say No. On the other hand, if you've ever been prone towards using manipulation on others—via guilt, for example— now may be when you see what you've done, and take steps to change it. You may alienate family members with this new attitude, or bring them closer to you. Something about the way you approach family situations will be altered dramatically. Since Pluto also coincides with times when we feel as life is forcing us to Let Go, when he touches the Moon, a child of some kind may also leave our lives. In fact, if ever there were a recipe for empty nest syndrome, this is it.

When Pluto touches the Moon by easier aspect, you begin to see just how powerful a tool changing your feelings can be. You'll still be transforming from the inside out, but the changes will come more easily. Your whole attitude about children in general and your Mom in particular will be drastically different. Although your home life and your relationship with your family will still be altered in some inevitable way, you'll be a bit more accepting of the situation, right from the beginning. You may plan a move across the country, contact your Mom after several years of stony silence, or begin an adoption process.

Most importantly, keep in mind that everything that happens to you now, whether you see yourself or the outside world as the choreographer of these events, is going to be a symbolic Instant Replay of the birth process you went through when you separated from your Mom's body—and of your reaction to what you instinctively knew she was feeling about your birth. Now, any physical birth is a tough process, full of immense joy and great fear. Although you don't remember it, both you and your Mom were terrified. She'd created a brand-new person—and now it was time to meet you. She was facing a time of tremendous responsibility, when she'd be in charge of another human's nurturing. And you were about to leave home for the first time, to separate from the safest place you'd ever lived to begin a brave new separate journey—towards fulfilling the purpose you chose when you decided to hop inside a human body. When you feel a push toward change in your present life coming along, then, think of it as a contraction of sorts, the end of a period of comfort and protection, but the beginning of a wonderful journey. And as the contractions come at closer intervals, (that is, as events start to pile up towards a new beginning), take deep breaths, and get ready to see a whole new world with entirely new eyes.

PLUTO/MERCURY

This combination, friends, is the technology behind Focused Thinking—in all its forms, for better or worse. Yes, if ever there were a time tailor-made for Concentration, this is it. Now, concentration can emerge in many ways. Through an ability to sit still and do intense research, perhaps—(and if you've got a project like that to get through, now's when you'll be able to throw yourself right into it, for as many solitary hours as it takes). Picture Pluto, dressed all in black, sitting in a black leather chair behind a dark mahogany desk, magnifying glass in hand. The room is unlit except for the desk-lamp, and it's completely silent. Now imagine how much you'll be able to absorb when you're able to do this type of intense, focused study. Needless to say, he's not reading comic books in there, either. He's poring over Dante's *Inferno*, or the chronicles of someone who profiles serial killers— and that's the lighter stuff. So you may now find yourself quite absorbed in studying people or topics you'd ordinarily dismiss as far too heavy—regardless of which aspect transiting Pluto makes to your Mercury.

When he looks up from his book, he'll want to discuss what he's learned. And that makes for very heavy conversations. Your ordinarily curious, talkative little Mercury, then, isn't going to want to chit-chat lightly for awhile. In fact, any type of light, social conversation just won't cut it. You'll want to examine, analyze, and meticulously scrutinize every detail of everything that crosses your mind. And it won't be easy for you to stop thinking, either.

With the tougher transits, in fact, you can become quite obsessive. What did she really mean by that? What's he got up his sleeve? Don't be surprised if thoughts like those keep you awake all night. No matter what crosses your mind, it's going to be tough to shake it. Under these more challenging times, it's also possible to either practice or become prey to mind control of the unsavory kind. First off, then, be careful not to force your opinions on others. This isn't their transit, it's yours. This applies especially to the rather rabid attitude some folks take on with regard to politics when Pluto touches Mercury by hard aspect. Remember, whoever you're talking to might be having a nice, optimistic, liberal Jupiter transit to their Mercury. Sure, you can initiate a good discussion—but don't threaten to assassinate them if they're still going to vote for the Other Team after you've delivered your speech. Be on guard against others who will try to use these same techniques on you, too. With Pluto here, you'll be extremely open to persuasion. If they're delivered skillfully enough, even the most far-fetched conspiracy theory or tale of governmental espionage will sound quite rational. If you find yourself pulling the shades down very tightly at night, wondering if you're Their next target, it might be time for therapy. Seriously.

Now, speaking of persuasion, when Pluto makes an easier aspect to your Mercury, expect to be very skilled in that art. Transiting planets in trine or sextile to Mercury add their input to all your communications without any resistance from what you used to think. Pluto's visits under these circumstances will enable you to sell ice cubes to Eskimos—or talk someone in off the ledge. You're a salesperson right now—so make sure you're selling a reputable product.

By the way, regardless of the aspect, now's a great time to quite smoking. Pluto rules purges, after all, and Mercury is in charge of your breathing mechanism. So do yourself a favor. Use Pluto's amazing ability to get you in touch with your personal power, and take a deep breath—smoke free.

PLUTO/VENUS

Picture The Lady Venus all dressed up in her sexiest black outfit, ready for an evening out. She's waiting for her date—who bears a very strong resemblance to Steven Seagal. She sees him pull up in front of her house in a black limo, and as he approaches the door, she notices that he has something in his hand. Flowers? Nope. Candy? Uh uh. It's a pomegranate—and as he hands it to her, smiling and looking right into her eyes, she wonders if she's ready for this.

That's how you're going to feel when Pluto taps on your Venus' door—because there will no longer be any casual dates. And be warned—anyone who comes to pick you up during this transit, whether or not they arrive in a black limo and hand you an oddly symbolic fruit, won't be there to play games. They'll be looking for a soul mate, a confidante, a partner who will absolutely become a part of them. Of course, that's what you'll be looking for, too—but will you be ready?

Well, yes and no. What you will be ready for is total, deep commitment. You'll be looking for someone who'll return your intense gaze and not look away. You'll be quite ready for Intimacy—on all levels. What you might not be ready for are the suitors you're not interested in who arrive with equally intense expressions on their faces. Remember, this is a three-year process—so even if you do fall in love when it first starts, that doesn't mean you can just turn this energy off. Pluto's transit to Venus turns you into a magnetic, sensual being—and magnets attract all kinds of things.

Now, when Pluto visits by conjunction, your Venus will be ready, willing, and able. If there's no one in your life, in fact, you'll be looking—no, hunting—for a partner. And the urgency you'll be feeling as you set off on that pursuit will be quite subtle, quite silent, but quite obvious—to everyone. If you are seeing someone, warn them before this transit arrives. Tell them they might expect you to become a bit more intense than you have been in awhile, in every possible relationship area. That includes the physical side of things—which they probably won't mind much at all.

On the other hand, when Pluto makes a tough aspect to Venus, you may not be ready at all. Whatever stirring you're feeling to Get Involved will still be there, but you may not be happy with the types you're attracting. The danger is that you may feel controlled or manipulated by someone you love during this time, or somehow drawn to someone who you know isn't good for you, who's dangerous in some way. You may feel as if you simply can't live without them. You can. And you should. It's easy to get involved with someone who really is dangerous under this transit. So please, please, resist the temptation to date someone who's involved in less than savory activities. That means no mafioso, no loan sharks, and no one with a previous history of violence—no matter how hard they try to tell you that You're Different and They've Changed. Do that for me, okay? Because if you're not careful, this is the type of transit that can coincide with the arrival of a Fatal Attraction thing. Even though you're looking for intensity, and they certainly can provide that, an obsessive suitor is not a good thing.

Now, I'm not telling you that you're about to be stalked, or attacked, or harmed in any way. Even Pluto's harder aspects to your Venus can simply be the oomph behind a wonderful, passionate affair. The problem is that Plutonian types of all kinds will be interested in you now—so confine your search to researchers, detectives, surgeons or FBI agents who can't tell you what they're working on right now.

Under the easier transits, you'll attract equally profound relationships, and your current One-to-Ones will need to be a lot deeper than they may have been. But you won't stand quite so much of a chance of literally being in danger. Again, as with the conjunction, your appetite for Intimacy on all levels will increase dramatically. (Yep—another tough transit.) Just take it easy on yourself, and on your partner. This type of intensity can scare anyone away.

Now, under any of these transits, jealousy can be an issue. You may feel as if someone is trying to take away a loved one, or wonder if your partner is seeing someone else, or be accused of infidelity by someone else. Jealousy is the lowest possible expression of love. It's not based on love; it's based on fear of loss. It's a crisis of self-confidence. Now, if you (or they) are afraid someone will leave you or find someone else, it may be because deep down inside you feel that you're not enough for them—in some way. And that means that you're not nearly as compatible as you think you are.

Needless to say, whether the surface reason is—unrealistic jealousy or real infidelity—someone may leave your life when Pluto touches Venus. If that's the case, as with all Pluto transits, just let them go. Your affections and attentions aren't for the faint of heart right now, and anyone who leaves just isn't up for the challenge. But there's someone out there who will be. So if you're experiencing a painful, tragic loss, and you're sure you won't be able to live without this individual, rest assured that you will. You'll get over it. Sooner than you think, too. All relationship endings can be absolute agony, but if Pluto breaks them, they wouldn't have been much good to you in hard times, anyway. Grieve, cry, and understand that the depth you're offering is worth waiting for The Best to come along.

Of course, Venus is also in charge of The Money and Possessions Department. So, depending on the type of aspect Pluto makes, you can expect to find the same issues present in your financial life. That means you may have to deal with jealousy, possessiveness, or power-struggles over money. Now, don't be afraid to defend what's yours—regardless of the aspect Pluto makes to Venus—and do be prepared to lose what isn't yours. The best ways to use this transit in a material sense are to honestly evaluate your financial picture, take steps that will put you in charge of your money, clean house, and get rid of what you don't need.

PLUTO/MARS

It's undeniable that Mars is one tough dude. First of all, he's the ancient God of War—and that's a pretty tough business. He's also in charge of muscles, strength, and adrenaline—the things you need to be physically tough. His favorite toys are weapons and tools—guns, knives, anything made of steel. Not exactly delicate objects, any of them. Oh, and his favorite color is red—not an especially wimpy color. Of course, black is also not a wimpy color—in fact, black and red are known as The Power Colors. Now, guess whose favorite color is black. Right. Ol' Darth just loves black—it helps him to remain invisible at night—his favorite time—and it's worn by any bad guy who's worth his weight in a cowboy movie.

Needless to say, then, putting these two dudes together in any combination is like mixing up an atom bomb in a laboratory. They're the Bad Boys of Mt. Olympus, and a most formidable pair when they join forces. Of course, they don't have to be super-villains. They can also be Batman and Robin—a pair of super-heroes. (One of whom dresses like a black bat, drives a black car, and has his office in a cave.) Regardless of what type of cartoon characters you create from this mix, what it amounts to in your life is this: you're about to be endowed with amazing, serious strength—on all levels. Especially physical.

Strength? Yes, indeedy. Even if you've never touched a weight in your life, you'll be astounded at what you're now capable of. This is a great transit to use for exercising, body-building, and weight-lifting. It's the type of charge professional athletes are born with—and win their Gold medals with. But even if you have absolutely no desire to walk into a gym, your strength of will is going to be just as tough. So if you've got a hard project to complete, or a situation that requires you to be tough as nails to get through it, this is the transit that will give you the technology. And God/dess help anyone who gets in your way while you're pumping up. All this will apply especially to Pluto's conjunction to your Mars. Remember, when any natal planet is touched directly by a transiting planet, it becomes fused with the symbolic energies of the visitor.

Under the harder aspects, you may be put in a position of having to pull out this new super-weapon—to defend yourself. Squares indicate conflict, and oppositions often play out in our relationships with others. This is not to say that you should stay home for three years, or imagine that every set of footsteps you hear behind you is a mugger waiting to pounce—but do be careful. And take some type of self-defense class. You probably won't need it, but it's a great way to use this mighty combination—along with your work-outs, of course.

On the other hand, there are lots of situations that require us to defend ourselves in other than physical ways—arguments, power struggles, and intellectual challenges, for example. If you're feeling threatened in some way, then, whether it's by an individual or an agency, find a way to do battle and take care of yourself. Take on a powerful ally, or hire a professional who's shrewd and combative when necessary. Just be careful not to become quite a bully yourself when these two come together. It's tough to know when to quit when you're feeling this super-charged—and these two can be just about unstoppable when they come together. If you're really spoiling for a battle, use your new super-powers to defend a worthy cause, or take on an adversary you know is harming or manipulating someone less powerful.

When The Bad Boys come together in an easy aspect, you can expect your personal power and magnetic appeal to be on High. You'll probably find that others will be drawn to you, and will ask for your help. And if you've got to rebuild something—whether it's a part of your life, an old home, or a career—this combination will be indispensable towards giving you the energy and the drive to tear it all down happily and start over.

In all, your best bet is to use these two to accomplish something that's not purely personal. It's a tremendous force to have tucked into your bat-utility belt, and Gotham City might just need you.

PLUTO/JUPITER

Well, now. Picture your favorite uncle Jupiter receiving a visit from Darth, Master of Power, Persuasion, and Passion. This is the same uncle, of course, who's never been famous for his gift for knowing when to quit, the guy who doesn't want one of anything, or a small anything. Okay. Now what's it going to be like when they get together?

First of all, your uncle's going to be a bit overwhelmed by his visitor. Sure, he's game for anything, but the type of stuff Pluto's whispering in his ear kind of gives him the creeps—at first. But Pluto and Jupiter have a couple of things in common. They both hate stagnation of any kind, and they both love power. Granted, their techniques are quite different. Pluto stops stagnation by ending a situation, while Jupiter stops it by promoting constant growth. Jupiter's kind of power stretches back to the fact that he's known mythologically as The King of the Gods—the original benevolent dictator, you might say. Pluto isn't exactly benevolent. His type of power comes from an urge to be Master of All He Surveys, totally In Control of Everything. These common interests, then, give them something to talk about. And the result is lotsa power, lotsa change, and lotsa ambition. And if you add Jupiter's natural gift for gab to Pluto's knack for knowing exactly what someone wants you to say, you've got the makings of a very influential partnership. It's a natural for politics—and yes, ba-ruthas and a-sistas, Evangelism as well.

Yes, if you need to Influence The Masses by the very power of what you believe, this transit is invaluable. Whether you're Spreading The World about politics (office-politics, real, live, governmental politics, or lobbying for your pet cause) or religion, or anything else you feel strongly is Important for The Masses to know, the easier aspects and the easier conjunctions from Pluto to your Jupiter can be absolutely wonderful. Pluto lends his persuasive abilities to Jupiter, and all of a sudden, you're a whiz at the art of Convincing Others. Jupiter's natural enthusiasm becomes super-charged when Pluto adds his fervor. Your Jupiter also knows quite a bit about networking—an essential tool in any campaign. Everybody loves Jupiter, too—and he's got a whole pack of favors to call in. Add Pluto's shrewdness and his talent for strategy, and you've got the skill and knowledge to talk anybody into anything. So no matter what you're involved in when Pluto touches your Jupiter kindly, it's going to be quite easy for you to rise to the top and take charge. People will want to see you in The Big Chair—you'll have more support than you'll know what to do with.

Also on a quite positive note, Jupiter's lotsa along with Pluto's power can also add up to Wealth. Talk about fund-raising—and, as They say, Money Talks. Pluto's long-time connection with Inheritances could mean that you receive a sizable bequest from a relative, a large settlement in a legal matter, or an endowment from an institution. But your Jupiter is also representative of your higher or spiritual side—so your concern and understanding of The Larger Issues will also deepen now, and you can do a lot of good for a lot of people if you use this transit well. Pluto just loves to reform things, and Jupiter is a very social kind of guy, very concerned with bringing folks together, and very skilled at Incorporation.

On the down-side, when Pluto makes a tough aspect to Jupiter, you also stand to lose a lot. Jupiter is the place where we're not at all afraid to take risks, and Pluto is often in the neighborhood when folks who try to manipulate you are, too. You could become so hungry for power that you develop a God-Complex, and become pretty darned obsessed with your Jupiterian beliefs. Remember, when these two get together in a square or opposition, the action-oriented aspects, the temptation to become quite full of yourself is a possibility. You're quite powerful now, but you're not omnipotent. Evangelists and politicians fall from favor all the time. Don't take on more than you can handle—and don't forget you're mortal.

PLUTO/SATURN

Saturn is the planet who loves to build permanent structures. He's the tool in our kit that we use to create a firm foundation for our lives—to set down roots that connect us to the planet. He's not a big fan of Change, either. He's the technology behind gridlock, and when he folds his arms and hesitates too much, he can get into a rut, or procrastinate so much that nothing gets done. But he's just doing his job. He represents the urge or need inside you that most wants to resist Change, to build a bigger wall when you see it coming. Pluto, on the other hand, loves Change. He knows that it's inevitable, if you're going to evolve. He's seen walls—and he has yet to find one that can keep him out.

When Pluto conjoins your Saturn, then, you may feel as if the Powers That Be are forcing you into a corner—and you may have to stand back and watch your foundation crumble. This can come along in many ways. Your business is downsized, leaving you careerless for the first time in your adult life. Or your apartment-house is purchased by a large company who wants to turn it into condominiums, and you've got 60 days to move—after living there for 15 years. Regardless of the scenario, Big, Drastic Change comes along, and you've got to start over. This is the type of transit that coincides with long-term, permanent shifts in your lifestyle. Although it doesn't always feel good while it's happening, there's a reason. It's Time. It's inevitable. You've been standing in the same spot for too long, and you've got to go now.

If any of these changes come your way, then, get your things together and go. Look at this as an opportunity to rebuild yourself, and don't be afraid. Something better always comes along when we cooperate with Change—especially Pluto's brand. Besides, you've probably been subconsciously feeling the urge to tear your whole life down and start over—and this huge push from the outer worlds is simply a reflection of what you've already been working on internally. Pluto's push to Saturn is inspirational in re-structuring anything.

And speaking of restructuring, think of what Pluto can do for Saturn's image. I mean, Pluto's quite a sexy guy—magnetic, even. Although Saturn hasn't traditionally been known as an especially sensual planet, when Pluto touches Saturn, the effect is to turn Icobod Crane into that sexy older teacher you had a crush on in high school. You loved him or her because they were so intelligent, so wise—and so experienced. After all, there's something very attractive about Experience. Now imagine yourself as becoming that teacher for awhile. Think of the ability you'll have to get the facts across—by charming someone with your knowledge.

Needless to say, this is a great transit to have if you're involved in The Business World. It's so potent, in fact, that you may become extremely successful during this transit—in the Career Department. And since Pluto wants it all, you may also become quite driven. See, Pluto wants you to take total control in the area of life he touches. When it's Saturn he's visiting, your public or professional self wants more—of everything. The conjunction and the easier aspects often point to a time when we reap the benefits of the hard work we've done in the past, when the Authority Figures in the world hand us the opportunity to write our own tickets.

Saturn is also quite good at details—and Pluto loves to research. So if you're involved in a tedious but important project at this time, you'll be well-equipped to finish it. And when you're done, you can expect a certificate, a dinner in your honor, and the recognition you deserve. But don't think it's going to be given to you. Wherever Saturn is in our charts is a place where we work very hard for what we get.

The tougher transits often indicate times when something like an implosion can occur in your professional life. The Forces That Be—that is, authority figures, superiors, etc.— may seem to push you quite relentlessly, force you to work harder, and take away what you haven't earned. In the end, any transit of Pluto to your Saturn will be a time of trial and effort, when you'll need to rework projects, rewrite your essays, and start over several times until you get it right—until you earn it. But you'll be up for it. Pluto's tough transits are times when we set to work eliminating what's wrong in our lives, and rebuilding what needs it. It's well worth it. After the purge, you'll have a stronger, more stable foundation—one that's quite long-lasting. Your best bet under any of these transits, then, is to Do It Right The First Time, and set to work refurbishing what needs it. Just don't give up until you've accomplished your goals. Saturn appreciates enduring effort—and Pluto won't let you sleep until you're done, anyway.

PLUTO/URANUS

Uranus represents the urge or need you were born with to be a radical, fight City Hall, and charge ahead into the future, regardless of what They think. Pluto brings along a strong dose of Intensity and Relentlessness—for better or worse. He sends the planet he touches off on a passionate quest—to Change Things by reforming, rejuvenating, or regenerating. In your own life, that means that you're about to begin a period of intense experimentation, trying out different types of behaviors to see which one will allow you to become totally free. Your goal is to become an Individual, in the truest sense of the word—and in typical Plutonian style, right now you won't care what it takes to get there. Remember, Uranus is the mad professor inside you—Pluto gives that professor the urge to research experiments tirelessly, to peer behind closed doors and investigate what used to terrify you. This is the technology that produced Frankenstein, kids—and although you probably won't be quite as drastic in your quest to reach your goal, your objective will be the same: to Build the Perfect Beast.

Now, in the process of assembling all the right pieces, you'll probably use your own life as a laboratory. And the more others try to stop you, the more determined you'll be to rebel—to do it your way. Uranus is where you just love to shock folks, anyway—to show them how different and unique you are. Pluto adds fuel to that fire, and an urgency, too. Just be careful you don't end up rebelling for the sake of rebellion, especially when the 'push' of the harder transits urges you on. Although it satisfies your need to Just Say No, it won't help you find out who you are. You may also incur the wrath of Darth's representatives if you push it too far, and end up fighting the IRS, or Internal Affairs.

Under the easier transits, you'll find that the world is quite supportive of your individuality and uniqueness—mainly because the techniques you'll use to express yourself will be less inflammatory—to society in general.

In all, when these two get together, you can become a powerful force for humanitarian causes that may seem just a bit too radical, or a few years ahead of their time. These causes will be popular at the moment, because everyone born within a year or two of you are having the same transit. You'll all be able to see that these causes aren't radical at all—and that there's really not a moment to lose. But remember—neither of these two give a good damn what anybody else thinks of their methods, and you and your mini-generation won't, either. Their common goal is simply to push forward—into the inevitable future. You're going to feel very much like you're an agent for drastic societal changes under any of these transits, much like Margaret Sanger or Jack Kevorkian, both of whom were profoundly opposed and seen as radical when they set off on their quests. Just be sure whatever you're taking on is for the good of everyone—and fasten your seat-belt.

PLUTO/NEPTUNE—AND PLUTO/PLUTO

When I sat down to write these last two entries, I realized that this combination is the most generational of all transits. Most of us born over the last 50 years or so arrived with a sextile between Pluto and Neptune, so when Pluto transits either planet, it's transiting both. That fact made this transit awfully hard to write about, but extremely illuminating personally after I figured it out. I've tried here to separate these transits, so that you'll be able to see how each part of you is responding to both personal and generational issues. However, in combination, these planets are nothing if not ethereal. Intense, but ethereal. So it was tough to define them in terms of specific situations that might come up. I've tried to give you both the feelings they'd inspire generationally, and the inner changes they'd coincide with personally. I hope you get something out of these delineations on both levels, then—even though these two are quite tough to talk about in my usual style.

Now, because Pluto is so far out there in the galaxy, with such a long, long orbit, for the next century or so most of us will only experience the sextile, square, trine, and opposition to both our natal Neptune and our natal Pluto. When you're looking at transits, it's best to begin with Pluto and the other Outers and work your way in. Look at the backdrop they're setting for the faster-moving planets. Since Pluto is the outermost planet that we're currently familiar with, it stands to reason that his transits to this sextile in your chart are among the biggest ones, the ones with the most potential to coincide with complete and total change to your life. This will be quite noticeable if the Pluto/Neptune sextile is connected to any personal planet in your chart, but much more subtle if it isn't. Either way, Big Stuff is happening to both you and those folks who are in your age group. Read on—and try to understand just how imbedded this aspect is in our generational attitudes. This aspect, like no other, reminds us that we're all in this one together.

PLUTO/NEPTUNE

Neptune represents a generation's opinion on drugs, alcohol, and religion—and any of the other ways we choose to escape reality—or alter it. But on a more personal level, she's the urge inside each of us to Connect with all life. Since she stays in one place for so long, then, when you feel the urge to cut out, the methods you use for your escape may be similar to what most of your peers (age-wise, at least), are also using. Every generation comes to a time when the reality of the moment doesn't suit them—when they turn their thoughts upward and look for more than what's in front of their eyes. When Pluto aspects Neptune, this amounts to the beginning of a quest. You're all going to be looking to put the ritual back into your spiritual life—through ceremonies and experiences with others that will bring the depth, magic and mystery of life right into your living room, right there in River City. Regardless of the aspect, these transits are times when you'll all investigate the more spiritual side of your nature, especially through religions that promote your connection with all life forms—like Buddhism, or Wicca. If you're already a member of a spiritual community, prepare to become intensely interested in it—and possibly drawn into the political side of it.

Yes, Religion and Politics are two issues that come face to face when Pluto and Neptune get together—for better or worse. That's something all of us already know. After all, we were born with this sextile, so we expect that connection to be there. When Pluto touches Neptune, whether or not you become formally involved in either of those groups, you may feel quite Divinely Inspired or Divinely Disappointed. Either way, you'll want to set off on a spiritual mission of some kind—something that will reflect your personal inner faith.

...AND PLUTO/PLUTO

You'll be especially fervent in seeking out a higher purpose for life, since you're also experiencing Pluto to Pluto. But let's look at just Pluto for a moment. Yes, here's the double-dose again. Whatever Issues your natal Pluto has given you to work on for life, you're about to have a test. Remember that this is a place in your chart where you're quite familiar with things being in a state of turmoil, where you're used to ongoing change and a constant shedding of your skin—all in the name of Evolution, which is what our higher purpose really is. When it's time to evolve through ending a situation and taking the next step, whether it's a relationship, a job, or someone dear to you that's passed over, your Pluto is the tool you reach for. So when Pluto touches Pluto, regardless of the aspect and the situations that come up, although Change is certainly coming, you're equipped for it.

No matter what the aspect, you'll experience a type of turmoil as your feel your life rearranging on every level. However, since Neptune is also involved, no matter what else happens, you're going to be very interested in seeking out the spiritual side of the changes. Your natal Pluto represents the urge or need to End Things. Neptune wants to feel the spiritual purpose behind that end, and understand what's next.

When the easy transits come along, then, as things pass away from you, you'll be quite peaceful with those changes. You'll realize that like it or not, life goes on—even after tremendous loss. This is the side of you who'll reflect on those losses down the road and try to make sense of them. It's also true that here is where you'll crave intense experiences—anything from horror movies to deep, honest, soul-baring conversation, to physical intimacy. And under the easy aspects, you'll have your share of intensity, but it won't be overwhelming, and you'll be ready for it. Most importantly, since Pluto rules life, death, and rebirth, no matter what happens, you'll understand the importance of process. You're already very strong where your Pluto is. He's a well of concentrated, transformative energy. When he aspects himself by transit, your willpower and strength stand to double, too.

In all, the combination of these transits is the combination that inspires complete spiritual overhauls—both personally and generationally. You'll be looking for a deep connection—with a faith, with an Other, with all life on the planet. You'll be quite focused on this quest, too. But when the Pluto/Neptune sextile is touched by Pluto, don't be surprised if, after looking everywhere for The Answers, you find that the most important connection you make is with yourself.

CHAPTER FOURTEEN

GOOD-BYE

And In Conclusion...

Well, that's it, folks. We've completed another segment in our journey together, this time into the future. I hope you enjoy this book, and that you find it worthy of revisiting often. That will make my Saturn happy—and God/dess knows, we all want happy Saturns. (I mean, consider the alternative...). I also hope you leave every passage with a positive feeling—because no matter which transit you're experiencing, there really are positive uses for it, and positive outcomes to expect. Besides, there's a great line from a country song that applies beautifully here: "Some of God's greatest gifts are unanswered prayers." That goes for transits of all the planets—but okay, especially Saturn.

Please remember (as my Uncle Jupiter says) that this wonderful planet of ours is a giant playground, full of new experiences and unexplored paths—and that our transits are like signposts along the way, showing us how best to travel, and which paths to take. Don't get stuck in negative places or in bad company, then, and don't ever just sit through a tough time, waiting for it to end. Give your tougher transits tough work to do—and concentrate on using up that energy in a constructive way. Give your easier transits projects, too—don't waste them.

If all else fails, think of the transiting planet as a visitor, and your natal planet as a host/ess. Imagine what they might do together that would make them both happy. And realize that your natal planet won't be the same after any transit. After all, the point is to learn another lesson, and if nothing changes, you haven't learned anything.

Also, please know that I appreciate your presence here. I wake up every day, turn on the computer, and thank Jupiter, God/dess, and Whoever Else of the Powers That Be who might be responsible for allowing me to continue to do what I love— but I also want to thank each of you, from the very tip of my Sagittarian toes (hooves?). And please let me hear from you. Drop a line, send an e-mail, or introduce yourself at a conference.

It's always wonderful to meet new friends.

See you next time, when our topic will be relationships—most likely viewed through the lens of composite charts.

Once again, the author wishes to mention that a percentage of the proceeds of this book will be divided between Critter Organizations, Resident Critters, Wild Winged Visitors and other causes and projects beneficial to The Animal Kingdom and Mother Earth, all of whom thank you for your support. Anything left over (this time) will be invested in plane tickets, books, supplies for yet another book, and—oh, yes—food and shelter.

**Now, a sneak preview from another recent release,
Unveiling Your Future: Progressions Made Easy,
by Maritha Pottenger and Zipporah Dobyns.**

Astrological peers are raving about *Unveiling Your Future*!
Here's what **Raymond A. Merriman, President of International
Society for Astrological Research**, has to say:

"How many times have you been asked by students:
'Can you recommend a good book on secondary progressions?' And how many times have you responded
with something like, 'Well, I learned about progressions
from ...., but as far as a book just on progressions,
I don't really know.'

"Most of the literature on secondary progressions is
contained in a single chapter within books on general or
predictive astrology. However, now comes a new book called
Unveiling Your Future: Progressions Made Easy, dedicated
entirely to the subject of secondary progressions by two of
the foremost professional astrologers today: Maritha
Pottenger and Zipporah Dobyns.

"The expertise of the authors truly stands out. Anyone
can write a reference book which interprets various
astrological signatures, but Pottenger and Dobyns have their
own unique style and insights. The crux of their analysis is
psychological, but even within that they offer a generous
grouping of events that are possible under each progression.
And unlike most books on astrological forecasting, this
one also includes delineations involving Chiron, the
Moon's Nodes, and the four primary asteroids: Ceres, Pallas,
Juno, and Vesta. Not only is this material different from
other books, but the interpretations also just happen to be
very good!

"There is a wealth of new material presented in this
wonderful new book. The interpretations are clear, sensible,
and insightful. The material is organized in a very practical
way, which makes it easy to use as a reference work. And
the later chapters include some case histories which
demonstrate exactly how the authors apply their techniques.

"Astrologers looking for an excellent book on secondary
progressions can't go wrong with *Unveiling Your Future:
Progressions Made Easy*. **It is probably the best book**

written on the subject, and will likely become the standard for secondary progressions for many, many years to come. Highly recommended."

Jeanne Long, financial astrologer, author and international lecturer, has this to say:

"**Maritha Pottenger and Zipporah Dobyns have done the impossible...they've made looking into the future easy!** *Unveiling Your Future* addresses the most mysterious and exciting area of astrological delineation – known as progressions, revealing it in such a way that looking into the future has never been more easy or clearly defined. The authors have pooled their vast astrological knowledge and compressed it into this valuable reference book. It is presented in a refreshingly clear and practical way, but more importantly, in a usable manner.

"Maritha and Zip never hold back astrological information; they always make a point of going to the limit in generously sharing their knowledge.

"Wonderfully, **this book has something for everyone**, from the student to the professional. It provides a solid foundation in a step-by-step format to keep the student on track. I especially like the keyword headings in many sections of the book, such as 'Sun in Leo or 5th House: Star Quality' and 'Venus in Aries or 1st House: Please Me!' I love it. A student will get the picture instantly.

"Advanced students and professionals will appreciate the wealth of information presented on [the] "big four" asteroids and Chiron showing how they function in the progressed chart. Much of this is new information including the section on house rulerships. The Case Studies Section presents a simple formula which combines long-term and short-term cycles with lunar cycles and progressed aspects to put all of the pieces into perspective.

"Most importantly, *Unveiling Your Future* shows how to put all the fragments of conflicting information together in a clear-cut and concise way, allowing you to explore the future in a surprisingly easy fashion. Finally, Maritha and Zip not only take you on an adventure into your future, but counsel and guide you as to the best use of the energies involved.

"Because this book offers a whole new world of easy progressions, you will want to **keep it handy for constant reference**. Thank you Maritha and Zip for taking the time to share!"

Carol Tebbs, MA, astrologer, teacher, and UAC Board Chair has this to say:

"Page one of *Unveiling Your Future* leads off with meaty stuff—a prioritized list of what to look for to interpret a secondary progression. And then, the well-experienced astrological mother/daughter team, Maritha Pottenger and Dr. Zipporah Dobyns, follows through with the goods — a detailed, humane interpretation of the various combinations formed by angles, planets, nodes, and yes, "the big four" asteroids and Chiron. **For student to professional, this book provides insight and depth to one of astrology's standard interpretive tools, the Secondary Progression. Consider it a must read.**"

From Chapter One, *Basics*

Priorities

A general "rule of thumb" in astrology is: the more often a pattern repeats in the sky, the less important a single occurrence is likely to be in your life. The rarer an astrological placement, the more significance should be given to it in your interpretations. Following is an outline which suggests priorities to follow when interpreting progressions. The chapters in this book will follow this outline and provide instant look-ups for the planetary placements discussed.
...

A change of sign or house by the progressed Moon. The progressed Moon is a major key to emotional needs, and where we seek safety. A new sign or house shows issues and needs in high focus for the next few years (average of 2-1/2 years per sign—time spent in houses varies due to size differences).

The Moon's changes of house and sign are interpreted in Chapter 9.
...

From Chapter Eleven, *Aspects of Progressed Moon*

MOON CONJUNCT JUNO (AND VICE VERSA)

Sharing, commitment, attachments and closeness are central themes now. You may be ready for a deeper level of association. You may further explore interdependency, especially in your partnership(s). Emotional support from and to a spouse/partner becomes more central. You may also get sustenance from beauty/ artistic activities.

Commitment is a central theme for this period. With the asteroid of marriage and the planet of home and family joining forces, thinking about "domestic bliss" is extremely likely. Usually, the urge is for a permanent love relationship, or for strengthening and deepening already-existing bonds. If the rest of your chart is very freedom-oriented, you could subconsciously attract a partner to express this very family-oriented side for you. Generally, this aspect suggests a strong focus on love, caring, emotional support and a solid home life.

Security, fidelity, commitment, support and protection are part of the picture. This can be a time when one spouse (or partner) depends a bit more than usual on the other (perhaps due to illness or other stress in the life). If carried too far, the partnership can become more like a parent/child association. If the spouses are able to take turns caring for one another, it is healthy, human interdependency. Each has something to give that the other can receive.

An urge to bring more beauty, grace, pleasure or aesthetic activities into the home is also possible. The desire for harmony and balance may be satisfied through artistic endeavors or "house beautiful" activities. In general, this is a time to explore the concept that "Love means being there for each other."

Your Horoscope
FREE!
Get A Complimetary Natal Chart Just by Sending Us This Order Form!
(Or a copy of your original sales receipt.)

ASTRO is making this offer because we would like you to know about our complete computer calculation service.

Send us your birth information & address, along with this page, or a copy of your original sales receipt, and we'll send you your natal chart right away.

We'll also include our free catalog that explains all of our special calculation services.

Ask for your FREE BWYAAC-BKALSF- an $8.00 value!

		am pm
Name	Birthdate (day, month & year)	Birth Time

Birth Place (city)	Birth Place (state)

Current Street Address City	State Zip Code

Astro Communications Services, Inc.
5521 Ruffin Road, San Diego, CA 92123
1-800-888-9983
Operators available Mon-Fri 8am to 5pm Pacific Time

Create YOUR FUTURE!

A Planetary Guide to Your Future

Your Horoscope written just for you! Be ready for each day with the insights this reading offers! Choose the most constructive and positive way to approach a trend and see how daily planetary changes play out in your daily life. Start each morning with your own personal daily horoscope! Specify starting month.

6 months 75-90 pages DTIX6-BKALSF **$32.95**
12 months 150-180 pages DTIX12-BKALSF **$49.95**

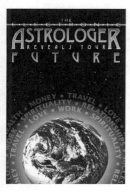

SOFTWARE:
The Electronic Astrologer Reveals Your FUTURE

"Best Program of the Year"—*American Astrology*
A program that takes you beyond today and puts tomorrow in the palm of your hand. Have you ever wondered which days would be best to ask for a raise, take a vacation, or get married? Be prepared for upcoming events! You choose the dates and **The Electronic Astrologer** does the rest. With this software you can pinpoint the exact time to make those important decisions. **IBMWEAF-BKALSF**............**$59.95**

Transit Calendar

For those of you who just want to know the planetary movements and their relation to your own chart, we offer the Transit Calendar. This personal calendar lists exact transiting aspects for that day, with the times they are exact. Transits in effect for longer than one day are listed on the right of each box. Outer planet transits are listed at the beginning and end. Available with or without the moon aspects. Specify the starting month.

All Calendar Transits CAT-BKALSF .... **6 mos. $17.95/1yr. $24.95**
Planets (no Moon) CT-BKALSF .... **6 mos. $9.95/1yr. $17.95**

1-800-888-9983

Astro Communications Services, Inc.

5521 Ruffin Road, San Diego, CA 92123
Operators available Monday through Friday, 8 am to 5 pm Pacific Time.
Prices subject to change. Shipping & handling will be added.